VIKING MERSEY

SCANDINAVIAN WIRRAL, WEST LANCASHIRE AND CHESTER

STEPHEN HARDING

Countyvise Limited, UK

First published 2002 by Countyvise Limited,
14 Appin Road, Birkenhead, Merseyside, CH41 9HH

Copyright © 2002 Steven Harding

The right of Steven Harding to be identified as the author of this work has been asserted
by him in accordance with the Copyright, Design and Patents Act 1988.

British Library Cataloguing in Publication Data.
A Catalogue record for this book is available from the British Library.

ISBN 1 901231 34 8

Printed by Birkenhead Press Limited, 14 Appin Road, Birkenhead CH41 9HH

A book commemorating the 1100th anniversary of the arrival and settlement of Vikings into Wirral and Merseyside in 902AD or shortly afterwards, and dedicated to F.T. Wainwright.

v

PREFACE

In the early 10th-Century a group of battle weary Viking adventurers, led by the Norseman Ingimund pleaded with the Queen of the Mercian English for permission to land and settle peacefully in a small peninsula between the Rivers Dee and Mersey in North-west England now known as Wirral. There then followed a migration of Viking peoples into the whole of the coastal region between the Dee and the Solway. These were initially Norsemen driven out of Ireland, but later joined by fellow Scandinavians from the Isle of Man, the Isles of Scotland and the Viking homelands of Norway and Denmark. In Wirral and Merseyside we are fortunate to have the only lasting historical record of this movement, which began in 902A.D. The settlements were indeed peaceful at first, but Vikings are Vikings however and it was not long before they were attacking Chester.

This book has been written to commemorate the 1100th anniversary of this movement and settlement, arguably one of the most significant events in the history of the region and yet an event that has never been given the coverage it deserved. It covers the Viking settlements and their influence past and present: the birth of Mersey Northernism, the settlements in Wirral, the extraordinary raids and then settlements in Chester, paralleled by the settlements in West Lancashire.

The Mersey Vikings were not only raiders and traders, but also farmers, fishermen, moneyers and parliamentarians with their special places of Assembly or "Things". They were not all heathens or pagans as the traditional image of Vikings are portrayed. There is some evidence of pagan burial mounds, but they were also Christians - with Viking churches. In the 14th-Century some were still naming their children the traditional Viking way, with names appearing with the suffixes -doghter "daughter of" and -sson "son of", just as in modern day Iceland which still preserves this tradition. The famous 14th-Century poem *Sir Gawain and the Green Knight*, considered by experts to have been written by someone from Cheshire, is pervaded by a large number of dialect words of Scandinavian origin, and the poem also takes Sir Gawain through Wirral. The book also surveys the increasing and impressive evidence for the location of the famous Battle of *Brunanburh* in the region.

Modern genetic methods, used in conjunction with surname and place-name information are being used to probe for descendants of these people in the area today. This combined approach may help address difficulties in interpretation caused by the large population increases and movements since the Industrial Revolution. *Viking Mersey* concludes with a review of two years of celebrations in the area to commemorate the 1100th anniversary of the settlements. Highlights included the opening of a new ferry link between Ireland and Merseyside with a new teminal in Wirral and the revival of the ancient Festival of St. Olave in Chester.

The book follows two others published in 2000 that were written specifically about Wirral: the scholarly text *Wirral and its Viking Heritage* by Paul Cavill, Stephen Harding and Judith Jesch published by the English Place-Name Society in 2000. This was accompanied by the more populace book *Ingimund's Saga: Norwegian Wirral* published by Countyvise Ltd. and written by Stephen Harding with a foreword by the well known Viking expert and TV personality Magnus Magnusson. *Viking Mersey* has been written to include the whole of Merseyside, and its environs, and focuses on Wirrral, Chester and West Lancashire. The treatment of the extensive settlements of West Lancashire has been reinforced by the inclusion of material by the late scholar Frederick Threlfall Wainwright based on a seminal article he wrote nearly 60 years ago. In fact this book has been compiled as a personal tribute to him. The present author owes a large part of his fascination with the Vikings to a chance discovery in a College Library in 1976 of Wainwright's book *Scandinavian England* whilst revising for final examinations... in Natural Science, Physics!.

Without the continuous encouragement and help of Judith Jesch - Professor of Viking Studies, and Paul Cavill, the Research Fellow of the English Place Names Society - both colleagues at the University of Nottingham, *Viking Mersey* would not have been possible. They have tried to ensure I have said nothing outlandish, but of course things might have slipped through their grasp! The author is also grateful to a large number of other people who have hoped with the project. Professor Gillian Fellows-Jensen of the University of Copenhagen advised on the Danish influence in the area and the *Things*, and painstakingly checked through large parts of the manuscript. Dr. David Griffiths, Fellow and Tutor of Archaeology at the University of Oxford together with Dr. Andy Towle of the National Museums and Art Galleries Liverpool were a great help with the Chapter on Meols. Dan Robinson, Keeper of Archaeology of the Grosvenor Museum was seminal in his help with the Chester material and checked through Chapter 6. Tinho da Cruz, at the University of Liverpool, Department of Geography helped with Chapter 7. Stephen Matthews (Honorary Secretary) and the Lancashire and Cheshire Antiquarian Society gave permission to reproduce the appropriate parts of Wainwright's article on Lancashire for Chapter 8.

Roger White of the Ironbridge Institute provided extensive help with the Neston stonework of Chapter 9. Dr. Nick Higham of the University of Manchester and the authority on *Brunanburh*, advised on Chapter 11 and also checked through the Chapter on the Things. Allan Alsbury, local historian from Higher Bebington, Gavin Hunter from Unilever Research at Port Sunlight and Susan Nicholson from the Bromborough Society were also a great help with Chapter 11. Professor Jan Ragnar Hagland, of the Norges teknisk naturvitenskapelige universitet - NTNU, Trondheim also advised on the Scandinavian Things. Professor Nils Lennart Johanesson, also at the NTNU kindly gave permission for use of his analysis of Scandinavian words in *Sir Gawain and the Green Knight* for Chapter 13, and Professor Thorlac Turville-Petre also advised. Brian Roberts provided valuable information about the Stanley family. Dr. Mark Jobling, Department of Genetics, University of Leicester was a great help with the material concerning Chapter 14 and the ongoing genetic survey. Stephen Roberts rediscovered the Henry VIII subsidy rolls - of all those paying taxes in 1542 - the surnames from which the new genetic survey of Wirral is based. Patrick Waite of the West Lancashire Heritage Association has also been of great support and provided a similar list of names based on inhabitants of West Lancashire "who promised to contribute to the stipend of the priest of the altar of Our Lady at Ormskirk, in the year 1366". Stuart Hornby drew my attention to the South Wirral 'ssons and 'doghters who were still filling in their rent books at the turn of the 15th-Century. John Harding helped with the artwork, including the front cover design. J.M. Davies of Amlwch provided the burning ship photograph for the back cover.

A special thanks is appropriate to everyone who helped me with the Anniversary celebrations of 2002 and the build up in 2001, which has been reviewed in Chapter 15. I would particularly like to thank John and Pauline Cocker, Mayor and Mayoress of Wirral in the period 2001-2002, Allan Brown, Howard Mortimer, Pippa Shedden, Deirdre Smith, Ian Ward, Wayne Richardson (all of Wirral Borough Council), Hrolf Douglasson, Vara Hrolfswiffe and other members of the Wirhalh Skip-Felag; Tony Foarde, Bagman of the Mersey Morris Men, Revd. Roger Clarke, St. Bridgets Church, West Kirby, Wirral, Revd. Paul Robinson of St.Hilary's Church, Wallasey Village, Revd. Graham Dalton, of the Cheshire Revival Centre at St.Olave's Chester, Peter Copeland of the Norwegian Consulate in Liverpool, Anne Ulset of the Royal Norwegian Embassy, Eyrún Hafsteinsdóttir and Jón Baldvinsson of the Icelandic Embassy in London, Andrew McCartney, Headmaster of Thingwall School and all the children who made a great success of the May 1st event at Thor's stone. A special mention also to the time, effort and enthusiasm of colleagues from Trondheim Norway: Liv Sandven, Deputy Mayor of Trondheim, Gerhard Dalen, Director of Cultural Affairs, Per Uddu, Director of the Olavsfestdagene and St. Olav Pilgrim Priest Kjell Skartseterhagen. Liv

Sandven in particular, who, despite taking over as "Acting Mayor" in 2002, was still able to come over for the events surrounding May 1st. Pastor Oddgeir Bolstad and members of the congregation of the Scandinavian Church in Liverpool all helped to revive the St. Olave tradition in Chester and members of the Norwegian, Icelandic and English Press, Radio and TV who helped disseminate news of the Anniversary, particularly Trine Andresen, Sigrun Davidsdóttir, Nick Baty, Louise Powney, Stuart Hughes, Mick Hornby, Dave Charters, David Harding, Pauline McAdam, Jimmy McCracken, 'Snelly' (Tony Snell), Roger Phillips, Rachel Bullock, Ralph Blunsom, Cathy Henderson, Nicola Dixon, Alan Urry and Mark Edwardson. Liz Murphy of the Norwegian Consulate and Norman Guard of Liverpool FC secured the interview with Per Anders Todal for Vegard Heggem, and a special thanks to Per Anders Todal for providing the transcript of both that interview and also one with Bill Housley, and providing many of the photographs.

We would like to thank the following people or organisations not mentioned above for permissions to reproduce their material: *The Daily Mail*, the *Daily Post, Adresseavisen*, Lichfield City Council, the John Rylands Library, University of Manchester; the Picton Reference Library, Liverpool; Wallasey Central Reference Library, Wirral; Liverpool Museum; Frank Biddle, Pasture Road, Moreton, Wirral, Warrington Museum, Manchester City Galleries, the Bibliothèque Royale in Brussels, the English Place-Name Society, the EEC Environmental Birds Directive, Chester & Cheshire Archives & Local Studies at Duke Street, and the Getty Foundation. Others helping to provide photographs included Bob Warwick, Richard Smith, Stan Strickland of Burscough FC, Arthur Gore of Skelmersdale United FC, John Byast, J.M. Davies and Barbara Jones of the Tranmere Rovers Rearguard website. The author was extremely lucky to have Patrick Trollope of the *Southport Reporter* volunteering to chase around Lancashire obtaining some of the photographs for Chapter 7, and more remarkably Ragnar Th. Sigurðsson running around Iceland obtaining pictures of the equivalent places in Iceland to Kirkby, Meols, Croxteth, Thingwall and West Kirby. He even found an East Kirby!

Finally without the support from Stein Thue of Trondheim Kommune and Ian Coles of Wirral Borough Council for the initial *Ingimund Project* we would not have been able to put the Vikings back on the Mersey Agenda and the Anniversary would almost certainly have been missed.

Stephen Harding
Nottingham, December 2002

Steve.Harding@nottingham.ac.uk

ABBREVIATIONS AND PRONUNCIATION

Abbreviations used:

ON	Old Norse (Old Norwegian)
OIr	Old Irish
ODan	Old Danish
OE	Old English
OF	Old French
ME	Middle English
MIr	Middle Irish
OSw	Old Swedish
OIcel	Old Icelandic
OESc	Old East Scandinavian
OWSc	Old West Scandinavian
AD	anno domini
JRC	John Rylands Charter
pers.n.	personal name

Pronunciation of Norse letters

j is pronounced as a y such as in young

v is pronounced as a w such as in will

ö is pronounced like the vowel in her or purr (ø in modern Norwegian)

æ is pronounced like the i in hike or mice

The accent above a vowel as in á, é, í, ó, ú and also ý means the vowel is long

The following additional characters are pronounced as in th:

Lower case form: ð, þ

Upper case form: Ð, Þ

ð, Ð is the "voiced" form of "th" as in "the"

þ, Þ is the "unvoiced" form of "th" as in "think"

CONTENTS

Chapter 1

BLOOD OF VIKING MERSEY

In 2001 the BBC launched the series "Blood of Vikings" with the intention of investigating the evidence for Viking influence in the British Isles. As part of that series 2000 men were tested to see if they had genetic material in their Y-chromosomes comparable to men in the Viking homelands of Norway and Denmark. In the final programme of the series the BBC presented Bill Housley from Wirral - a small peninsula in the North-west of England between the Rivers Mersey and Dee, as one of their best examples of a match with men surveyed in Norway.

Was this a sheer coincidence, or is there something about the history of Merseyside, Chester, West Lancashire and indeed the North-west of England as a whole that makes the finding about Bill's Y-chromosome perhaps not so surprising?

The first clue comes from Bill's home village - Meols, near Hoylake. Meols is an old Viking name or, to be more precise an "Old Norse" name, from "*melr*" meaning "sandbank". "Norse" is used as a term to describe Vikings originating from Norway,

Found on the Wirral, a man with the blood of a warrior

Daily Mail Headline, 5th December 2001. Courtesy of Lawrence H Sear, Managing Editor.

BILL Housley went to the dentist an ordinary fisherman and emerged a fully-fledged Viking.

The 63-year-old grandfather was asked for a saliva sample as part of a scientific study into the Norse invaders of Britain.

Amazingly, it proved he is a direct descendant of the sea-faring warriors who plundered the north

By **Adam Powell**

found - in Scotland - and their genetic heritage was not as strong.

Mr Housley, from Meols, Wirral, said: 'I always thought we were an ordinary fishing family which could be traced back 150 years.

'I was utterly amazed. I didn't know what I was going to be told but it certainly wasn't that I was a Viking. It means that my sons and

2,000 men from Britain, Ireland, Norway, Denmark and northern Germany who took part in the random survey.

Their Y chromosome, which gives information about ancestry, was compared to DNA markers common in Scandinavians.

The research revealed that Norwegian Vikings settled in Scotland, Cumbria, the Isle of Man and as far south as Merseyside.

Norse code: Bill Housley is a true Viking

distinguishing them from Danes. In fact Old Norse (abbreviated as "ON") is very similar to Old Danish (ODan) - although there are subtle differences as we shall see later, and is not too dissimilar to Old English (OE), the language of the early Anglo-Saxon invaders from Northern Germany. The place-name element *Meols* also appears in West Lancashire as North Meols and Meols Hall, all near Southport. And it is no coincidence it also appears in Iceland several times - as *Melar*. So: Vikings in Merseyside and Lancashire? Most definitely yes!

The place-name element most people are aware of as typically Viking is the ending *-by* which means "settlement": and the second clue they were here

Distribution of the bys in England and South Scotland. Adapted from Gillian Fellows-Jensen[1]

YORK

DERBY

	Marsh and alluvium	•	Place-name in -*bý*
	Land over 250m above sea-level	\	Southern boundary of the Danelaw as drawn in the treaty of about 886

[1]G. Fellows Jensen (1992) Scandinavian Place-Names of the Irish Sea Province. In
J. Graham-Campbell ed. *Viking Treasure from the North West*, Chapter 4, National Museums and Guides on Merseyside, Liverpool.

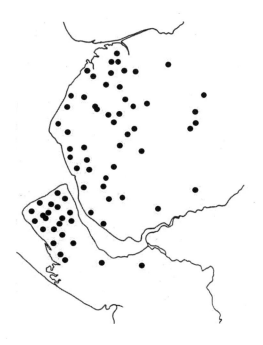

Distribution of place-names in Wirral and West Lancashire bearing Scandinavian or Irish elements.

comes from a consideration of the distribution of place-names in Britain with this element. Experts now regard the place-name *-by* as more typical of Danish as opposed to Norwegian Vikings. If we look at the distribution of all place-names of village and towns which can be traced to Danish, Norse or Norse-Irish roots, the evidence for significant Viking influence in Merseyside and West Lancashire is beyond dispute.

And the influence extends to some surprising quarters. The connoisseur of Association Football may be surprised to learn that at least three of its teams in the area carry the flag of Viking names: the most senior of these is Tranmere, a village in the north of Wirral, which surprised many in 2000 by reaching the final of the English Football League Cup at Wembley Stadium. Across the Mersey into West Lancashire, another Viking village, Skelmersdale reached the final, also at Wembley, of the FA Amateur Cup in 1967, and reached the final again in 1971 to win the trophy. Nearby Burscough FC, which also sports a Viking name, are one of the top sides in the North-west of England outside the Football League.

January 2000:
Tranmere Rovers players celebrate
after winning 4-0 on aggregate in the
semi-final to play at Wembley
Stadium in the English League Cup
Final in front of a capacity 76,000
crowd. Not bad for a Viking village
team!

February 2000:
Viking village team at Wembley.
David Kelly scores the memorable
equalising goal for Trani-melr
against the Premiership giants of
Leicester.

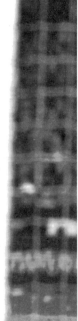

Photographs courtesy of
the Getty Group.

June 1967: Action from Skelmersdale United's (dark shirts) appearance in the FA Amateur Cup Final in 1967. The penalty by Alan Bermingham, watched by 75,000 spectators at Wembley stadium, was saved and the team from Skjaldmarrsdalr lost the replay. They returned however in 1971 and won it. Again not bad for a Viking village team! Courtesy Arthur Gore.

The connection of the area with Scandinavia has surprised many latter day Scandinavians who visit or work in the area. None more so than the many Scandinavian players - past and present, who have plied their trade with Liverpool or Everton Football clubs. In an interview with Norwegian reporter Per Anders Todal of *Dag og tid*, Liverpool FC's Norwegian international Vegard Heggem said the following:

> I found it fascinating to learn about the old Viking settlements. Someone at the Consulate mentioned the Ingimund book to me. I found it interesting to read about the way they moved inwards from the coast towards Bromborough. I have read some of the Norse sagas before. To learn about all the Viking names over here was enjoyable. I don't think a lot of people are aware of this part of the history.

Liverpool FC's Norwegian footballer Vegard Heggem was fascinated by the historical connection. Photo by Per-Anders Todal. Courtesy of Norman Guard and Liverpool FC.

Trani-melr (Tranmere). Water painting of cranes near a sandbank by Serge Nicolle and reproduced with the permission of the EEC Environment/Nature directive.

Trani-melr, Burh-skógr and Skjaldmarrsdalr

Tranmere is in fact a pure Norwegian construction and comes from the elements *trani* - crane, and *melr* - sandbank. The cranes were not of the sort found at the Cammell Laird Shipyard but of the bird type. So we have "crane sandbank", or "the sandbank frequented by crane birds" and the word *trani* is still used in modern Scandinavia for birds of this type: *trane* in Norway and Denmark, and *trana* in Sweden. Also, one of the most influential of the 20th-Century Scandinavian politicians was Martin *Tranmæl* (1879-1967), a key player behind the Norwegian Labour or Socialist movement. The place-names *Tranbjerg* and *Tranebjerg* "crane-bird hill" occur quite frequently in Denmark. The place-name Burscough comes from *Burh-skógr*, the latter element Scandinavian for a "wood" and Skelmersdale from *Skelmerrsdalr* or *Skjaldmarrsdalr* "Skjaldmarr's valley", after the personal name Skelmer, which probably comes from the Old Norse personal name *Skjaldmarr*.

Martin Tranmæl, 20th-Century leader of the Norwegian Socialist movement

Duald's Three Fragments

So, the place-name evidence is pretty convincing. Furthermore, although we know from such evidence that the Vikings settled all over the North-west from the River Dee up to the Solway Firth, the only surviving documented records of Vikings settling in the North-west refer to the Merseyside area, and in particular the Wirral peninsula. These records are ancient Irish annals referred to as the "*Three Fragments*" because of the state they were in when they were rediscovered by the Irishman Duald MacFirbis in the 17th-Century. A surviving copy is kept in the Royal Library (*Bibliothèque Royale*) in Belgium. The settlement these records record - and the date of their arrival - 902AD or thereabouts are now taken as genuine historical fact by scholars.

902AD, Beer mats, Green Knights and "doghters."

The event of 902AD has even captured the imagination of a famous local brewery, who bedecked Merseyside with posters and beer mats, the front side of the latter reminding pub patrons when the last "attack" occurred, the flip-side warning people of what to do just in case they come back again.

The pervading influence of the Scandinavians extended to well after the Norman conquest: Not only are there traces of their language in place-names long afterwards, but we know there was a significant proportion of their words in the speech of the area in the 13th and 14th centuries, as

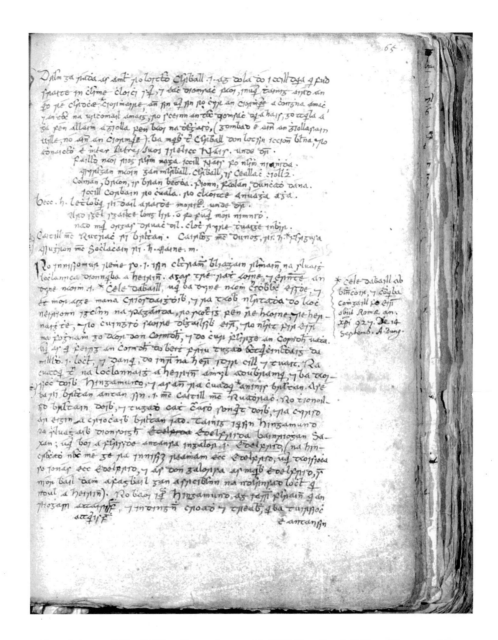

Part of the copy of Duald's Three Fragments, now at the Bibliothèque Royale, Belgium. The names of the holy man, Cele Dubhaill, the Norse leader Ingimund and the King and Queen of the Mercian English - Æthelred and Æthelflæd - are underlined by the scribe.

*Danish Name in a
Norwegian village.*

preserved in poems such as *Sir Gawain and the Green Knight*.[2]   And even as late as 1398 we have evidence of children being named in the Scandinavian way, with people like Mabilla Raynaldesdoghter, Agnes and Johanne Hondesdoghter, and Richard Hondesson paying rentals in Wirral.   And surnames and place-names sometimes make a fascinating combination as the illustration from Scarisbrick shows. So, the discovery about Bill Housley's Y-chromosome may not have been a fluke.

This book now considers all the evidence for the Vikings in Wirral, West Lancashire and Chester, and the fascinations that have gripped people in the whole area with this great Heritage over the years, a fascination encompassed in a movement once known as Mersey Northernism.

[2] J.D. Bu'Lock (1972) Pre-Conquest Cheshire, 383-1066 (in *History of Cheshire, III*), Chester.

Famous beer mat depicting the last Viking arrival and
settlement of 902AD (top) and what to do if they come
back again (bottom).
Courtesy of Cain's brewery, Liverpool.

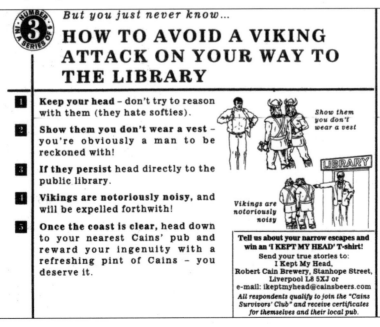

Chapter 2

MERSEY NORTHERNISM

Legend and Reality

Since Viking times, centuries simply passed by as successive generations of the local people lived and generally went about their own business unaware of the region's Viking past. For many life was tough, and the existence for example of all the places surrounding them with the ending *-by* held no real significance for them as they struggled to eke out living. Then by the dawn of the 19th-Century and the growth of the port of Liverpool and its environs, a powerful middle class was emerging, with a burning desire to learn and disseminate facts and stories about the past. This fascination with things gone by was sometimes coupled with a capacity to romanticize and speculate. It is the Victorians for example who propagated the notion that Vikings wore horns on their helmets, and it was two particular local legends - one concerning the Norse god Thor and his association with a rock at Thurstaston, the other concerning the Danish King Canute and his attempt to turn back the tide - which particularly captured their imagination. It was the Victorians on Merseyside who rediscovered the historical tradition of the settlements of the area 1000 years previous. It was the Victorians who also developed the tool of Philology - linguistic and place-name analysis - which became a powerful indicator of the extent of Viking settlements in the North West. It was also the Victorians who were responsible for the significant archaeological finds at Meols, and Cuerdale. Finally it was from the Victorian age that much of the significance of ancient stonework found in the Mersey region was realised. In this Chapter we look at the contribution these Mersey Northernists have made and also the local legends of years gone by that inspired many of them.

Anna Seward

Anna Seward and John Stanley

One of the first to rekindle this spirit and rediscover the Viking or "northernist" past was the poetess Anna Seward (1747-1809), much sought after even in her declining years by the gentlemen of the time, including the novelist Sir Walter Scott. Anna and Scott were friends of the powerful Stanley family who had a great influence on Merseyside in the 18th/19th Centuries: Stanley Park separating Liverpool and Everton football clubs is just one small example. Another is Stanley Road, Hoylake, home of the Royal Liverpool Golf Course in Wirral, which occasionally hosts the British Open Golf Championship. Seward was particularly friendly with Sir John Thomas Stanley. Seward, Stanley, Scott and his friend the Victorian writer William Morris all had one thing in common: they were fascinated by all things Viking… and also all things Icelandic, a language very similar to that once used by the old warriors. As we shall consider later, the Stanleys influence on the area in fact penetrated back much further with Sir John Stanley (1350-1414), Lord of Storeton Hall and also of Lathom, and, supposedly an ancestor of the author.

The 18th-Century Stanley family built a new hotel which opened in Hoylake in 1792: Seward herself, a native of Lichfield, came to the opening jamboree and from then on became a frequent visitor to the Wirral. The awesome atmosphere of the former colony of the North and its Thingwall and Thor was still lingering enough to inspire her to produce two significant Viking works: these were draft paraphrases of two Viking Age poems[3]: *Herva, at the Tomb of Argantyr* - which tells of a Viking woman who seeks revenge for her father's death by using the sword Tifting, and *Harold's Complaint. A Scandinavian Ode*, about Harald Sigurðason ("Harald Hardrada") the Norwegian king killed at the Battle of Stamford Bridge in 1066. Mersey Northernism was born.

Andrew Wawn, who contributed a Chapter on Vikings and Victorians, for "*Wirral and its Viking Heritage*"[4] says the following

> During the Napoleonic wars Icelandic woollens, skins, eider down, whale oil and dried fish were familiar sights and smells on the quayside at Pier Head, while Icelanders stranded by the Napoleonic wars would head for home up the Mersey on the brig 'John Thomas Stanley'. At the beginning of the Century few native Merseysiders or embarking Icelanders would have realised that some of those distant homes among the lava and lyme grass of sixty-six degrees north were closely linked by name with equivalent locations on the Wirral - as with West Kirby and *Vestri-Kirkjubær*, Meols and *Melar*.

[3] W. Scott, ed. *The Collected Poems of Anna Seward* III, 90-103.

[4] P. Cavill, S.E. Harding and J. Jesch, (2000) *Wirral and its Viking Heritage*, Chapter 9, English Place-Name Society, Nottingham, 2000.

To this list could be added others such as North Meols and Croxteth of West Lancashire (*Króksstaðir* in Iceland), Thingwall in Wirral and Thingwall Hall of West Lancashire (*Thingvellir* in Iceland) and also the Kirkbys of Wirral (old name for Wallasey Village) and West Lancashire (*Kirkjubær* in Iceland). The lack of awareness about the northern past was thus soon being addressed as the interests of more and more on both sides of the Mersey were steadily being kindled. Another of John Stanley's colleagues was Henry Holland from Chester who "travelled widely in, and wrote influentially about, Iceland before assuming his twin roles as Queen Victoria's favourite Physician and mid-Victorian Britain's best connected supporter of Icelandic causes and culture."[5]

The Earls of Derby, the Custs and the Canute Legend

Besides the Stanley family, another family which had a great influence on Merseyside were the Earls of Derby, who in fact were also descendants of the Stanleys. The 5th Earl was responsible for the construction of Leasowe Castle in 1592, the sands outside being host to the Derby races before moving to Newmarket and then Epsom. By the early 19th-Century the property came into possession of the Boode family, and Mary Anne Boode married Sir Edward Cust K.C.B. from Belton, Lincolnshire, in or sometime near the year 1821. The Custs apparently picked up on a local tradition that it was at some, unspecified location along the seafront between Meols, Lingham and Moreton Shore that Canute, King of England 1017-1035, of Denmark and Norway, undertook his famous attempt to turn back the waves. "*Sea come not hither nor wet the sole of my foot*" was carved on the back of the so-called Canute Chair. This was once on the sea-front at Leasowe Castle before being destroyed by vandals and used as firewood, as recorded by the local writer N.F. Ellison in 1955.[6]

Stopping the flooding at Meols and Moreton shore: Canute turning back the waves. Vikings depicted as having horned helmets, a modern tradition from the Victorians. Illustration by Frank Hampson[7] and reproduced courtesy of Peter Hampson.

[5] Andrew Wawn, ed. *The Icelandic Journal of Henry Holland, 1810*, Hakluyt Society, 2nd Series, 168 (London).

[6] N.F. Ellison (1955) *The Wirral Peninsula*, Redwood Burn Ltd., Trowbridge & Esher, U.K.

[7] In L. du Garde Peach (1968) *Kings and Queens of England*, Wills & Hepworth Ltd., London.

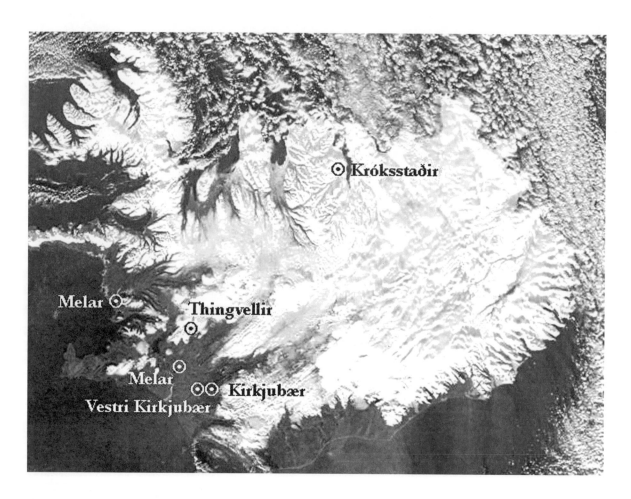

Satellite map of Iceland (taken February 2nd 2002), showing Króksstaðir (Croxteth),
Thingvellir (Thingwall) Vestri Kirkjubær (West Kirby) and Kirkjubær (Kirkby) and two
Melar, one at Borganes (top) the other at Fluðir.

*Signpost to Melar "Meols"
in Fluðir, Iceland.*

Farm at Melar.

Signpost to Kirkjubær "Kirkby" in Iceland.

Sunset over Vestri Kirkjubær "West Kirby" in Iceland.

Photographs courtesy of Ragnar Th. Sigurðsson.

"N.F. Ellison seated on chair 1923. The chair was then situated on the sea-wall of the castle by the entrance gates to the sea. On the back was carved: SEA COME NOT HITHER NOR WET THE SOLE OF MY FOOT. Vandals partly destroyed the chair and when I made enquiries at the castle when I was gathering information for my Wirral book, I was shown at the boiler house a remnant. The chair had been chopped up to fire the boiler. This would be in 1950".

A similar fate of vandalism had earlier befallen a Norse cross in Wallasey Village, which was apparently "a monolith standing twelve feet high and covered with curious cuttings" and was destroyed by vandals in the seventeenth-Century: the interested reader can read a chapter written by J.D. Bu'Lock in *Wirral and its Viking Heritage*.[8]

The Cust family may well have catalysed the propagation of the legend on Merseyside, although the speed of propagation might also show the affection in which the Scandinavian heritage of the area was held locally. The Canute story is recorded by Henry of Huntingdon in the 12th-Century without specifying the place, and Henry's language is echoed by the inscription on the Wirral seat. Henry records Canute saying to the sea,

> I command you therefore not to rise on my land, nor to presume to wet the clothing or limbs of your master.[9]

Leasowe Castle, Wirral. Home of the Earls of Derby and then the Cust family. Photography taken in 1917, showing the central tower built in 1593 by the 5th Earl.
Courtesy of Iain Boumphrey

Also in the 12th-Century, the Anglo-Norman historian Geoffrey Gaimar mentions that Canute tried to stem the waves, but the place is given as Westminster, on the tidal estuary of the Thames.[10] Magnus Magnusson writing in *Vikings!*[11], points out that contrary to popular belief, Canute did not think he could turn the tide back; he staged the charade on the seashore as a parable for his arrogant courtiers, to show that only God had power over the sea, and over them - including kings and courtiers.

Clearly the story is legendary, but it would have a particular relevance for the medieval inhabitants of Wirral[12] who were suffering periodic tidal inundation: not even the great Canute, King of England and more than half of Scandinavia could turn back the waves. In view of this, a medieval origin for the Wirral tradition is not unimaginable.

8 P. Cavill, S.E. Harding and J. Jesch (2000) *Wirral and its Viking Heritage*, Chapter 6, English Place-Name Society, Nottingham.

9 D. Greenway ed. (1996) *Henry, Archdeacon of Huntingdon Historia Angolorum: The History of the English People* (Oxford), iv, 8, pp 366-8.

10 A. Bell ed. (1960) *L'Estoire des Engleis, by Geffrei Gaimar* (Oxford), lines 4693 f.

11 Magnus Magnusson (1980) *Vikings!* Elsevier-Dutton Pub. Co., Amsterdam, Holland/London, U.K./ New York, USA, 180 p 275-276. Second Edition, 2000 (Harvill Press).

12 This happened right up until the 20th-Century reinforcement of the sea defences. The home of the author's mother's family at Pasture Lane, Moreton Shore, also suffered such periodic flooding.

King Canute's chair at Leasowe with N.F. "Nomad" Ellison. The inscription "Sea come not hither nor wet the sole of my foot" can just be seen.
Photograph courtesy of Frank Biddle.

Flood Scene, Kerr's Field, Moreton, 1912. Despite Canute's unavailability to help on this occasion, everyone still seems happy!

Sir James Picton and the Thor stone legend

Perhaps the greatest symbol of Mersey Northernism is the impressive Thor's stone at Thurstaston common, Wirral. Notwithstanding the much greater historical significance of nearby Thingwall and Meols, it is Thors stone that Wirralians and Merseysiders treasure as their outstanding focal point for their Viking heritage. And it is indeed impressive, befitting the great northern god himself as he rides through the heavens protecting the world from the Frost Giants.

The stone itself - a huge outcrop of sandstone - is considered to represent the hammerhead of *Mjöllnir*, Thors hammer. In 2001 it was the scene of a visitation by the Deputy Mayor of Trondheim in Norway, Ms. Liv Sandven, and the Director of Cultural and Religious Affairs, Mr. Gerhard Dalen, an event recorded in the Norwegian newspaper *Adresseavisen*. The

Thors's Stone, Thurstaston. Its size can be gauged from two of the author's sons (Thomas and Matthew) on top of it.

article reported that the Norwegian delegation were happy that the former colony was still looking after their hammer. This was one of a number of articles appearing in Norwegian and Icelandic papers and TV and radio broadcasts surrounding the publication of *Wirral and its Viking Heritage,* and *Ingimund's Saga, Norwegian Wirral.* Ms Sandven, Mr. Dalen and the Ambassador of Iceland were guests of honour at the official launch of the books at Birkenhead Town Hall on February 23rd.

The antiquity of the legend is impossible to determine. It was the Victorians, and one in particular, who let their imaginations flow. Just as the Cust family developed an apparently local tradition about Canute, it was Sir James Picton (1805-1889), a pillar of the Liverpool community who developed the local tradition about Thor's stone in a series of prominent lectures and writings. Picton propagated the story that the rock was once used by the Vikings as a sacrificial altar in honour of Thor[13]

> This record of Danish heathendom… the gigantic rock altar

P. Sulley in his books *The Hundred of the Wirral* (Birkenhead, 1889) and *History of Ancient and Modern Birkenhead*, (Murphy, Liverpool, 1907) wrote

---

[13] J.A. (Sir James) Picton (1877) The Great Stone of Thor, *Notes and Queries* 5th Series 8, 364-5: Besides musing on its possible sacrificial role, he welcomes the news that the site was to be preserved from developers.

Thór, with his chariot, his goats and hammer Mjöllnir, confronting the Frost Giants. 1872 painting by Mårtin Eskil Winge. Reproduced, courtesy of the Swedish National Museum, Stockholm.

The great stone of Thor was reddened with the blood of
priests and captives.

Hilda Gamlin who wrote the books *Memories/The Chronicles of Birkenhead: the
Scenes and People of its Early Days*, (Holwell, Liverpool, 1892) and *'Twixt Mersey
and Dee* (Marples, Liverpool, 1897) made the fascinating connection with the
battle of Brunanburh:

The stone was probably raised by the Danes to
commemorate the great battle of Brunanburh.

There has been a lot of discussion concerning whether the stone we see
today was actually there in a similar form back in Viking times. There is
some indication of quarrying in the area during medieval times, and some
have argued that Thor's stone is what was possibly part of the area that was
left unquarried. We just don't know. One thing we can say with some
certainty - if the settlers did, like the latter day Merseysiders, associate this
place with Thor then it would not have been used for
sacrifices - the settlement period was quite late in
the Viking period when that practice was rare.
Scandinavian settlers arriving from Ireland
would have been at least partly
Christianized during their stay in Ireland.

*Sir James Picton, Victorian
antiquarian. Photograph courtesy of
the Picton Reference Library,
Liverpool.*

The stone is situated at the highest
point of Wirral - Thurstaston Common -
and it is well known that this part of
Wirral is most prone to lightning strikes
during thunderstorms. It is not
unimaginable that Viking settlers in this
area, whilst working the farmstead of
Thorsteinn, made the connection with their
pagan god after witnessing such an event over a
millennium ago.

Stephens and Sephton

On the other side of the Mersey, a growing band of Liverpudlian
northernists were promoting Norse scholarship. Familiarity with Icelandic
and the Old Norse tongue was not considered an oddity in Victorian
Merseyside. Quite the contrary, and one of these was the Copenhagen-based

scouser Professor George Stephens (1813-95) whose most notable contribution was his translation of Frithiof's Saga (*Friðþjófs saga*) from Icelandic into English.[14]   Another Mersey scholar of Old Norse and champion of the North was the Reverend John Sephton, Reader in Icelandic at the newly founded University College of Liverpool. Sephton[15], like Stephens, also produced widely used translations of Norse Sagas, namely Sverri's Saga and Olaf Trygvasson's Saga (*Ólafs saga Tryggvasonar*), and like Picton was well known on Merseyside for his public speaking on all things Viking. Indeed, Sephton's house was frequently visited by many of the Viking and Icelandic Scholars of the time, the most notable being the Oxford Professor of Icelandic Guðbrandur Vigfússon. Sephton made the astonishing identification of the place *Hlíðarendi* in another Old Norse saga - *Njals Saga* with Litherland in Liverpool.[16]

Francis Tudsbury and the Battle of Brunanburh

Francis Tudsbury was another Victorian bitten by the spirit of Thingwall and Thor. A former Oxford undergraduate he became a close friend of the Cambridge-based Icelandic scholar Eiríkur Magnússon. Magnússon was responsible for translating several Norse Sagas into English, but both were convinced that the *Brunanburh* of the famous battle must have been Bromborough, years before the penetrating analysis of John McNeal Dodgson[17] and others, and Tudsbury published the arguments in 1907[18].

Fergusson Irvine - The Cheshire Sheaf.

The *Cheshire Sheaf* was a monthly journal started in the late 19th-Century and provided until recently a useful forum for historical and other discussion about Chester and Wirral. Many of the articles from the *Sheaf* of relevance to the Scandinavian settlements were considered in *Ingimund's Saga*. For example one concerned a place called *The Arno* in Oxton - linked to a Viking burial, and another three concerned a series of field names in Caldy (including the *Kneckyn* - the old name for Caldy Hill), and the West Kirby area of Wirral. Many involved penetrating detective work presumably undertaken by the Birkonian William Fergusson Irvine, a very prominent local historian at the turn of the 19th-Century. One such piece by him appeared in the 1902 volume. It quoted and commented on part of a 16th-Century rental of the Earl of Derby which identifies in Bidston, Wirral, two former thwaites or

[14] A. Wawn (1995) George Stephens, Cheapinghaven, and Old Northern Antiquity. *Studies in Medievalism 7*, 63-104

[15] A. Wawn, see footnote 4

[16] J. Sephton (1904) Notes on South Lancashire place-names in Domesday Book, *Otia Merseiana 4*, 65-74

[17] See Chapter 5 in P Cavill, S.E. Harding and J. Jesch (2000) *Wirral and its Viking Heritage*, English Place-Name Society, Nottingham, and Chapter 11 in S.E. Harding (2000) *Ingimund's Saga, Norwegian Wirral*, Countyvise Ltd, Birkenhead.

[18] F.W.T. Tudsbury (1907) *Brunanburh A.D. 937* (London and Chester).

þveits, long since lost: Uttertwaite (ON: *úttar* or *utar* "outer" and *þveit* "clearing") and Indertwaite (ON: *innar* "inner").

> FROM CHESHIRE SHEAF, VOL. 4, MARCH 1902, PAGE 23-25. EXTRACT FROM ARTICLE 589: RENTAL OF THE (2ND) EARL OF DERBY'S PROPERTY IN WIRRAL, 1521-2
> Uttertwaite and Indertwaite or as we should now call them Outer Thwaite and Inner Thwaite, are probably represented by the modern Tassey's Thwaite, Whinney Thwaite, Spencer's Thwaite and the rest of the group of fields known as the Thwaites down on the Bidston Moss… Wm. Fergusson Irvine.
>
> The rental: "Hankyn Hycoke and another for one close called Uttertwaite containing 40 acres of land, 40s 0d; Richard Smyth for a close of land called Indertwaite containing 24 acres of land, 24s 0d".

More examples can be found in *Ingimund's Saga*.

W. G. Collingwood

Perhaps the Liverpudlian to make the greatest contribution to Northern

W. G. Collingwood 1854-1932

antiquarianism was William G. Collingwood, born in 1854. He was a brilliant artist, and was inspired by many trips he took as a youngster with his father to the Lake District. Later as a student at Oxford he was influenced by the works of the earlier Northernists, particularly William Morris, author of the *Story of Sigurd the Volsung and the Fall of the Niblungs*, and this combination of artistic skill and Viking fascination proved most powerful.

Like the other Mersey Northernists he found trips to Iceland irresistible, and based on a visit in 1897 he produced some 150 water paintings that now reside in the Icelandic National Museum. His experiences prompted the publication of a book with Jón Stefánsson[19] in which he makes the remarkable comment about one of the Icelandic Sagas which he had helped illustrate:

[19] W.G. Collingwood and Jón Stefánsson (1899) *A Pilgrimage to the Saga-steads of Iceland* (Ulverston).

Kormak's own home had been founded by his father on the Meols, as the gravelly shore-banks would be called on the coast of Lancashire, and was thence called Mel, now Melstad[20].

He was an expert in Northern crosses and ancient stonework. In 1927 he published *Northumbrian Crosses of the Pre-Norman Age,* illustrated with his own drawings, followed the next year by *Early Monuments of West Kirby* - again illustrated with his own drawings, including the remarkable hogback tombstone of West Kirby. This article was reprinted as Chapter 7 in *Wirral and its Viking Heritage*. In the Lake District, where he lived for many years, the large but attractive war memorial erected in 1919 in the churchyard of St. Michael & All Angels' Church, Hawkshead, was designed by him. He also wrote a novel set around his home next to Lake Coniston *Thorstein of the Mere, A Saga of the Northmen in Lakeland*. Collingwood proved a powerful ambassador for both the Lake District - his new home - and Merseyside - his birthright. Upon his election as President of the Viking Society for Northern Research, he ensured that one of the handful of areas considered powerful enough in Viking roots to have a representative on the Society's Council, was Wirral, Merseyside.

---

[20] This was *Kormak's Saga*. See Chapter (9) by Andrew Wawn in P. Cavill, S.E. Harding and J. Jesch (2000) *Wirral and its Viking Heritage*, English Place-Name Society, Nottingham.

Chapter 3
902A.D.

902AD is the year recognised as the start of the migrations of Scandinavians into the North-west of England, stretching from the River Dee to the Solway Firth. 902AD corresponds to the mass expulsion from the old Viking kingdom of Dublin following a significant defeat inflicted on the Vikings by the Irish. The only surviving record we have of this wholesale exodus across the Irish Sea is in an ancient Irish Annal now referred to as *The Three Fragments,* but this has been reinforced by contemporary reports from the *Annals of Ulster,* and the Welsh chronicles: *Annales Cambriae* and *Brut y Tywysogion,* and indirectly by the *Anglo-Saxon Chronicle.* The *Three Fragments* describe the expedition of the Norseman Ingimund who established Wirral as a Scandinavian colony.

Ingimund origin

Although the Norse Viking expeditions had started in the 8th-Century - and raids in Ireland from about 795AD - the great exodus of peoples out of Norway is said to have followed the unification of Norway from 880AD onwards, by Harald Harfagre - *Hárfagri,* the fine hair - which saw them move to other lands, many never to return. Whereas the Danes largely came into England along its eastern coast as an attempted military conquest, the Norwegians who were either expelled by Harald or who were just following a great thirst for adventure - a characteristic of these peoples - headed westwards, settling in the Orkneys, Shetland, Faroes and Iceland. From there some headed further west to Greenland and North America (as recorded in the Vinland sagas). After passing northern Britain, a large number then headed south, some stopping at the Isle of Man, and many ending up in the newly founded Viking kingdom of Dublin.

It was from here, as recorded in the *Three Fragments,* that Ingimund's men were expelled in 902, which would have been some twenty years after the initial departure from Norway. Although the bulk of the migrations probably happened in the first two decades of the 10th-Century, fresh waves of settlers continued to come in, many based on trading via the seaport of Meols and the new financial centre of Chester. Not all the Scandinavians were from Ireland and it may be that the proportion of Danes to Norsemen was much larger than originally thought. The final major expulsion of Norsemen from Ireland at the Battle of Clontarf in 1014AD probably

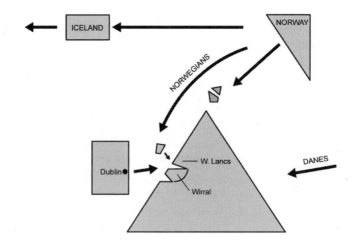

The exodus from Norway.
Drawing by John Harding.

marked the last of the exodus of Scandinavian settlers into the North-west.

The following is extracted from some old Irish annals called the *Three Fragments* which describe the arrival of the first group of Scandinavians led by Ingimund (called Hingamund by the Irish) into the Wirral peninsula at the start of the 10th-Century. These were people who had been driven out of Ireland by Caerbhall, leader of the Leinster Irish in the year 902AD. Then they made a brief but unsuccessful attempt to settle in Anglesey, but were driven out of there too - then received permission from "Edelfrida, queen of the Saxons" (Æthelflæd, daughter of Alfred the Great) to settle in "lands near Chester" later identified as Wirral.

THE STORY OF INGIMUND
(from "Fragmenta Tria Annalium Hiberniæ", Bibliothèque Royale, Brussels, MS. 5301-5320, fo. 33a-fo. 34b).

We have related above, namely in the fourth year before us, of the expulsion of the Norse hosts from Ireland; through the fasting and praying of the holy man, namely Céle Dabhaill, for he was a saintly, devout man. The Norsemen, then, departed from Ireland as we have said and Hingamund was their leader, and where they went to was the island of Britain[21]. The king of Britain at this time was the son of Cadell, son of Rhodri. The

[21] Island of Britain = Anglesey

men of Britain[22] assembled against them, and they were driven by force from the territories of the men of Britain. Afterwards Hingamund came with his forces to Edelfrida queen of the Saxons, for her husband, that is Edelfrid, was that time in disease (let no one blame me although I have already mentioned the death of Edelfrid, and it was from the disease that Edelfrid died, but I did not wish to leave unwritten what the Norsemen did after going from Ireland). Now Hingamund was asking lands of the queen in which he would settle, and on which he would build huts and dwellings, for at this time he was weary of war. Then Edelfrida gave him lands near Chester, and he stayed there for a long time. The result of this was, when he saw the city full of wealth and the choice of land around it, he desired to possess them. Afterwards Hingamund came to the leaders of the Norsemen and the Danes; he made a great complaint in their presence, and he said that they were not well off without good lands, and that it was right for them all to seize Chester and to possess it with its wealth and its lands. Many great battles and wars arose on account of that. This is what he said: "Let us beseech and implore them first, and if we do not get them willingly in this way let us contest them by force". All the leaders of the Norsemen and the Danes agreed to do this. Ingimund then came to his house, with an assembly following him. Though they made this council a secret, the queen came to know of it. Therefore the queen collected large forces around her in every direction, and the city of Chester was filled with her hosts.

The armies of the Danes and Norsemen assembled towards Chester and, since they did not get their consent by beseeching or supplication, they proclaimed battle on a certain day. On that day they came to attack the city; there was a large force with many freemen in the city awaiting them. When the forces who were in the city saw, from the wall of the city, the great armies of the Danes and Norsemen approaching them, they sent messengers to the king of the Saxons who was in a disease, and on the point of death at that time, to ask his advice and the advice of the queen. This was the advice they gave: to make battle near the city outside, and the gate of the city should be wide open, and to choose a body of horsemen, concealed on the inside, and those of the people of the city who should be

---

[22] Britain = Wales. The Vikings called Wales *Bretland,* 'Land of the Brits'.

stronger in the battle should flee back into the city as if in defeat, and when the greater number of the forces of the Norsemen came inside the gate of the city the force hidden yonder should close the gate after this band and not admit any more; capture those who came into the city and kill them all. This was all done accordingly, and complete slaughter was thus made of the Danes and Norsemen. Great, however, as was that slaughter, Norsemen did not abandon the city, for they were stubborn and vicious, but they all said that they would make many hurdles, and put posts into them, and pierce the wall under them. This was not delayed; the hurdles were made, and the forces were under them to pierce the wall, for they were eager to take the city to avenge their people.

Then the king (who was on the point of death) and the queen sent messengers to the Irishmen who were among the pagans (for there were many Irish among the pagans), to say to the Irishmen: "Life and health to you from the king of the Saxons, who is in disease, and from his queen, who has all authority over the Saxons, and they are certain that you are true and trusty friends to them. Therefore you should take their side; for they did not bestow any greater honour to a Saxon warrior or cleric than to each warrior and cleric who came to them from Ireland, because this inimical race of pagans is equally hostile to you also. It is right, then, for you, as you are trusty friends, to help them on this occasion." This was the same as if it was said to them: We have come from faithful friends of yours to address you so that you ask the Danes what token of lands and treasures they would give to those who would betray the city to them. If they accept this, to bring them to swear to a place where it will be easy to kill them; and when they will be swearing by their swords and by their shields, as is their custom, they will lay aside all their missile weapons. They all did accordingly, and they put away their arms. And the reason why the Irishmen did this to the Danes was because they were less friends to them than to the Norsemen. Many of them were killed in this manner for large rocks and large beams were thrown down upon them; great numbers also [were killed] by darts and spears and by every other means for killing man.

But the other forces, the Norsemen, were under the hurdles piercing the walls. What the Saxons and the Irishmen who were among them did was to throw large rocks so that they destroyed the hurdles over them. What they did in the face of this was to place large posts under the hurdles. What the Saxons did was to put all the ale and water of the town in the cauldrons of the town, to boil them and pour them over those who were under the hurdles so that the skins were stripped from them. The answer which the Norsemen gave to this was to spread hides on the hurdles. What the Saxons did was to let loose on the attacking force all the beehives in the town, so that they could not move their legs or hands from the great numbers of bees stinging them. Afterwards they left the city and abandoned it. It was not long after that [before they came] to wage battle again.

Translation by the late Professor I.L. Foster, of Jesus College, Oxford.

The story or saga of Ingimund thus tells of his departure from Ireland with his fellow band of Norsemen, then an aborted attempt to land in Anglesey followed by his arrival in the Wirral in or soon after 902AD after securing an agreement with Æthelflæd, queen of the Mercian English. It tells of his subsequent restlessness and of continued attempts of the new Scandinavian colony - which comprised of Norwegians, Danes and Irish - to acquire by force the city of Chester. The story ends with the note

It was not long after that before they came to wage battle again.

The Ingimund saga is not only beautifully preserved in the Irish annals but is also supported by Welsh Chronicles which in *Annales Cambriae* and *Brut y Tywysogion* record the aborted attempt to settle in Anglesey. *Annales Cambriae* (entry for year 902AD)[23] :

Igmund came to Mona (Anglesey) and took Maes Osfeilion (Osmeliaun).

Brut y Tywysogion (entry for 900AD)[24] :

900 was the year of Christ when Igmund came to the island of Anglesey and he held Maes Rhosmeilon.

Although there is no direct record of him by the Anglo-Saxon Chroniclers - who were more preoccupied by the Danes in the East - they do record the

[23] see J.D. Morris, translator (1980) *Nennius. The British History and the Welsh Annals* (Chichester).
[24] see T. Jones, editor (1952) *Brut Y Tywysogion, or the Chronicle of the Princes* (University of Wales, Cardiff).

refortification of Chester by Æthelflæd in 907AD, which corresponds with the attacks. This was followed by construction of further forts in the area, including Eddisbury (914AD), and Runcorn (915AD) thereby containing the growing and restless colony from spreading deep into Cheshire: its growth, together with the steady build up of Norse power in the North country resulting in the establishment of the Norse kingdom of York sparked a need for containment. J McNeal Dodgson says the following[25]

> The urgency of the need for fortification on this frontier cannot have been lessened by the existence upon the frontier itself of restless Norse colonies, whose territories would serve as excellent beach-heads for any expedition striking down into Mercia along a short, direct and strategic route from Mersey.

Apart from the largely Danish-led movements from the East, the Wirral settlement - recorded in Irish and Welsh annals - is the only Norse settlement into North-west England which is documented as such in medieval times.

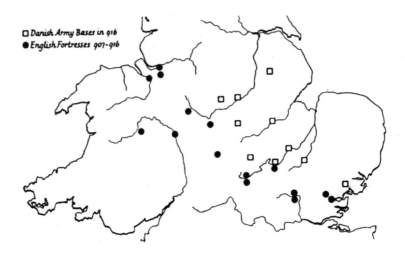

□ Danish Army Bases in 916
● English Fortresses 907-916

Containing the menace of the Wirral Norsemen[26]. The bulk of the English defences were designed to contain the Danes to the East and North. Three forts constructed at Chester (907), Eddisbury (914) and Runcorn (915) were built for different purposes: to contain the Mersey Norsemen.

[25] J. Mc N. Dodgson (1957) The Background of Brunanburh, *Saga-Book of the Viking Society 14*, 303-16. See aso footnote 6.

[26] From F.T. Wainwright (1975) Aethelflaed Lady of the Mercians. In P. Clemoes ed, *The Anglo-Saxons: Studies in Some Aspects of their History and Culture Presented to Bruce Dickens* (Bowes and Bowes, London), pp53-70.

Timeline Ingimund

We can map out a timeline for Ingimund and the Norse invaders in the forty year or so period from 870AD until 907AD and beyond:

870AD: Expulsion from Norway by Harald Hárfagri.
                Settlement of Dublin.
902AD: Expulsion from Dublin.
                Attempted settlement of Anglesey.
                Battle of Osmeliaun or Ros Meilon: expulsion by the Britons.
                Permission to settle in Wirral from Æthelflæd, Lady of the Mercians.
907AD: Meeting of Wirral Norse and Danish chiefs at Thingwall
                Refortification of Chester by Æthelflæd.
                Attacks on Chester commence.
Post907AD: Scandinavian community established in the south of the city.

The Ingimund manuscripts

The transcripts describing the story of Ingimund have themselves had a fascinating history. The particular part of the Irish annals containing the Ingimund story became known as the *Three Fragments*, which themselves became lost. A vellum manuscript of unknown antiquity came into the possession of a certain Dubhaltach or Duald MacFirbis who made a copy. This then came into the possession of a Nehemias MacEgan. Although that particular copy was also subsequently lost, another copy that had been made eventually found its way to a John O'Donovan who edited and published the story with the Irish Archaeological and Celtic Society in 1860. For the last 140 years the story which has come from "a copy of a copy of a vellum manuscript of unknown antiquity" has been under the scrutiny of scholars worldwide, but the general consensus now is that, despite the fictional nature of some of the text, the essence of the Ingimund story must be true. This conclusion is largely thanks to a penetrating and exhaustive study by F.T. Wainwright in two papers: North-west Mercia, and Ingimund's Invasion, published in the 1940s, and both reprinted in 2000 in *Wirral and its Viking Heritage*. It fits in exactly with all the Scandinavian place-names and name-elements in the major and minor names of the area, which include Irish names such as Irby (Old Norse: *Ira-býr* "settlement of the Irish"), Liscard (Old Irish: *lios na carraige* "hall on a rock") and Noctorum (Old Irish *cnocc-tírim* "hill that's dry"). The same element *cnocc* appears to be present in *Kneckyn* which is now Caldy Hill. We know there were also Danes in the area from Denhall "Danes' spring", from Old Norse *Danir*, or Old English *Dene* "Danes", and there is a growing body of support for the suggestion that the large number of place-names, past and present, with the ending element *-by*, are indications that most of the Scandinavian speakers on Wirral would have come from somewhere other than Ireland: this is considered further in the following Chapter. We even have a fairly good idea about the site where Ingimund may have discussed with his fellow Norsemen and Danes plans for expanding the community to incorporate Chester: an emergency meeting of the Thing at Thingwall.

Ingimund and his fellow settlers are historical fact. What was the nature of the Scandinavian community - and its composition - all those years ago. And what was its relation with the surrounding English and Celtic communities?

Thingwall, Wirral.
Photograph courtesy of Trine
Andersen.

Chapter 4

INGIMUND'S WIRRAL

So having arrived in what has been described as "mass migration numbers" into a previously empty Wirral from 902AD and beyond, where did all these new colonists get to? Hundreds of place-names provide us with a clue as to how far they penetrated - and at what density. To assist, the illustration below shows a 19th-Century map of Wirral parishes - a map which has remained little changed since the time of the Vikings and Domesday - and on it we have indicated the boundary demarking the limit of of what is believed to have been the original settlement area: this boundary is essentially that suggested by the Oxford Archaeologist David Griffiths based on the distribution of major place-names of Scandinavian origin, and also by the place-name and linguistic expert or "philologist" John McNeal Dodgson based on manors held by Scandinavians at the time of the Domesday survey (1086AD), instigated after the Norman conquest of England.

The Wirral Parishes and the Scandinavian enclave. The 19th-Century distribution of parishes has remained remarkably unchanged since Viking times and Domesday.

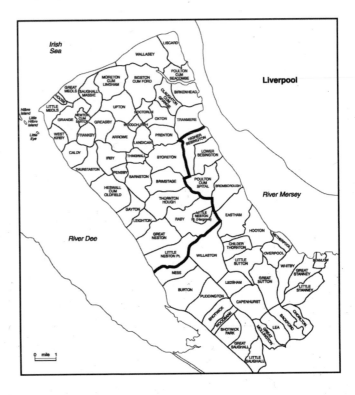

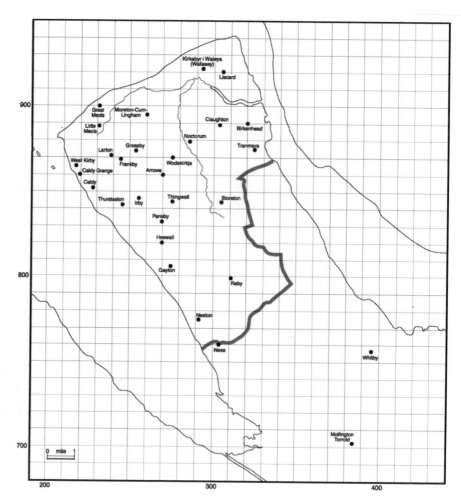

Major Wirral Place names with
Scandinavian elements.

Parishes to the north and west of the boundary shown in the illustrations represent the main Scandinavian enclave whose bounds are defined by the River Dee, Neston/Raby, Lower Dibbinsdale, Storeton Hill and Tranmere, the River Mersey and the the Irish Sea.

We can further assess the significance of this boundary by looking at the distribution of all the names in the Wirral - major and minor - of Scandinavian or Irish-Scandinavian origin. The minor names include field names and topographical features like hills and slopes (ON *brekka*, OIr *cnocc*), hillocks and mounds (ON *haugr*), hollows or "slacks" (ON *slakki*), projecting rocks (ODan *klint*), ravines or dips (ON *gil*), lanes or rakes (ON *rák*), marshes or carrs (ON *kjarr*[27]), and islands in marshy areas (ON *hólmr*). To achieve this data, although earlier researchers such as J. McNeal Dodgson in his exhaustive treatise on the place-names of Cheshire had identified the origins of virtually all of the place-names in Wirral, their precise locations in terms of Ordnance Survey coordinates were provided for only a fraction. To pin down the other coordinates the present author spent many a day visiting the Chester Record Office to compare 19th-Century Tithe maps and Apportionments with modern day Ordnance Survey maps; visits to the John Rylands Library in Manchester, to view some of the ancient Wirral Charters now stored there, were also necessary. The result shows a higher density of minor names in the north of the peninsula, although clearly the Scandinavian influence is seen to stretch across the whole of the peninsula. However, it is important to realise that names for most of the minor field-names as

Distribution of all the Wirral names with Scandinavian elements. The □ marks Þingvöllr (Thingwall). The battle sign marks a suggested site for the battle of Brunanburh, 937AD.

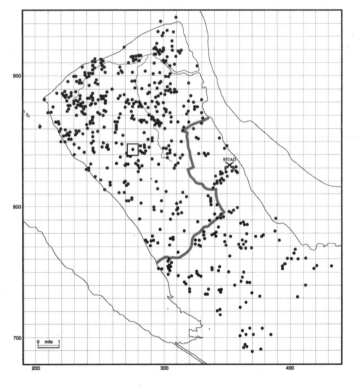

recorded, would have been assigned centuries after the initial settlement period: the presence of Scandinavian elements in these names would probably have arisen from dialect words that had still remained in the local 'Middle English' language.   *In short what a comparison of the major name distribution and the minor name distribution appears to be showing is that the initial settlement area was in the north of the peninsula, but subsequently spread to the whole.* There are however alternative views as to where the initial settlement of Ingimund may have been before the enclave in the north end had been established. As discussed recently by Judith Jesch in *Wirral and its Viking Heritage*, Margaret Gelling has suggested that the initial settlements were on the outskirts of Chester. Ingimund and the initial settlers became overlords near Chester, thereby creating a "safe haven" for subsequent waves of Scandinavian settlers coming in from Ireland, the Isle of Man and the Western Isles, and the Danelaw who then took over the northern end of the Wirral peninsula. This is an example of what is called the Kenneth Cameron theory of "secondary migration".   An archaeological dig is currently underway at Heronbridge, south of Chester to look for possible evidence of Ingimund's supposed initial settlement site.

We can also see from this distribution how sensible was the choice by the settlers of a suitable place for the Thing: Thingwall is right in the centre of the Scandinavian enclave. Significantly the boundary cuts round the parish of Raby, a name which comes from the Old Norse *rá-býr* or Old Danish *rá-bý*[28] meaning "border village or settlement". Moving northwards from there it follows lower Dibbinsdale (or "Plymyard Dale"), Mickledale (from *Mikill-dalr* meaning "great-valley"), and then along the boundary between the north of Raby, Thornton, Brimstage and Storeton parishes with the "English" Poulton and Higher Bebington parishes - following the ridge of high ground, including what is now Prospect and Storeton Hills, up to "Norse" Tranmere parish as the Eastern extent. Raby, Hargrave/Little Neston and Neston parishes form the southern de-limiter, with the old boundary probably not too far off from where Mill Lane and Damhead Lane now run.

The South-eastern boundary region covering the Raby, Hargrave and Willaston areas is particularly interesting, and the subject of several articles in the Cheshire Sheaf, recently reviewed in *Ingimund's Saga.*[29] Hargrave itself, although an English name, was a manor owned by a Scandinavian at least by the time of Domesday, with a gentleman by the name of *Ásgautr* recorded by the Domesday scribes as "Osgot", the pre-conquest lord. The English name for Hargrave ("the hoar wood" from OE har and græfe) also conveys a boundary. J. McN. Dodgson, in Part IV of *The Place Names of Cheshire* writes on page 228:

[28] Opinion seems moving now in favour of the Old Danish form, *bý*.

[29] S.E. Harding (2000) *Ingimund's Saga, Norwegian Wirral.* p116, Countyvise, Birkenhead.

Hargrave was a manor in the same hands as Little Neston. The element *har* is probably used here in the sense 'boundary' hence 'the boundary wood', cf. Raby. Boundary marks and territory would tend to be left undisturbed for fear of trespass, and an unbroken wood or an untouched boundary stone would grow mossy, venerable and 'hoary' with age.

It is also interesting to note that the current boundary for Wirral Metropolitan Borough also cuts along the southern edge of Raby and Hargrave, although the full extent of the modern cut across Wirral is from West to East and excludes Leighton and Neston, whereas the conjectured Scandinavian boundary cuts South-west to North-east and includes Leighton and Neston but excludes Bebington, Bromborough and Eastham from the main Scandinavian enclave. We can therefore use the boundary mark for the main enclave shown in the illustrations with some confidence although there is clearly a case also for the inclusion of Ness parish and parts of Bromborough. It is interesting that in the Storeton/Bebington/Bromborough "boundary" area one encounters former place-names like le Gremotehalland (1330, ON *Griða-mót* - place of a meeting under a truce), Lathegestfeld (1412, ON *Leið-gestr*[30] - unwelcome guest) and le Dedemonnes Greue (1323 - dead man's wood).

The Major Place-Names of Wirral

For the enthusiast, to find these places a 1:50000 scale Landranger Ordnance Survey map is sufficient.

Arrowe Park today. Members of the re-enactment group Wirhalh Skip-Felag set up camp. Courtesy: Pip Shedden.

Arrowe, SJ270860. "A shieling", or "At the shieling" from ON *erg*, or *argi*. Early forms include Arwe (1240-1249) and Argh (1296). This refers to summer pastureland away from the farmhouse. This practice of sending cattle away from the farmhouse thus saving the local pasture for winter fodder is known as "transhumance" and is still practiced in modern Norway (see Chapter 1 by J. Jesch in *Wirral and its Viking Heritage*[31]). The preponderance of many field names in the locality bearing the Arrowe element, as recorded in the 19th-Century tithe maps, suggests this practice was followed in Wirral until at least 150 years ago.

---

[30] Suggested by J. McN. Dodgson in *The Place-Names of Cheshire Part IV*, page 244. More recent interpretations have been 'Visitor's guide' or 'Visiting guide's' - see *Ingimund's Saga* page 81.

[31] P. Cavill, S.E. Harding and J. Jesch, *Wirral and its Viking Heritage*, English Place-Name Society, Nottingham, 2000.

[32] See J. McN. Dodgson in *The Place-Names of Cheshire Part IV*, p314.

Signpost to the past. This signpost in Irby, Wirral, also points to the Scandinavian past of the area, as all the names on it have Viking roots. From right to left: West Kirby: "The west settlement of the Church" - named after St. Bridget's Church, founded by the Vikings in the 10th-Century, and distinguishing it from Kirkby, the old name for Wallasey. Thurstaston: "Thorsteinn's farmstead". Thingwall: "Assembly field" - The site of the Wirral Norse parliament. Arrowe Park: Arrowe comes from "erg" or "argi" meaning pastureland/farmland away from the farmhouse. Heswall: "Hazel spring" - although originally Saxon, influenced by the Viking "hesli". Pensby: "Settlement at a hill called Penn". Irby itself means "Settlement of the Irish" or "Settlement of Vikings who came from Ireland".

Birkenhead, SJ320890, **Birkenhead Priory**, SJ328885, **Birkenhead Ferry**, SJ330885. *Birki-höfuð* "Headland growing with birch trees", from OE *birce*, influenced by ON *birki* and OE *heafod*, influenced by ON *höfuð*[32]. Early forms include Byrkeheveht (1259) and Birkheued (1260). The Priory of sixteen Benedictine monks was founded sometime near 1150 by Hamo de Massey. The ferry (ON *ferja*) was defunct by 1882.

Caldy (formerly Little Caldy) SJ228852, and **Caldy Grange** (formerly Great Caldy, now Grange), SJ220860. *Kald-eyjar* "Cold-islands" from ON *kaldr* or OE *cald*, and ON *ey or eyjar* (plural). Early forms include Calders (Domesday), Caldei (1182), Kaldeya (1239). OE *cald-ears* (instead of *ey*) has also been suggested, lit. "cold arse". Prudery about the latter even at an early date renders such an interpretation to be unlikely - to the relief of local Estate Agents! E. Ekwall and J. McN. Dodgson[33] both provide convincing arguments for *Kald-eyjar:*

---

[33] See J. McN. Dodgson, p283 & references to Ekwall and Mawer cited therein.

Caldei (-e, -a), Calder(a) would mean the district of the cold islands' denoting a territory including the islands of Hilbre and the opposing high ground on the Wirral mainland occupied by Grange, Caldy and West Kirby townships. A parallel case of a mainland village named after a coastline or offshore feature occurs at Tranmere[34]. Within such a district Calders would be the name of a mainland hill and the settlements upon it. After the separation of West Kirby and Hilbre from the original territory, Caldy would in fact consist only of the Calders part (i.e. the hill of Grange and Caldy), there would be no need to distinguish the part from the whole, and the name Calders would fall into disuse. This would explain the alternative forms of the place-name. It would also reveal another name 'cold islands' for Hilbre.

Claughton, SJ304889. *Klakkr-tún* "Hamlet on a hillock" from ON *klakkr* (hillock) and ON *tún*, or OE *tun*. Early forms include Clahtun (1260) and Claghton (1272).

Denhall, SJ300748. Denhall House (SJ297759), Denhall Quay (SJ289759). From ON or ODan *Danir* "The Danes" and OE *wella* "spring". Early form Danewell (1184). Possibly the nucleus of the Danish community which joined Ingimund in the raids on Chester?

Frankby, SJ245869. *Frankisbýr* "Franki's (or Frakki's) village or settlement" from ODan pers.n. *Franki* and ODan *bý* (settlement, village) or ON *býr*. Dodgson originally believed this as "Frenchman's farmstead"[35] although more recent philological opinion appears to favour the former, i.e. the settlement of Franki the Dane. G. Fellows-Jensen considers this as key evidence for Danish settlers possibly coming via Isle of Man[36]. J. McN. Dodgson made the comment "the old Danish personal name Franki would be remarkable in a Norse-Irish district like this", although the consensus of opinion is the Danes were in Wirral in more than inconsiderable numbers, particularly if the unusually high number of *bys* in the area are to be explained. These matters are considered in some detail by Judith Jesch in Chapter 1 of *Wirral and its Viking Heritage*.

Gayton, SJ275806, Gayton Sands, Gayton Hall. *Geit-tún* "Goat farmstead", from ON *geit* and ON *tún*, or OE *tun*. Early forms include Gaitone (Domesday), Gayton (1237).

Greasby (SJ254874), Greasby Bridge, Greasby Copse, Gresby Brook. From OE *græf* (stronghold) and ON *býr* or ODan *bý*. Scandinavianized form of OE *Gravesberie*, with the Scandinavians changing OE *byrig* (wood) to ON *by* or *býr*. Early forms include Gravesberies (Domesday) and Grauisby

---

[34] see below.

[35] J. McN. Dodgson, p.287.

[36] G. Fellows-Jensen (1992) Scandinavian Place-Names of the Irish Sea Province. In J. Graham-Campbell ed. *Viking Treasure from the North West*, Chapter 4, National Museums and Guides on Merseyside, Liverpool.

"Welcome to Viking Mersey". Motorists just about to enter Wirral on the M56 are greeted by Helsby or Helsby Hill.

(1096). This is a good example of the Scandinavian settlers taking an existing English place-name and modifying it to what for them would have been a more understandable or pronounceable form.

Helsby, SJ490755. *Hjalli-býr* Village at the ledge" from ON *hjall* and ON *býr* or ODan *bý*. Helsby is just at the entry point for Wirral and was probably a significant outlier of the main Scandinavian enclave to the North-west of the peninsula: it is recorded in the Domesday Book. Helsby can be clearly seen from the M53 motorway on the southern side. The village lies on the side of an impressive steep and prominent hill overlooking the Mersey. E. Ekwall[37] and F. T. Wainwright[38] suggest the first element to be *hellir* - cave.

Heswall, SJ270820. "Hazel spring" from OE *hæsel*, reinforced by ON *hesli* with OE *wælla* (spring). Early forms rule out ON *hestur* (horse) and *völlr* (field): Eswelle (Domesday), Heselwall (1200).

Hinderton SJ305780, **Hinderton Brow, Hinderton Hall**. "The part of the village which lies more to the back", or "the hinder part of the town (Neston)", from ON *hindri* (at the back). Earlier form Hinder-town (1621). Another Hinderton, now lost, was formerly near Tranmere.

Irby, SJ256846. *Íra-býr* "Settlement of the Irish", or possibly "Settlement of Scandinavians from Ireland", from ON *Írar* and ON *býr*, or ODan *bý*. Early forms include Irreby (1096), Ireby (1181), Herby (1515) and Erby (1646). Irby has promoted considerable discussion as to the nature of the Scandinavian community in the district. If the origin of the name is "settlement of the Irish" this is clear indication some Irish settlers came over the Irish Sea with the Norse settlers (as corroborated by the Ingimund story, "Hiberno-Norse" stonework and the Irish place-names of Noctorum and Liscard). If however it was "settlers of the Norsemen from Ireland", this means the surrounding Scandinavian community - who gave it this name - would have come from somewhere else, such as the Isle of Man[39] , and may, since -*by* was most common in Danish settled areas rather than Norse, have been Danes.

[37] E. Ekwall (1960) *The Concise Oxford Dictionary of English Place-Names*, p122.
[38] F.T. Wainwright (1942) North West Mercia 871-924, *Trans. Hist. Soc. Lancashire and Cheshire* 94, 3-55.
[39] see Judith Jesch's Chapter 1 in P. Cavill, S.E. Harding, J. Jesch (2000) *Wirral and its Viking Heritage*.

Kirkby í Waleya (now Wallasey Village), SJ294922. *Kirkju-býr* "Village with the Church in Wallasey" from ON *kirkja*, ON *í*, and ON *býr* or ODan *bý*. The Scandinavian settlers approaching the north Wirral coastline from the Irish sea would have seen the wooden Saxon church of St. Hilary's: they gave the name to this place as Kirkby. Early forms: Kirkeby in Waleya (1180), Kirkeby (1254), Kirkby (1354) Kirkeby Waley (1398), Kirkeby in Walesee (1459).

Larton, SJ239871. *Leir-tún* "Farmstead at a clayey place" ON *leir*, ON *tún*. Early forms Layrton (1291), Lairton (1345).

Lingham (now part of Moreton), SJ252910. *Lyng-hólmr* "Heather island on a marsh" from ON *lyng*, ON *hólmr*, or "long marsh" from ON *lang*. What is now the Moreton Shore area. Until the construction of 20th-Century sea defences this area was always prone to inundation from the sea, and it was in this area that the legend of King Canute turning back the waves was fostered.

Liscard, SJ305920. "Hall at the rock" from OIr *lios na carraige*. This links the place-name with other evidence for Irish and Hiberno-Norse settlers in Wirral. The site of Liscard Hall (SJ312914) is now in Central Park, although the original manor house was probably off, or at one end of, what is now Manor Road. R. Coates has recently considerd the Irish origin of the place-name Liscard in some detail.[40]   Early forms include Lisnekarke (1260), Lisecair (1277).

Meols, **Great** (SJ232900) and **Little** (SJ232888).   From ON *melr* (sandbank, sandhills). The old seaport of the Viking community on Wirral (see Chapter 5) and the site of many key archaeological finds. A place-name of identical origin exists in Iceland (*Melar*). Same origin as North Meols, Ravensmeols and the former Argarmeles on the West Lancashire coast, although now pronounced differently: The Wirral Meols as "mells", the West Lancashire Meols as "meelz".

Mollington Torold (now Gt. Mollington), SJ385703. Although Mollington is an English name "Moll's farm", the manorial affix is a Scandinavian name "Thorot" from ON pers.n. *Þóraldr*, who owned land in Mollington from 1271. The land was in possession of the Thorot or Torold family also in the 14th-Century. Early form: Molynton Thorot (1286).

Ness, SJ304760 *Nes* "Promontory" from ON nes or OE *næs*. F.T. Wainwright has said[41] "ON *nes* is in many ways more probable than OE *næs* as the element which is found in Ness and Neston".

Neston, SJ292775. *Nes-tún* "Farmstead at or near the promintory" from ON *nes* or OE *næs* and ON *tún* or OE *tun*. Early forms include Nestone (Domesday), Nesston (1348). In Viking times - well before the change in coastline - Neston would have been accessible by the River Dee. Medieval

---

[40] R. Coates (1997-8) Liscard and Irish names in northern Wirral, *Journal of the English Place-Name Society*, 31, 23-6

[41] F.T. Wainwright (1943) North West Mercia 871-924, *Trans. Historic. Soc. Lancashire and Cheshire* 94, 3-55.

Neston was the main town in Wirral, and in 1348 the author's namesake was accused of killing a dog and damaging hedges:

Extract from "Calendar of Cheshire Trailbaston Proceedings 1353" ed. P. Booth in *Cheshire History* (vol. 12, 1983): Henry Cherleton v. Robert Poole and Thomas Harding. Henry Cherleton complained that Robert Poole and Thomas Harding killed his dog at Great Neston, Wirral on Friday 1st Feb. 1348 and broke his hedges. They denied guilt. Jury verdict - Not guilty.

The Wheatsheaf Public House at Raby.

The Church of St. Mary and St. Helen is also the home of some remarkable Viking stonework, as will be considered in Chapter 9, indicating a Scandinavian population. The Viking rather than the English origin for Neston would thus appear to be preferred.

Noctorum, SJ286879. *Cnocc-tírim* "Hill that's dry" or "Dry Hill" from OIr *cnocc* (hill) and OIr *tírim*. Old forms include Cnoctyrum (1119), Knocktirum (1535).

Pensby, SJ270832. "Village or settlement at a hill called Penn" from ON *býr* or ODan *bý*. The first element is either the name of the hill or a Celtic word meaning "top, end". Old forms include Penisby (1229), Penesby (1261).

Raby, SJ311799, Raby Mere. *Rá-býr*, "Village at a boundary" from ON *rá* and ON *býr* or ODan *bý*. Settlement at the Norse/English boundary. With Hargrave signifying the English side of the boundary this Norse name indicates the limit, or initial limit, of the Scandinavian enclave in Wirral. Early forms include Raby (1096).

Storeton, SJ305844. *Stór-tún* "The great farmstead" from ON *stórr* and ON *tún*. Early forms include Stortone (Domesday), Storeton (1070). The same element is in Storting, "the Great Assembly" - the Norwegian Parliament. Another early form is Stortton and Dodgson has suggested the first element might possibly come from ON *storð* 'a young wood, a plantation, land growing with brushwood'. This is probably the more likely.

Thingwall , SJ276844. *Þing-völlr,* "Assembly field", or "Assembly fields" from ON *þing* and ON *völlr*. Meeting place or parliament for the Norse community in the Wirral. This is situated right in the centre of the Scandinavian enclave, and is the site where Ingimund may have planned the 907AD attack on Chester with his fellow Norse and Danish chiefs. Early forms include Tinguelle (Domesday), Thingwelle (1278). Cross Hill, the site associated in local antiquarian tradition with the Thing, is located at SJ282842. Another Thingwall is situated on the opposite side of the Mersey (Thingwall Hall) and would have served the Scandinavian community in South-west or West Lancashire.

Thurstaston, SJ246842. *Þorsteinns-tún* "Þorstein's farmstead" from ON pers.n. *Þorsteinn* and ON *tún*. Many locals believe the name is derived from Thors-stone, "Thor's-stone-ton" from the large outcrop of sandstone on Thurstaston common, although this is incorrect. Old forms include Thurstantona (1119), Thorstanton (1202).

*Tranmere Rovers FC.
Photograph by
Per-Anders Todal.*

Tranmere , SJ325875. *Trani-melr,* "Cranes' sandbank" from ON *trani* and ON *melr*. Sandbank with the crane-birds. These birds apparently singled out this part of the Mersey shore as their favoured spot, and the Vikings were quick to see this. There was also **Tranmere Pool**, now lost, formerly between SJ330882 and SJ322885. This would have been the site of the previously named Raynildes Pool, as recorded in 1330, from the ON woman's name *Ragnhildr*, and nearby Gonnille Pool, at SJ330872, named after another Scandinavian woman, *Gunnhildr*. Old forms of Tranmere include Tranemel (1290) and Tranmer (1393). As we have seen earlier in this book, Martin Tranmæl was a famous 20th-Century Norwegian politician, a champion for workers rights and the Socialist movement.

West Kirby, SJ218865. *Vestri-Kirkjubýr*, "The west village of the church" from ON *vestri*, ON *kirkja* (church) and ON *býr* or ODan *bý*. The "west" distinguishes it from the other Kirkjubýr in Wallasey. The Church is St. Bridgets, founded by the Scandinavians. All that remains of the original

Reverend Roger Clarke, with the Hogback tombstone at St. Bridgets, West Kirby. Photograph by Per-Anders Todal.

West Kirby, Wirral. Photograph by Per-Anders Todal.

Farmers repair a hut at Eystri Kirkjubær "East Kirby" in Iceland. Photograph courtesy of Ragnar Th. Sigurðsson.

Vestri Kirkjubær "West Kirby" in Iceland. Photograph courtesy of Ragnar Th. Sigurðsson.

church is the famous hogback tombstone, which now resides within the present church building. Early forms include Kyrkeby in Wyrhale (1137), Westkyrby (1287). As we have seen earlier, the same place-name, as *Vestri-Kirkjubær*, exists in Iceland, and there is even an *Eystri Kirkjubær* "East Kirby".

Whitby, SJ396757 "The white manor or village". From ON *hviti* (white) and ON *býr* or ODan *bý* (settlement). F.T. Wainwright has suggested the first element may be the ON personal name *Hviti*. Early forms include Witebia (1096), Witebi (1188), Whiteby (1241). The Scandinavian second element has replaced a previous OE element, and in this regard Whitby has a parallel with its namesake in North Yorkshire.

Wodekirkja (now Woodchurch), SJ276870 "Wooden church" or "Church in a wood". From ON *kirkja*. Predecessor of what is now Holy Cross Church. Early elements include Wodekirke (1250).

Brimstage, Crabwall, Oxton and Shotwick.

Following work of W.G. Collingwood[42] F.T. Wainwright[43] has made the additional suggestions:

> Brimstage may preserve the ON personal name *Brúnn*, and Crabwall may possibly represent ON *krapp-vollr*, "narrow field" as was suggested by Collingwood. It has also been declared by Collingwood that the first element of Oxton is Scandinavian. Finally a derivation of Shotwick from ON *vík*, "a bay", is very strongly supported by a definite creek cutting inland from the old level of the Dee.

Minor Names

> "Wirral has more rakes than Alan Titchmarsh and more carrs than Michael Schumacher".

Besides the major names, a study of the minor names - field, road and track names, can throw light on the nature of the settlements. Unfortunately field names as recorded usually don't, unlike major names, go back to the Viking Age - most are from the last few hundred years, well after English - as Middle English and then the modern English we know today had become the language of daily life. However Scandinavian dialect words did penetrate the later language of the locals and we can see the clear results of this in for

---

[42] W.G. Collingwood. *The Saga Book of the Viking Club*, II, part II, p145.

[43] F.T. Wainwright. See footnote 38.

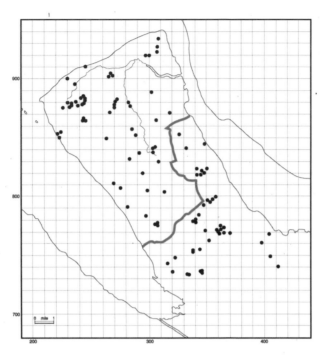

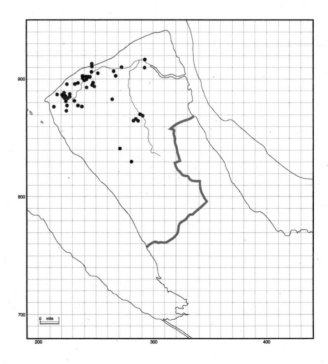

Distribution of the 100 or so rake's (top) and 50 carrs (bottom) in Wirral.

example the large number of rakes and carrs in the area. The carrs come from ON *kjarr* "brushwood in marshland" and most of the fifty or so in Wirral are distributed about the Rivers Birket and Fender. The rakes have a more interesting history - from ON *rák* "stripe, lane" and the interested reader is referred to Chapter 10 of *Wirral and its Viking Heritage* which describes how this became an accepted dialect word for the Scandinavian and the surrounding English communities. The interested reader is also referred to *Ingimund's Saga* where distributions of other name elements such as holm, slack and kirk are considered. N.J. Higham, writing in *The Origins of Cheshire*[44] wrote the following:

> That Scandinavian was still spoken in the region long after the Norman Conquest helps to explain this mélange of linguistic influences and the widespread minor- and field-names of Scandinavian origin in the area.

Whats in a name? Clues to the origins of the Wirral Invaders

The Ingimund story tells of a Scandinavian settlement. Although initially peaceful, the report of the later attacks on Chester give an interesting insight into the composition of the setters. Although Ingimund himself was a Norseman - possibly born in Ireland, and possibly also with an Irish wife, the story indicates he was leader - or a leader - of a mixed Wirral community of Norsemen, Danes and Irishmen. His saga makes it clear where at least many of the early Invaders of 902AD came from:

> "We have related above, namely in the fourth year before us, of the expulsion of the Norse hosts from Ireland; through the praying and fasting of the holy man Céle Dabhaill."

Later in the story, the Chronicler informs us:

> "Afterwards Ingimund came to the leaders of the Norsemen and the Danes..."
> "All the leaders of the Norsemen and the Danes agreed to do this"
> "The armies of the Danes and Norsemen assembled towards Chester"

So by 907AD - the commencement of the attacks on Chester - the Danish population in the peninsula must have been significant[45]. As to how the

---

[44] N.J. Higham (1993) *The Origins of Cheshire*, Manchester University Press, p.108.

[45] Unless this group was an organised army arriving from the Danelaw to help the Norsemen.

Danes got to Wirral - and the proportion of Norsemen to Danes - this has remained a subject of considerable discussion and speculation, although a consensus opinion appears to be emerging.

A study of place-names, or "philology" can throw some more light on this. Distinguishing Irish from Scandinavian or English is not a problem - the language is very different. Old Norse and Old Danish however were very similar, and also not too dissimilar from Old English. This is not surprising, since all three languages derived from the same continental source. A Norseman could easily understand a Dane, and would also be able to understand much of the speech of an Anglo-Saxon. However, there are certain test word elements which distinguish Old Norse or Old Danish. Elements such as *brekka, slakki, gil* and *rák* are characteristic of Norsemen, whereas *-by, klint* and *-thorp* are more characteristic of the Danes. Other words such as *carr, holm* and *thveit* could equally well be either, and word elements like "dale" and *-ton* could be either Scandinavian or Anglo-Saxon.

Even "late" Field-Names are still useful indicators of Scandinavians

Unlike in the case of the major names, it is very difficult to assign the antiquity of many of the minor names, i.e. field-names, road or track names etc. back to the time of the settlements. Indeed, the earliest records we can find for many are in the Tithe Maps and Apportionments of the early 19th-Century. This is because, although changes to the names of major places were rare (apart form spellings), field names could be changed simply by the wishes and whims of a new owner. However, as pointed out by F.T. Wainwright and others, this can be extremely important for another reason: it shows that even if a field-name with a Scandinavian element belongs to a later period, nonetheless that element or dialect word was still in active use at the time someone or some persons assigned that name: this would apply for example to many of the minor "Arrowes" in Wirral. But we can now take the lists of these place-names, compiled in *Ingimund's Saga*, and see how these fit into the Norse/Danish/Irish or "unresolved" categories. The lists are based on place-names recorded in the 19th-Century Tithe Map and Apportionments or earlier records bearing these elements. Where the name had fallen out of use at the time of the Tithe maps, the latest recorded date of use is given in brackets. The enthusiast wishing to find the places listed is referred to *Ingimund's Saga*, which gives the six-figure Ordnance Survey coordinates for each.

Norsemen: The Wirral Arrowes, Rakes, Brecks, Gills and Slacks

These five test word elements which occur in a large number of Wirral minor names all indicate settlers with a Norwegian rather than Danish background, and have the following origins:

Arrowe: from ON *argi,* meaning "summer pastureland away from the farmhouse", and used by Norsemen coming from Ireland.

Rake: from ON *rák,* literally meaning "stripe", and adapted to mean "lane". So the evolution of Viking tracks as road names in several parts of modern day Wirral as "Rake Lane" literally mean "Lane Lane"! New Brighton Rakers FC - former Football League side - were once the champion for this name. Perhaps more interestingly *rák* is quite frequent in the Isle of Man - used to denote paths for cattle and sheep etc.

Breck: from ON *brekka,* meaning slope on a hillside.

Gill: from ON *gil* meaning "dip" or "ravine". Could be ODan: Gil is found in Denmark but less common than in Norway because of the nature of the landscape.

Slack: from ON *slakki* meaning a "hollow or cutting" through e.g. some high ground or possibly a wood.

Additional Scandinavian elements appearing in conjunction with argi, rák, brekka, gil or slakki are indicated:

The Barnston Gil. The dip down to the Fender valley at the end of Gills Lane.

Arrowe Parish: *Rake Lane, Top Rake Field. Arrowe Brook & Arrowe Brook House, Arrowe Hill, Arrowe Bridge, Youd's & Bennet's Arrowe, Brown's Arrowe, Bithel's Arrowe, Harrison's Arrowe, Wharton's Arrowe, Widing's Arrowe.*

Barnston Parish: *Le Rake* (1347), *Slack Road* (now Milner Road, which at Heswall becomes the "Heswall Slack"). *Gills Lane/ Ghylls Lane.* Near a definite ravine or steep dip at the junction with Thingwall Road (Fender Valley). See also the entry for *Gills Field & Meadow* in Pensby below.

Bidston Parish: *Hoolerake.*

Brimstage Parish: *Rake Ends, Rake Shute* .

Bromborough Parish: *The Rake, Mark Rake, Rakehouse, Rake Hey, Rake Croft, Ellis' Lower Rake Hey. The Slack* (1731) - at the top end of what is now Eastham Country Park, is recorded on the 1731 Mainwaring Estate map, but not on the 1834 Tithe map. *Acre Slack/ Acre Slack Wood* (ON *akr* - field, acre):

not connected to *"The Slack"* but on the western side of Bromborough, across the railway line, south of Bromborough Rake railway station.

Burton Parish: *The Church Rake, Rake Hey, Rake Croft. Slack Lake (& Field).*

Caldy Parish: *The Rake, Rake Hay.*

Childer Thornton Parish: *Rake or Goose Pasture, Rake Croft, Rake Part, Old Rake, Rake Lane (1831).*

Claughton Cum Grange Parish: *Flaybrick Hill (Flaga-brekka* "Hill/slope with a flagstone" - ON *flaga* - flagstone). *Gill Field, Little Gill Field, Gill Field Moss, Gill Brook* (now the name of a housing estate), *Gill Brook Basin* (an inlet in the docks at the mouth of a lost stream).

Eastham Parish: *Eastham Rake, Rake Inclosure, Rake Hey.*

Frankby Parish: *Second Rake Hay, Near Rake Hay, Garden Rake Hay, Rake Hay Brow.*

One of the many roads or lanes in Wirral bearing the name "Rake": Eastham Rake.

Grange Parish: *Long Rake Lane* (Now Heron Road), *Rake House* (at 1847), *Rake House Farm, Long Rake Farm, Rake Field, Rake End, Rake Hay* (1639), *Further Rake Hey* (1780), *Little Rake Hey, Middle Rake Hey, Rake Hey Meadow.*

Greasby Parish: *Wimbricks (Hvin-brekka* "Gorsey slope on a hill" or "Gorse bank" - ON *hvin* "gorse").

Great Saughall Parish: *Slack Croft.*

Great Stanney Parish: *Rakemore Field* (1600).

Heswall & Gayton Parish: *The Slack* (now Milner Copse & the site of the public house called Sandon Arms - formally "The Slack"). *Slack Road* (now Milner Road). *Wall Rake, Rake Ditch.*

Higher Bebington Parish: *Rake Hay.*

Irby Parish: *Rake Hey.*

Landican Parish: *Rakes, Rake Shoots.*

Ledsham Parish: *Badgersrake* (Covert) (see also entries under Puddington and Willaston below)

Leighton Parish: *Le Rake* (1280).

Liscard Parish: *Breck Hey, Breck Road, Cambrick Hey (Kambr-brekka* - ON *kambr* "ridge"), *Rake Lane, Rake Hey.*

Little Stanney Parish: *Rake Hall.*

Little Sutton: *Old Rake, Rake Croft, Rake, Rake Lane* (1831).

Lower Bebington Parish: *Le Rake* (1357) .

Moreton Cum Lingham Parish: *Rake Hey, Rakes Meadow.*

Neston Parishes(Great & Little): *Raby Rake, Rake Ends, Rake End Croft, Rake End Enclosure.*

Newton Cum Larton Parish: *Newton Rake, Rake House, Long Rake Farm. Newton Breken.*

Noctorum Parish: *Rake Hey, Big Rake Hey.*

Overchurch/Upton Parish: *Rake Lane* .

Pensby Parish: *Breck Place, Breck Hey. Gills Meadow, Gills Field:* near the bank of the Fender - see also entry for Gills Lane in Barnston.

Poulton Cum Spital Parish: *La Stopelrake* (1406) "Lane or path to the stepping stones" Stepping stones are in the stream at Raby Mill/Mere at the Poulton boundary.

Puddington Parish: *Badger Rake* (see also entries under Ledsham and Willaston) *Higher Rakeside, Lower Rakeside, Green Rake, Great Green Rake, Little Green Rake.*

Prenton Parish: *Rake Hay, Rake Hey. Slack Hey, Slackey Field.*

Saughall Massie Parish: *Long Rake Lane* (Now Heron Road). *Wimbricks* (see Greasby above)

Storeton Parish: *Rake Lane, Rake Hey, Rake Ditch, Ransel* (Rauncelrake at 1323 - ON *raun, reynir* "rowan tree"). The charter of 1323 and its translation describing Rauncelrake are given in *Ingimund's Saga*, Chapter 8.

Thornton Hough Parish: *Rake Hey.*

Tranmere Parish: *Slack Field, Kirks Slacks* (*Kirkja-slakki* "Hollow or cutting near the church" - ON *kirkja*). *Rake Hay.*

Wallasey Parish: *The Breck, Breck Hay, Field under Breck., Stony Rake, Le Scheperake* (1281 - "the sheep rake"- this lane was probably near Stony Rake: the "Liscard" rakes are too far away). *Le Rake Milne* ("Mill by the lane").

West Kirby Parish: *Slack*

Whitby Parish: *Bymans Slacks, Badgersrake Lane, Rake Meadow.*

Willaston Parish: *Badger's Rake* (see also Ledsham and Puddington above), *Eastham Rake*, (see also entry under Eastham), *Rake End Field, Rake End Croft, New Rake Hey, Rake End Meadow, Rake End & Hey.*

Woodbank Parish: *Slack Croft.*

Another place-name signature for Scandinavian invaders from Ireland was the Irish Patron Saint St. Bridget (*Bridget, Brigid*). The church is in West Kirby, but there are also field names in Eastham:

Road sign at the Wallasey Breck, from ON brekka. The nearby boundary with Bidston has many thwaites, from ancient clearings. The road also leads to the Granny Rock or "ye Clynsse" as recorded in 1642 (ODan klint).

Bridgets (Lower & Higher), Nearer Bridgets, Big Bridgets. All these minor names support the view of a significant Norse population, and reinforce the major place-name evidence in names like Meols, Storeton, Thingwall and Tranmere which are clearly Norse.

Danes: The Wirral -bys and thorps

The place-name ending *-by* is an old Scandinavian word element for "settlement" or "village" and there are eight existing in Wirral: Frankby, Irby, West Kirby, Pensby, Greasby, Raby, Whitby and Helsby and considered above. All are inside what is believed to have been the original Scandinavian enclave, denoted by Raby, the "boundary settlement", apart from Whitby, now part of Ellesmere Port, and Helsby, which lies just outside the peninsula. In addition there is Kirkby "the village of the church" the former name for Wallasey Village. The bys and another place-name element *thorp* are more typical of settlements of Scandinavians speaking Old Danish rather than Old Norwegian, and this has prompted some interesting discussion as to the strength of the Danish proportion of the 10th-Century Scandinavian

Distribution of the Wirral bys. 1=Frankby, 2=Greasby, 3=Irby, 4=Kirby in Wallasey, 5=Pensby, 6=Raby, 7=West Kirby, 8=Whitby. The following no longer exist: 9=Haby, 10=Eskby/Hesby, 11=Warmby, 12=Kiln Walby, 13=Stromby, 14=Syllaby. Another -by, Helsby lies just outside Wirral and is not shown.

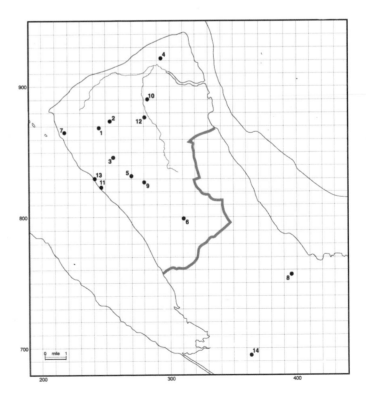

community. The view that the Danish population was not insignificant is reinforced if six further *bys* are taken into account although these were presumably smaller settlements as they no longer exist.

Haby, SJ280827. *Há- bý* "High-settlement" from ON *hár* (high) and ON *býr,* or ODan *bý.*

Hesby/ Eskeby, SJ283890. *Askr-býr,* "Farmstead at a place growing with ash-trees" from ON *askr* (ash trees) and ON *býr* or ODan *bý.*

Warmby, SJ247823. *Varmr-býr* "Warm settlement" from ON *varmr,* ON *býr* or ODan *bý.*

Kiln Walby (Gildewalleby), Top Kiln Walby, Kiln Walby Meadow, Lower Kiln Walby, SJ281877, SJ275868, SJ281880, SJ279880 *Gildi-býr* "Guildsman's settlement", "Settlement at the Guildsman's spring" from ON *gildi* (guildsman), ON *býr* (settlement) or ODan *bý.* Also OE *wælla* (spring).

Stromby: Stromby Hay, SJ241829. *Straumr-býr* "Settlement by a stream" from ON *straumr* (stream, current), ON *býr* or ODan *bý.*

Syllaby: Syllaby Butt, Syllaby Croft & Field, SJ364695, SJ363693. *Syllasbýr* "Sylla's settlement" from ON pers.n. *Sylla,* ON *býr* or ODan *bý.*

Another Haby as "Haby Town" has been quoted in the 1846 Tithe Apportionment for Raby Parish at SJ310798, but this is presumably a transcription error. A further *-by* has been quoted, Signeby, but F.T. Wainwright has pointed out this was due to a further transcription error. Four of the lost -bys we don't have records of prior to the Tithe Maps. Of the lost bys only two we know for sure go back to medieval times: Eskeby and Kiln Walby (the latter listed as Gildewalleby). For the other four the earliest records we have are the 19th-Century Tithe Maps and Apportionments. Although there were many bys, there is only one, possibly two, thorps:

Calthorpe (Bidston parish: SJ288887) *Karl-* (or *kald-*) *thorp,* "Karl's (or cold) settlement" from ON pers.n. *Karl* or ON/ODan *kaldur* (cold) and ODan *thorp* (settlement)

Winthrop (Claughton: SJ294884) *Vindr-þorp* "Windy settlement" from ON/ODan *vindr* (wind), and possibly ODan *thorp* (settlement).

The place-name *Denhall* also indicates the influence of Danish invaders and this was perhaps were some of them were based during the Ingimund years: *Denhall Field* (SJ320747), *Denhall Hay* (SJ303749) in the Burton/Ness areas.

Route for the Danes into Wirral and South West Lancashire

As we have seen in Chapter 3 we have a good idea for the route of many of the Norwegian settlers into Wirral and the North West in general - via Ireland or the Isle of Man. Deciphering the route of the Danes into the Mersey area is more tricky. One route favoured by the scholar Gillian Fellows Jensen is a migration starting from the northern Danelaw which is essentially now Yorkshire. The route is based principally on the distribution of bys in England and southern Scotland shown in Chapter 1. The Danes are postulated to have moved in an *anticlockwise* direction as follows:

1. From the northern Danelaw (Yorkshire), where there is a large number of -by place-names, moving across the Pennines

2. Down the valley of the River Eden to Carlisle and the North Lake District, where there is also a large number of *-bys*.

3. Spreading northwards into eastern Dumfriesshire, to Galloway, and southwards along the coastal plain of Cumberland.

4. Across the Irish Sea to The Isle of Man - where there are 28 place-names with *-by*.

5. Back across the Irish sea to Wirral -where there are 15 place-names with -by (including Helsby) and South-west Lancashire,

Route for the Danish settlers moving from the Danelaw of Yorkshire and the East Midlands into Wirral and South-West Lancashire, from a proposal by G. Fellows-Jensen. This proposed route is based on the distribution map of -bys in England and Southern Scotland given in Chapter 1, and other evidence.

---

[46] G. Fellows-Jensen (1992) Scandinavian Place-Names of the Irish Sea Province. In J. Graham-Campbell ed. *Viking Treasure from the North-West*, Chapter 4, National Museums and Guides on Merseyside, Liverpool.

where there are six (Crosby, Formby, Greetby, Kirkby, Roby, West Derby).

So this is where the Danes may have come from. Interestingly, in North-west England, there is a high concentration of *bys* in Wirral and South-west Lancashire. Moving northwards there is a gap (apart from a few isolated examples) until the North Lakes when they reach a significant density again. This would appear to support the Fellows-Jensen theory. In her 1992 paper she also says the following, with specific reference to Frankby and Irby:

> The specific of Frankby may be a Scandinavian personal name *Franki*, which seems likely to have been introduced to Wirral from (the Isle of) Man for its earliest recorded occurrence is in a runic inscription on the shaft of a cross at Braddan dating from the late tenth or early eleventh-Century[47]. Taken in conjunction, the names Arrowe, the two Thingwalls and Frankby, together with the two possible *staðir*-names, Toxteth and Croxteth, suggest that the Írar or 'Irishmen' recalled in the Wirral place-name Irby may have come from Man rather than Ireland.

General Scandinavian names

We now give a list of place-names, as recorded in the 19th-Century Tithe Map and Apportionments or earlier in Wirral bearing place-name elements which could be either Norwegian or Danish in origin.

Carr: From ON *kjarr* Although literally meaning "brushwood at marshland" it was used by the Viking settlers to denote any marshy area.

Clints: From ODan *klint* or possibly ON *klettr* denoting "projecting rock" or "large standing stone". The Danish form is more likely, and its occurrence several times could be taken as further evidence of significant Danish presence.

Holme: From ON *holmr* or ODan *holm* denoting an "island in a marshy area", i.e. part of a marshland that could be used, e.g. for agricultural purposes.

Intack or Intake: From ON *inntak*, denoting "enclosure", and is associated with farmsteads.

Kirk: From ON *kirkja* or ODan *kirk,* meaning "church".

Skog, Scough: From ON *skógr* meaning "wood".

Thwaite: From ON *þveit,* ODan, *thveit*, meaning "clearing", e.g. clearing of woodland for farming activity.

---

[47] G. Fellows-Jensen (1983) Scandinavian settlement in the Isle of Man and North-west England: the Place Name evidence, in C. Fell et al. editors, *The Viking Age in the Isle of Man*, London pp37-52

Barnston Parish: *Intake, Small Flat.*

Bidston Parish: *Bedestoncarre* (at 1306: now Bidston Moss), *Grass & Little Hoveacre* (ON/ODan *kjarr* rather than ON *akr*), *Olucar* (1347) (ON *ölur* - Alder and ON/ ODan *kjarr*). *Holmegarth* (*Hólm-garðr* - ON *garðr* "enclosure"). *Intake Meadow, Oxholme, Thwaite Lane, The Cornhill Thwaite, The Great Thwaite, Marled Thwaite, Meadow Thwaite, Salt Thwaite, Spencer's Thwaite,, Tassey's Thwaite, Whinney's Thwaite, Inderthwaite* (1522 - ON *innar* -inner), *Utterthwaite* (1522 - ON *útar* - outer). *Boscus De Grescow* (1357 - *Grjót-skógr* "Gravel wood" - possibly one of the present Woods on Bidston Hill, such as Park Wood, Silver Birch Wood and/or Taylor's Wood).

Bromborough Parish: *Lathegestfeld* (1412) The place-name expert John McNeal Dodgson[48] has suggested "Unwelcome guests field" from ON *leiðr* or OE *lað* (unwelcome) and ON *gestr* or OE *gest* ('a stranger, a traveller, a visitor'). He says also "Professor Sørensen suggests that Lathegest may represent an ON pers.n. *Leiðgestr* , ('the unwelcome visitor'), analagous with

The Bromborough klint at Brotherton Park.

the similar ON pers.n. *Leiðulfr* - ('the unwelcome wolf')." These interpretations may refer to some local conflict in the area. More recent opinion however[49] suggests the first ON element is *leiða* "to lead", so *Leiðgestr* means "visitor's guide". *The Clints, Wood Clints* (projecting rocks in Brotherton Park overlooking the R. Dibbin), *Intake, Brocks Dale* (ON *dalr* "valley"), *Flatts, Rawnesfeld* (1440, "Ragnald's field" from ON pers.n. *Ragnaldr* or "Raven's field" from ON *hrafn* "raven". See also entry for "Rawnuesfeld" in Whitby area), *Le Skereyorde* (1412, "Fish trap at the skerry" from ON *sker* "skerry"). *Ingimund's Saga* (Chapter 8) gives the 1412 charter and its translation, identifying both Lathegestfeld and le Skeryorde.

Burton Parish: *Fiddlestone, Fiddleston Plantation, Fiddleston Hay* (from ON pers.n. *Fiðill*, and possibly ON *tún* "farmstead"), *Moore Flat, Crooked Flat.*

Caldy Parish: *Intake (Further, Higher, Middle, New), Further Intake. Ascow* (1454 - "ash wood" (ON/ODan *skógr*, ON/ODan *askr* - ash).

[48] *The Place-Names of Cheshire*, Part IV, Page 244

[49] Suggested by Magnus Magnusson. Professor Jan Ragnar Hagland agrees and has indicated this would also fit in with the few other names of *Leið-* that have been recorded.

Capenhurst Parish: *Intake, Ingriessiche* (1340, "Ingrid's stream" from ON pers.n. *Ingríðr*).

Childer Thornton Parish: *Lowfields & House* (from ON *lágr* "low". Links with Loghfeld in Little Sutton parish), *Crook Croft* (1704, from ON *krókr* "crook". Links with Croketcroft in Eastham).

Chorlton Parish: *Ross Croft* (ON *rauðr* "red").

Claughton cum Grange Parish: *Lower Flat, Further Flat, Top, Lower, Further Flat* (1824), *Flat Cow Meadow* (1824). *Near Holmes Wood, Further Holmes Wood* (1824), *Intake* (1824), *The Taskar* (1546 - the site of this is now on Bidston Avenue opposite Alderney Avenue - ON *skógr*) *Seals* (1824 - ON *selja* "willow"). *Vfeldesgrene* (1340 - "Úfaldi's green or wood" from ON pers.n. *Úfaldi*. Probably part of what is now Birkenhead Park).

Eastham Parish: *Lower Flats, Croketcroft* (1440, from ON *krókr* "crooked" or ME *croked*. Links with Crook Croft in Childer Thornton).

Frankby Parish: *Hillbark, Hillbark Farm* (ON *bjarg* "cliff"), *Birch Hey* (ON *birki* "birch"). *Larton Hay, Larton Hey Farm* (ON *leir* "clay").

Grange Parish: *Carr and, Carr Farm, Carr Field. Larton Hay, New Larton Hay* (links with the Larton place-names above), *Mecca Brook* (ON *mjúkr* "gentle, mild"), *Wyhon Flatt* (adjoins the Flatts in Newton), *Scamblants* (ON *skammr* "short").

Greasby Parish: *Broad Flatt, Little Flatt, Long Flatt, Flatts, Kirkeway* (1639), *Kirka Loons, Top Kirka Loons.*

Great Meols Parish: *Caldey Hay* (ON *kaldr* "cold", ON *ey* or *eyjar* "island/s", *Intake, Carr Side Field, Carr Hall Farm, Carr Farm, Carr House, Carr Lane.*

Great Mollington Parish: *Torrald Fyeld*, now Townfield Lane ("Thorald's field" from ON pers.n. *Þóraldr*).

Hillbark Hall, Frankby, situated on the site where Franki probably had his "by". Photograph taken in 1929. Courtesy of Iain Boumphrey.

Great Saughall Parish: *Dales* (ON *dalr* "valley"), *Bark Corner, Bark Gate* (from ON *bjarg* "cliff", *gata* "street").

Great Stanney Parish: *Holmlake* (links with Holmlache in Stanlow).

Heswall & Gayton Parish: *Scarbrook Hill, Scarbrook* (ON *skarð* "bluff or scar". The brook once ran down Scarbrook Hill before the construction of the culvert), *Stack Yard* (ON *stakkr* "stack/ pile"), *Town Flatt, Lower Flatt, Harrowe Hay* (1293), *Haerri-haugr* "The higher hill enclosure" from ON *haerri*

One of the many road or field names in North Wirral bearing the name "Carr".

(higher) and ON *haugr* (hillock, burial mound). OE *hearg* "heathen shrine" has also been suggested: see Chapter 9.

Higher Bebington Parish: *Storeton Hill* (ON *stór* or ON *storð* -see above, ON *tún* or OE *tun*". May have marked boundary with main Norse enclave). *Le Schamforlong* (1300, "The short furlong" from ON *skammr* "short"), *Rock Ferry* (ON *ferja* "ferry", but unknown if it goes back to the settlement period).

Hilbre & Dee Estuary Parish: *Tanskey Rocks: Tönn-sker* "Tooth skerry rocks" from ON *tönn* (tooth), ON *sker* (skerry).

Hooton Parish: *Stack Wood*, now Church Wood: ("Stack or pile wood/ Pillar wood" from ON *stakkr* "stack, pile or pillar"), *Le Sker en Hooton,* now Poole Hall Rocks (from ON *sker,* "skerry"); *Ketilspol* (1402, "Ketill's Creek" from ON pers.n. *Ketill.* Site of what is now Riveacre Park).

Hoylake Parish: *Arnolds Eye* (1819). "Arnald's sandbank" from ON *eyrr* (a sandbank). Represents the northerly end of the Dee estuary on the Wirral side. The corresponding element appears in the name *Point of Ayr* at the end of the Dee estuary on the Welsh side. Could also be ON *eyjar* (islands).

Tonn-sker: Tanskey Rocks, just off the West Kirby shore near Hilbre island. Courtesy of Richard Smith.

Irby Parish: *Heskeths* (Hesta-skeið, "Horse race-track" from ON *hestur* "horse", ON *skeið* "track"). *Intake Meadow, Young's Intake, Mickansedge* (ON *mikill* "great, large").

Landican Parish: *Carremedowe* (Carr Bridge Meadow), *Carr Bridge Field,* Near *Carr Bridge Field, Storeton Field Hey, Far Storeton Field Hey.*

Heskeths in Irby. Horse race-track (hestaskeið) for the Vikings at SJ257844 seen from the bottom of Woodlands Road at Arrowe Brook looking towards Thingwall Road. Other Heskeths are in Thornton Parish and in West Lancashire near Southport.

Svart-sker. Black rocks on which Fort Perch Rock is now situated. Photograph courtesy of Bob Warwick.

Ledsham Parish: *Crook Loons* (ON *krókr* "crook"), *Flat Hey, Little Flat Hey, Big Flat Hey, Coopers Flat, Inntak, "Intack & Long Croft"*.

Leighton Parish: *Homes Hays, Raby Yate* (1569 - ON *gata* "street" or OE *geat*), *Flat*.

Liscard Parish: *Swarteskere* (now Fort Perch Rock, Black Rock: "Black skerry" from ON *svartr* "black", ON *sker* "skerry"); *Long Golacre, Further Golacre* (*Góligr-akr* "Fair/Pretty-field" from ON *góligr, gólegur* "fair/pretty" and ON *akr* "field, acre"), *Stonebark* (now Stoneby Drive: "Stoney cliff" from ON *bjarg* (cliff), *Le Gatebut* (1398 - ON *gata*), *The Shambrooks* (1654 - from ON *skammr* "narrow/ short". Possibly the site of what is now Central Park).

Little Meols Parish: *Carr, Carr Lane Field, Carr Field , Carr Side Hey, Carr Hey.*

Little Saughall: *Kirkland Ho, Kirks Field.*

Little Sutton Parish: *Loghfeld* (1432, from ON *lágr* "low". Links with Lowfields in Childer Thornton parish), *Le Clyntes* (1440, from ODan *klint* "projecting rocks". Appears to be none in the parish which fits the bill. However, *klint* is also taken to mean "tough large stones": there are some at the village golf course).

Lower Bebington Parish: *Kirket Lane* (Church Road), *Intake, Hellelond* (1300: now Ellens Lane. "Land at or near a flat rock" from ON *hella* "flat rock", ON *lundr)* "grove". The same first element along with ON *býr* possibly gives its name to the Scandinavian village of Helsby lying just outside Wirral, although J. McN. Dodgson suggests ON *hjallr (*a ledge) and F.T. Wainwright ascribes the origin as ON *hellir* "holes, caves".

Moreton cum Lingham Parish: *Lingham, Lingham Lane* (*Lyng-hólmr* "Heather-marsh island" from ON *lyng* "heather", ON *holmr*), *Dangkers* (now Danger Lane, from ON *kjarr*), *Bottom O' Th' Carrs* (now the site of Wallasey School, formerly Wallasey Grammar School), *West Car, West Carr Meadow, West Carr Hay, Holme Itch, Little Holme Hay, Big Holme Hay , Holme Intake, Intake* (at what is now the M53 Motorway interchange).

Ness Parish: *Mickwell, Mickwell Brow, Mickwell Covert* (from ON *mikill* "great, large" and OE *wælla* "spring"), *Great & Little*

Dale, Pit Dale (1831, from ON *dalr* "valley"), *Stack Yard* ("Stack or pile yard/ Pillar yard") from ON *stakkr* "stack, pile or pillar"), *Hate Flat*.

Neston Parishes (Great & Little): *Stone Stupes* (ON *stólpi* "post/pillar"), *Holmes Heys, The Inntack, Intack, Sour Flatt, Flatt Heath*.

>   *Blakeley/ Hargrave district of Little Neston Parish* : *Piladall* (*Píll-dalr* "Willow valley" from ON *píll* "willow", ON *dalr* "valley". Connects with Pellerdale in Raby and Piledale, in Willaston area), *Mickledale* (now Plymyard Dale), *Mikill-dalr* "Great-valley" from ON *mikill* "great, large", ON *dalr* "valley", *Mickle Moor Meadow* (1711 - ON *mikill* "great, large").

Newton cum Larton Parish: *Fornall Bridge, Fornall Green* (ON *forn* "old", ON *haugr* "hillock, burial mound"), *Newton Car* (at 1842) , *Sally Carr Lane* (now footpath - ON *selja* "willow"), *Carr Lane, Carr, Carr Meadow, Holmesides, Near Flatt, Far Flatt, Sawghon Flat, Great Flat, Little Flat, Banakers* (ON *akr* "field, acre" and ON *kjarr*).

Noctorum Parish: *Shirbeck* (ON *bekkr* "stream"), *Flat* .

Overchurch/Upton Parish: *Kill Flatt* (1666 - from ON *gildi* "guildsman", ON *flatr*), *Greasby Flat, Moreton Flatt, Flatts, Salacres, Salacre Lane* (*Selja-akr* or *Selja-kjarr* "Willow field" or "Willow marsh" from ON *selja* and ON *akr* or ON *kjarr*), *Lanacre* (from ON *akr*), *Hough Holme* (ON *haugr* "mound"), *Le Kar* (ON *kjarr*), *Overkirk Hill*.

Oxton Parish: *Arnehow* - now Arno Hill, *The Arno* (*Árni-haugr* "Árni's hillock/ burial mound" from ON pers.n. *Árni*, ON *haugr*), *Spath, Little Spath* (ON *sporðr* "fish-tail"), *Crook Loon* (ON *krókr* "crook"), *Holm Lane, New Home* (1831), *Home Field, Home Hey, Little Home, Carr Bridge Meadow, Carr Field Hey* , *Higher & Lower Flats*.

Pensby Parish: *Intake, Carr House Croft*.

Poulton cum Seacombe Parish: *Seacombe Ferry* (ON *ferja* "ferry").

Prenton Parish: *Kirk Hay, Intake, Stack Yard* (ON *stakkr* "stack, pile or pillar"), *Five Acre Holme* (ON *akr* "field, acre"), *Bridge Holme, Top Holme, Lower Holme, The Holme, Higher Holme*.

Puddington Parish: *Flats*.

Raby Parish: *Flatt Hey, Kirkett Hey* (ON *kirkja*, ON *gata* "street"), *Rake Hey, Pellerdale* (*Píll-dalr* "Willow valley" from ON *píll* "willow", ON *dalr* "valley". Connects with Piladall in the Hargrave/Blakeley part of Little Neston parish, and Piledale in Willaston parish).

Saughall Massie Parish: *Carr Farm, Carr Houses, Carr Meadow, New Carr, Carr, Carr Hay, Old Carr Meadow, Old Carr, Carr Lane, Ufilys Brow* (ON pers.n. *Úfaldi*).

Stanlow Parish: *Holmlache* (1209, links with Holmlake in Great Stanney), *Intack* (1554).

Storeton Parish: *Great Storeton, Little Storeton, Storeton Hill* (see above for comment on ON *stór*), *Le Gremotehalland* (1330 - *Griða-mót* "Place of a meeting under a truce" from ON *grið* "truce", ON *mót* "meeting"), *Flat, Flattbutts, Upper Flat, Lower Flat, Hill Flat, Sour Flats* (M53 motorway now cuts straight through Sour Flats), *Intack*.

Thingwall Parish: *Thingwell* (field-name), *Thingwall Brook, Cross Hill* (from ON *kross* "cross". Site believed to be that of the þing "Assembly"), *Shocking Dale, Dale Shoot, Dale Hay, Dale Heaps, Dale End Brook* (ON *dalr* "valley"), *Intake*.

Thornton Hough Parish: *Intack, Hesketh Grange* (*Hesta-skeið* "Horse race track" from ON *hestr* "horse", ON *skeið* "track").

Thurstaston Parish: *Thurstaston Hill, Thurstaston Common* (ON pers.n. *Þorsteinn* "Thorsteinn"), *Meckansedge* (ON *mikill* "great, large". Connects with Mickansedge in Irby parish). *Steyncolesdale* (1298, Later Tinkers Dale. *Steinkelldalr* from ON pers.n. *Steinkell*, ON *dalr* "valley"), *Crook Corner* (ON *krókr* "crook").

Tranmere Parish: *Hinderton, Hinderton Lane* (*Hindri-tún* "Rear farmstead" or "Back of the farmstead" from ON *hindri* "back, rear", ON *tún* "farmstead"), *Asker Dale* (from ON *askr* "ash", ON *dalr* "valley"), *Intake, Kirket Hay, Far Storeton Field, Near Storeton Field* (ON *stór* "great", ON *tún* "farmstead"), *Raynildes Pool* (1323 - "Ragnhildr's Pool" from ON pers.n. *Ragnhildr*. Ragnhildr's Pool was lost in the construction of the docks, with the drained stream above it now the site of Dingle Road and the Valley Lodge in Devonshire Park), *Gunnel Pool* (1800 - from ON pers.n. *Gunnhildr*. Gunnhildr's Pool, recorded in 1529 as Gonnille Pool, represents another creek in from the Mersey now lost).

Wallasey Parish: *The Clynsse* (1642 - "The Projecting Rock" from ODan *klint*. Large rock outcrop at the Breck (SJ305908) and/or the large sandstone rock at Red Noses (at SJ298942). The significance of this place is discussed in detail in Chapter 14 of *Ingimund's Saga* in connection with a 1642 Parish Register recording the deaths of two girls from a fall of a rock onto them. *Stone Bark* (ON *bjarg* "cliff". See also entry for Liscard area), *Kirkway* (now Church Hill), *Wallacre Road* (probably formerly Waley-Carr. From ON *kjarr*

or ON *akr* "field, acre"), *Fearney Flat, Intake, Wynny Hey* (ON *hvin* "gorse"), *Kettle Well Garden* (from ON pers.n. *Ketill*), *Tokesford* (1397- "Tóki's ford" from ODan or ON pers.n. *Tóki*). Old crossing point on Wallasey Pool at SJ309909. Possibly the same Tóki was responsible for the landing place at Toxteth on the other side of the Mersey. The name is typically Danish. *Seurydzis Alfland* (1281 - "Sigríðr's half-land " from ON pers.n. *Sigríðr*), *Le Crocishind* (1280 - ON *krókr* "crook").

West Kirby Parish: *The Rugs* (ON h*ryggr* "ridge"), *Kirbymount, Mickell Brook, Mickenbrook* (ON *mikill* "great, large").

Whitby Parish: *Crooklands, Crookloons* (from ON *krókr* "crook"), *Intake, Near Intake, Far Intake , Rawnuesfeld* (1440, from ON pers.n. *Ragnaldr*, or ON *hrafn* "raven". See also entry for Rawnsfeld in Bromborough area), *Flat, Halwoods Flat.*

Willaston Parish: *Intake, Little Intake, Top Intake, Stack Yard* (from ON *stakkr* "stack, pile or pillar"), *Ness Acre, Big Ness Acre, Ness Acre Croft* (from ON *akr* "field, acre"), *Leicherichewalledale* (1309, from ON *dalr* "valley"), *Mickeldale* (1309, from ON *mikill* "great, large", ON *dalr* "valley"). *Piledale* (1309, *Píll-dalr* "Willow valley" from ON *píll* "willow", ON *dalr* "valley"). Connects with Pellerdale (Raby Parish) and Piladall (Blakeley/Hargrave part of Little Neston).

Woodbank Parish: *Grymisgreue* (1463, "Grímr's wood" or "Óðinn's wood" from ON pers.n. *Grímr*: The same name appears in a list of pre-Domesday landowners from the Wirral. Grímr was also a personal name or by-name of Óðinn, the northern god), *Le Storrgreveson* (ON *stór* "great, large").

Woodchurch Parish: *Stack Yard* (ON *stakkr* "stack, pile, pillar"), *Lower Ackers, Higher Ackers* (ON *akr* "field, acre" or kjarr).

Place name evidence for Irish Settlers

Place names like Arrowe point to Norsemen coming from Gaelic speaking areas, probably the Western Isles of Scotland, or Ireland. Irby is also evidence for Irishmen or Norsemen coming from Ireland, although as we have seen above, there is an argument to suggest that Irby originates from settlers from the Isle of Man. However, there is unambiguous place-name evidence for Irishmen further reinforcing the Ingimund story: Noctorum (*cnocc-tírim* "Hill that's dry") and Liscard (*lios na carraige* "Hall on a rock"). To these could be added *Kneckyn* and *Knuckyn* (both cnocc-) "hill that's small", the old names respectively for Caldy Hill and the hill separating Irby and Thurstaston (last recorded use 1323). Both Noctorum and Liscard are now regarded as clearly Irish, although there is a difference of opinion whether Kneckyn and Knuckyn are Irish or Welsh in origin[50].

50   The Irish form is identified by W. Fergusson Irvine. John McNeal Dodgson suggests the equivalent Old Welsh *cync* rather than Old Irish *cnocc*. A similar name *Knukyn* is recorded in 1307-23 in Irby.

Language of the Settlement

This was without question Scandinavian. This was aptly described by the place-name expert Richard Coates who, in his recent (1997-8) article appearing in the *Journal of the English Place-Names Society* about Liscard wrote: "The impact of Scandinavian on the local dialect, and especially microtoponymic, vocabulary, as analysed by Wainwright and Dodgson, leaves no doubt which was the conversational language". We shall see later how clues from surprising sources - such as rental agreements with tenants and a Middle English Poem - that many Scandinavian customs, such as the method of naming children and large numbers of dialect words, survived at least into the 15th-Century.

Chapter 5

WIRRAL'S VIKING SEAPORT: MEOLS AND THE RIVER DEE

Sea and river communications were naturally significant for the Vikings. Apart from Thingwall, probably the most significant place for the Wirral Scandinavian community would have been Meols, its main trading port. The site had earlier been used by the Romans before being abandoned, but was quickly revitalised by the Vikings upon their arrival, and was probably the main entry point of the settlements.

The coastline in the ninth and later centuries of the medieval period was rather different from that of today. There used to be a significant coastline promontory at Dove Point which over the centuries has been eroded away. In the 19th-Century however very low tides, assisted by erosion of the covering sand, revealed the former settlement together with the remains of a forest of earlier times which have also gone. This was apparently the location of the medieval trading port and thousands of archaeological finds were made between 1810 and 1900. Although these discoveries have not yet been fully published they are clearly highly significant and compare with the finds in Chester and West Lancashire we consider later in the book. Judith Jesch, writing in *Wirral and its Viking Heritage*[51], says the following:

> Finds of coins and metalwork from Meols dated to the tenth and eleventh centuries show regular trading contacts with the rest of England, the Irish Sea and beyond. While Chester was an official port and mint for the (English) kingdom of Mercia, Meols seems to have operated as a trading centre for the politically separate Norse enclave on the peninsula, serving its own local Anglo-Scandinavian community. It has even been suggested[52] that a mint, producing 'Viking-style' imitations of official English coins, operated there in the 1010s and early 1020's.

A team of researchers, led by Dr. David Griffiths of the Department of Continuing Education, University of Oxford and Dr. Robert Philpott, Curator of Roman and Later Archaeology at the Liverpool Museum (National Museums and Galleries on Merseyside) are in the process of

[51] P. Cavill, S.E. Harding and J. Jesch, (2000) *Wirral and its Viking Heritage*, Chapter 1, English Place-Name Society, Nottingham.
[52] M. Blackburn (1996) 'Hiberno-Norse and Irish Sea imitations on Cnut's Quatrefoil type', *The British Numismatic Journal* 66, pp1-20.

Meols, today and past. LH top: Meols, high tide. RH top: Meols low tide (courtesy, Per-Anders Todal). Bottom: Old photo (courtesy of Frank Biddle) from the late 19th-Century of very low tides, showing remains of the old forest.

producing a full digital catalogue, site analysis and historical assessment of Meols[53]. This will be followed by "Phase 2" of the project involving Dr. Silvia Gonzalez of Liverpool John Moores University which will be a field investigation of the North Wirral landscape to define its continuing archaeological potential.

A recent article by David[54] highlighted the significance of the earlier discoveries, which includes the largest collection of Viking-style metalwork and coins in the North-west of England, but which at the moment is still less than has been found at York. He says the following:

> From around 1810, people from the local villages of Great Meols and Hoylake began to find small metal brooches, mounts, pins, tokens, seals, pilgrim badges, coins and knives, glass beads, pieces of leather and worked wood, iron weapons, knives and keys, sherds of pottery and flint tools, all as far as they could see from within the remains of the 'Ancient Forest'. The finds created a stir of interest in the isolated fishing community. Some of the Roman brooches were used as toys by local children, and other objects were kept as curiosities. A boy described as 'deaf and dumb' was one of the more prolific collectors. More people went down to the beach to search, and word got wider afield.

Griffiths then goes on to describe how people were able to build up impressive personal collections. As early as 1817 the first of these collectors was a P.B. Ainslie of Liverpool, and another notable collection appeared in the home of the Vicar of Hoylake, Reverend Longueville. A visiting rector from Liverpool, the respected antiquarian Revered Abraham Hume, was shown these by Mrs. Longueville, and this inspired him to attempt the first catalogue of these objects. Hume subsequenly presented a paper at a congress in York on these findings, and a book *Ancient Meols* was then published in 1863, shortly after J.J.A. Worsaae had produced his monumental work in Denmark on the *Danes and Norwegians in the British Isles*, and O'Donovan had published his discovery of the *Three Fragments*. Victorian Merseyside was bubbling with excitement. Hume himself was collecting objects, whilst paying a few pennies to anybody else who found interesting objects. Others making collections included Henry Ecroyd Smith, Curator of the Museum in Liverpool and a Charles Potter. Both Potter and Ecroyd Smith published the results of their finds in the *Transactions of the Historical Society of Lancashire and Cheshire*. However the collections were becoming scattered, and some objects were becoming lost to Meols and Merseyside altogther. Griffiths highlights the problem:

[53] D. Griffiths and R. Philpott (2003) *Meols: the Archaeology of the North Wirral Coast*, Oxbow Monograph Series, Oxford (with contributions by M. Adams, J. Axworthy, S. Bean, E. Callender, H. Cool, R. Cowell, G. Egan, S. Gonzalez, D. Higgins, J. Laughton, K. Matthews, P. Ottaway and D. Parker). A more popular book dealing with Wirral archaeology from the Mesolithic to post-medieval periods will follow, but focusing on the Meols story.

[54] D. Griffiths (2001) 'Meols' *British Archaeology* 62, p8.

There was some personal rivalry amongst the antiquaries, and their collections, like those of the locals, were their own private possessions. Ecroyd Smith was the first to donate his discoveries and purchases to a museum, principally to the early holdings of Liverpool Museum, but in 1858 he also sent a small parcel of 'representative objects' to the British Museum (where it lay almost forgotten until it was rediscovered deep in the museum archive last year). Potter donated his collection to the Grosvenor Museum, Chester, where it remains the largest of the groups of Meols objects. Mayer's collection was, like Ecroyd Smith's, donated to Liverpool Museum.

But what happened to the other collections, and in particular, Hume's? There is some evidence that Potter may have purchased some of Hume's objects, explaining the unusual variety and richness of his donation to Chester Museum. Other pieces probably never found their way into museums. As the owners died, some after moving to other parts of the country, the objects may have ended up almost anywhere, including sadly in the dustbin.

Smaller groups of objects from Meols (otherwise termed 'The Cheshire Shore', 'Hoylake' or 'Leasowe' after the neighbouring villages) have been identified in museums in Warrington, Birkenhead and even Verulamium. It is still possible that further objects from the site are lying forgotten in museum archives or private homes.

In his article, Griffiths explains how the impressive 19th-Century finds were reinforced by further discoveries in the 20th-Century. He says that these finds are broadly consistent in type and date with the previous ones, and show that traces of the ancient site may still remain amongst the sands. Griffiths also highlights the great new lease of life that the Viking settlers and traders had given to Meols:

The Saxons and Vikings gave Meols a fresh lease of life as a port, especially after the Wirral was densely settled by Scandinavians in the 10th-Century AD. Hiberno-Norse ringed pins and a small bronze bell, strap ends, mounts, coins and over 20 Anglo-Saxon silver pennies are evidence that the site participated in a trading network which extended to Dublin, York and Scandinavia during the early medieval period….. A recently re-identified group of iron weapons in the antiquarian collections, including a sword, a deliberately-bent spear head, an axe and a shield boss, suggest the presence of at least one pagan Viking grave at Meols. This could possibly link with some of the descriptions of burials.

The article by Griffiths highlighted the significance of the finds and also reflects on the point that for various reasons they have been dispersed over a wide range of museums and personal collections: the good news however is that the full database, when complete, will enable the documentation about the finds to be fully accessible to researchers.

The Vikings preferred the River Dee, not the Mersey
Like Meols the coastline on the River Dee side of Wirral was also different in the Medieval period: the present sea-front has been seriously affected by silting, accelerated by the colonisation over the last 150 years by Spartina grass from the USA brought in by ships from America[55]. Parkgate (from where Handel departed for his tour of Ireland in 1741), Neston and indeed Chester itself were once thriving sea-ports, and there was even a ferry to Gayton. As we will see in Chapter 11, the River Dee appears to have played a special role in the Battle of *Brunanburh* which took place in 937AD, and has been proposed as the legendary "Dingesmere" in that battle. The Dee was also the scene of a special boat trip upon which the English King Edgar took Celtic chiefs on in 975AD, the significance of which is also discussed in Chapter 11 in relation to Brunanburh. If local folklore is to be believed, post Brunanburh, the traffic along the Dee would have been further enhanced since the Vikings considered the River Mersey as cursed. The Dee may also have been crossed by Sir Gawain on his route from North Wales to Wirral in search of the Green Knight: a famous 14th-Century poem notable for its Norse dialect.

The change in the visible topography of the area may have resulted in some names being lost along with the physical features on all sides of the peninsula. One of the casualties of the change in sea-level on the Mersey side of the peninsula was the monastery at Stanlow which was inundated and finally abandoned by the end of the thirteenth-Century.

[55] R. and M. Freethy (1992), *Discovering Cheshire* (Edinburgh), p33. It has also been suggested that the Spartina was deliberately planted by John Summers Ltd. at Shotton steelworks to reinforce their partly reclaimed site for further construction. This unfortunately got out of control and the whole of the upper Estuary became infested.

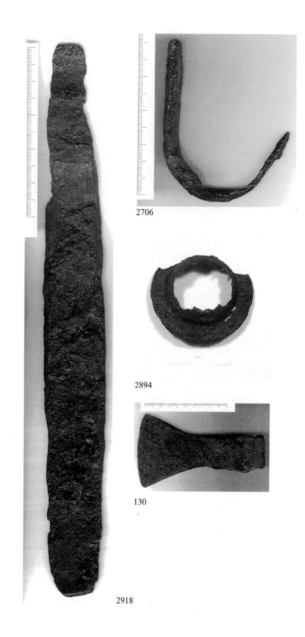

2706

2894

130

2918

Iron weapons found at Meols, including a shield boss (2894), axe (130) and deliberately bent spear head (2706) are probably from a Viking grave. The large object on the left (2918) had been considered to be a sword although there is now considerable doubt. © *The Meols Project.*

Conflict with the Welsh

In John of Trevisa's translation of the *Polychronicon* of Ranulph Higden[56], dating from about 1400, he notes the folklore probably going back to the Vikings which had arisen in relation to the Dee:

> Below the city of Chester runs the River Dee, which now separates England and Wales. The river often leaves the established channel, and changes the places shallow enough for fording every month, as the local people tell. Whichever side the water draws closer to, that side will have the disadvantage in war and be overthrown in that year, and the men of the other side will have the advantage and get the better of them. When the water changes its course in this fashion, it presages these events.

The drawing closer of the water in this tradition might well be an allusion to the progressive flooding of parts of Wirral, which would weaken the ability of the people to fight in the minor continuing conflicts since the settlement period. The new Scandinavian community of Wirral had however an earlier agenda: Chester.

---

[56] Text from K. Sisam, ed. (1985) *Fourteenth-Century Verse and Prose*, revised edition (Oxford), translation by Paul Cavill.

Chapter 6

VIKING CHESTER

The highly repected Cheshire historian and place-name expert, John McNeal Dodgson (1928-1990), made the following assessment of the aftermath of the 902AD settlements in the Wirral peninsula[57]:

> The Wirral colony began a programme of vigorous and occasionally armed expansion almost immediately after its establishment, towards the better lands of the English districts to the south.

Having settled in Wirral and, save the occasional skirmish with the English, kept their promise to Æthelflaed of not causing trouble, did the Vikings keep to their permitted area, presumably demarked by Raby? A perusal of the distribution of minor names of the area bearing possible Scandinavian or Irish roots reveals otherwise.   The large number of places with Viking roots not only inside the boundary of the original Scandinavian enclave but also outside demonstrates that after settling in the less fertile areas of North-west Wirral, the Scandinavian community of Wirral was soon exercising its muscles and engaging in an active programme of expansion towards the rest of Wirral and the surrounding hinterland - this included the coastal areas across the shores on the Wales side of the Dee (e.g. Talacre in Flint). This programme of expansion also extended towards Chester.

Viking designs on Chester

Ingimund's story - as described in the previous chapters - tells of Scandinavian Wirral's repeated attempts to secure Chester, by military means, working with its Danish and Irish allies and starting in 907AD - some five years after the start of the settlements. This was not the first time that the former Roman fortress had been subjected to attacks or occupation by Vikings or other germanic invaders. The Anglian tribes led by an *Ethelfrith* had first acquired Chester from the Britons in a battle recorded by the famous scribe Bede. This battle was assigned by him to a date of 613AD, although latter-day scholars have suggested a slightly later date. The historian F.T. Wainwright says[58]:

[57] J. McN Dodgson (1957) *Saga Book of the Viking Society* 14, 303-316
[58] F.T. Wainwright (1941) The Anglian Settlement of Lancashire, *Transactions Historical Society of Lancashire and Cheshire*, 93, pp 1-45.

Ethelrith consolidated the Anglian power in northern England. Not only did he weld Northumbria[59] into a powerful, if temporary, unity, but he made the first and most spectacular advance against the Britons in this area. He penetrated to the West coast of England. Of two discernible movements, the first culminating in the battle of Degsastan, AD603, by which an Anglian wedge was driven between the Strathclyde Britons of the remote North-west and their kinsmen of Lancashire and the South. The second thrust was towards Chester, and this seems to have brought the Lancashire plain under Anglian control. Bede describes the Battle of Chester, which was an annihilating defeat for the Britons. The usual interpretation is that the battle of Chester opened Lancashire to the English settlers who now flowed across the Pennines to take possession of their conquests. Archaeology has as yet no comment to make upon this view that Ethelfrith's was the first step towards the colonization of Lancashire.

280 years later in 893AD it was the Vikings - Danish Vikings - who were in Chester. At that time the Danes had control of Eastern England - the Danelaw - and had intentions on Mercia. The Anglo-Saxon Chronicle records how, late in 893AD the Danes moved rapidly to "a desolate town in Wirral which is called Chester", and stayed there until probably 895AD before embarking on a Welsh campaign. The ancient Welsh annals known as the *Annales Cambriae* and *Brut y Tywysogion* recall:

> *Nordmani venerunt et vastaverunt Loyer et Bricheniaue et Guent et Guinnligiauc.* "And then the Northmen devastated England, Brecheiniog, Morganwy, Gwent, Buallt, and Gwenllwg".

RH. Hodgkin, writing in the *History of the Anglo-Saxons* states: "The Danes then broke out of Chester, for a time ravaged in North Wales before returning to Essex through Northumbria and East Anglia", and it has been suggested that on their return they passed through Chester again. A most interesting point however is the reference by the Anglo-Saxon Chronicle to the desolate and wasted state of Chester before the Danish arrival in 893AD. Wainwright says the following:

> It has been suggested that the desolation dates from the Battle of Chester, 613AD. This would mean that for 280 years, the

[59] Northumbria in medieval times was different from today and included what is now Yorkshire, Lancashire and part of the Lake District.

seventh, eighth and ninth centuries, the town of Chester has no history worth the name. It may be, however, that the desolation was more recent: it may have been due to some raid of the Norsemen who had been plundering along the Irish and Welsh coasts for years. Chester, if it had recovered from Ethelfrith's campaign, was not likely to have escaped from the attention of these ubiquitous sea-rovers.

A few years later there was a movement of far greater significance: the new and powerful Scandinavian settlements of Wirral were flexing their muscles in the direction of Chester: the English had in the meantime refortified the city by 907AD, and were waiting for the Vikings to strike.

907AD and after

The previous Chapters described in detail the settlements and subsequent attacks based on the *Three Fragments,* now accepted by scholars as accurately recording the settlement and dates of the attacks on Chester. Although the detail of the skirmishes themselves has been open to question, the account presents a fascinating cycle of measure and countermeasure: "we did this so they did that". The full account has been given in Chapter 3 but we summarise the essence of the attacks on Chester here.

Although there has been five years of peace, the settlers have had to put up with poor quality land for their farms; so Ingimund calls together an emergency meeting of the Norse and Danish chiefs, presumably gathering them at Cross Hill, Thingwall. They agree they want action: a request is made for possession of Chester, which until recently has been a relatively deserted city, at least as found by the Danes some fourteen years previous. The English respond negatively, and re-fortify the city, expecting trouble. The first wave of attack is launched by a combined Norse, Danish and Irish force. They are tricked into going inside the city where many are trapped and killed. We are told that they regrouped and came back to attack again, but this time the English persuade the Irish contingent of the Wirral force to turn on the Danes which they do, killing some of them whilst they are off guard. The Norsemen, however, press on again, trying to ram down the gates. The English throw spears and boulders at them, so the Norsemen come back with hurdles to protect themselves as they batter away. Then the English throw boiling ale over them. The Norsemen counter this by covering the hurdles with hides. Then the English respond by setting bees on their attackers! The story finishes with the Vikings retreating back to Wirral.

910AD: Raiders to Traders - and then Settlers

Although the Scandinavians had not succeeded, the Ingimund story, as recorded in the *Three Fragments* ends with the tantalising statement "*but it was not long after that before the Norsemen came to do battle again...*" We do not know

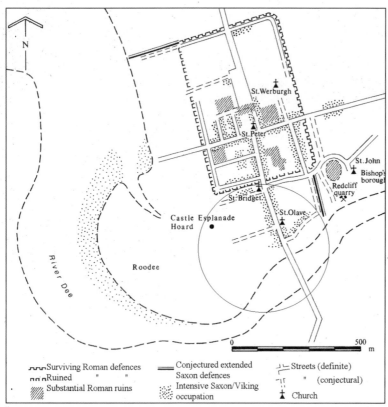

what this refers to, but eventually they were to achieve considerable success at Chester by abandoning aggression. Adopting a more peaceful approach seems to have paid dividends, with a trading community developing in the south of the city paralleled by an active involvement in the financial organisation of not only Wirral but also Chester. Scandinavians like Kolbein, Thorald and Othulf played a major role in developing the Chester Mint, prolific in the 10th and 11th Centuries.

Chester, first revived by Æthelflæd in 907AD following the Viking settlements of Wirral, grew during the 10th-Century into a major trading port, with the Dee as its major waterway, and the old Roman roads giving links to the Midlands and to York. The Dee, Wirral and Chester were conveniently on the axis between the major Viking centres of Dublin and York: Dublin was rapidly recovering as a Viking power base again after the expulsions of 902AD. Chester thus found itself on the southern edge of a vibrant, if unruly, Viking world with huge opportunities for trade. This Viking world stretched out from the Dee and across the seaways to Dublin and Ireland, the Isle of Man and Scottish Isles, Scandinavia and Iceland, and later to Greenland and, for a short period, even to North America. The desolate, deserted city, as found by a marauding Danish army only some two decades previously, had now found a new life. And it seems that, after the disagreements with Ingimund's Wirral had been settled, this time the Scandinavians were here to stay.

Plan of 10th-Century Chester, areas of densest settlement and the most substantial Roman ruins. The main Scandinavian community was the southern part of the city as indicated by the circle, although there appears to have been considerable integration. Approximately 25% of the population were thought to have been Scandinavian.

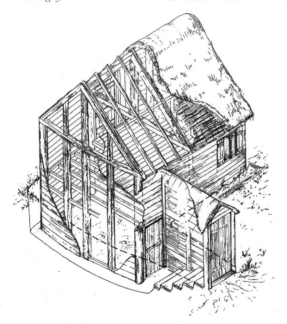

A reconstruction drawing of a Scandinavian-style timber building found during excavations in Lower Bridge Street in the 1970's. Note the typical cellar. Reproduced by courtesy of Chester City Council/ Chester Archaeology; drawing by Peter Alebon.

The Scandinavians in Chester

A significant number of the Chester Scandinavians had come from Ireland. We know this because a proportion of the 10th-Century moneyers from the area bore clear Irish-Norse origins with the name of *Irfara* (ON derivation "Ireland journeyer") and others included *Oslac* and *Mældomen*. But these were just three of a large number of moneyers bearing Scandinavian names from 910 onwards - three years after the start of the feuds with Ingimund. It appears the main enclave was in the south of the city, in the area from what is now Grosvenor Street and the Grosvenor Museum area, extending eastwards to at least the corner of Bridge Street, where St. Bridget's church (now gone) once stood, and down Lower Bridge Street to where St. Olave's church is located (on the same site as the original wooden church), and extending south beyond the city walls into Handbridge. St. Olave's was dedicated to the patron saint of Norway, and St. Bridget's to the patron saint of Ireland.

Integration between the Scandinavians and Saxons

This community would have existed side by side with the English who were within the old Roman Fortress area. The discovery of Saxon "Chester Ware" pottery in the Scandinavian area, together with Scandinavian and Hiberno-Norse metalwork such as ring headed pins and a brooch with an exact parallel in Dublin found in the Saxon area, suggests considerable integration between the two communities: the recent indiscretions by the raiders appear to have been forgiven or forgotten.

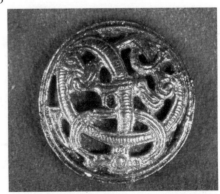

Viking disc brooch of silvered bronze in the form of an interlaced serpent, found in the ruins of a Roman building in Hunter Street, Chester. It is in the Jellinge style and dates to the 10th-Century. Reproduced by courtesy of Chester City Council/ Chester Archaeology.

A ring-headed dress pin made of bronze from Chester. This style of dress fastening was adopted by the Vikings who settled in Ireland; an almost identical example was found at L'Anse-aux-Meadows in Newfoundland, the only known Viking settlement in America. Reproduced by courtesy of Chester City Council/ Grosvenor Museum.

The Chester Mint

The 10th-Century saw Chester emerge as one of the main mints, in fact the fifth largest in England, with a prolific output of silver pennies. This growth was fuelled by the rapidly expanding trade with the Viking North through the River Dee. Chester, along with Meols at the top end of Wirral, was booming as a trading port, and a measure of this activity is that silver pennies and pottery from Chester were soon to be common in Dublin, as archaeological finds there have shown. Unfortunately we do not know the actual location of the mint in the city.

The Dublin connections proved particularly important, and the increased trade was the catalyst for further growth of the Scandinavian community in Chester. In 921AD a pair of dies had been cut at Chester for a coin of the Dublin Viking leader Sithric. Sithric was succeeded in 927 by Guthfrith, whose son Ólaf came face to face with Æthelstan's English at the Battle of Brunanburh, as we consider in detail later in this book. The mint and ties with Dublin continued to flourish throughout the 10th-Century. There would no doubt have been a lull at the time of Brunanburh in 937AD, and then there was another lull in the 970's for reasons that are not properly understood, although it might be connected with King Edgar taking British chiefs rowing on the Dee in 975AD (reminding them of Brunanburh?), or a major Viking raid into the area which took place around 980AD. The mint did, however, revive near the end of the 10th-Century, and was thriving again during the period when the Danish King Cnut (Canute) (1017-1035) and his sons Harald (until 1040) and Harthacnut (1042) were in control of England.

Besides silver coins from this period, modern discoveries in Chester have included 'hacksilber' (= scrap silver), and silver ingots. One of the latter, presumably from Chester, was found in 1995 in a farm in Ness, Wirral, and described by Simon Bean[60]: the shape is similar to two stone moulds found in Chester. A more impressive discovery had been made in 1950 at Castle Esplanade in the South-west area of the city: *The Castle Esplanade Hoard* consisted of a large number of coins (at least 520) marked with the names of Scandinavian and English moneyers. These were stored in a Saxon pot, together with a quantity of hacksilber and a number of fragmentary or whole silver ingots of the Ness type. The hoard has been dated at c965AD, and its total value has been estimated at some 1300 pennies, a very considerable sum of money for the 10th-Century! The find spot - between the Saxon area and the river - has led to the theory that the hoard belonged to a Viking trader, presumably from Dublin, who had left his ship and hidden his fortune in a safe place before entering the Saxon town. For some unknown reason he never came back to retrieve it.

[60] P. Cavill, S.E. Harding and J. Jesch. (2000) *Wirral and its Viking Heritage*, English Place-Name Society, Nottingham, pp. 19-20.

Part of the Castle Esplanade Hoard, consisting of silver pennies, ingots and hacksilber - pieces of jewellery chopped up to act as currency. Everything was contained in the small cooking pot which stands in the background. The hoard was lost by a Viking trader some time around 965AD. Reproduced by courtesy of Chester City Council/Grosvenor Museum.

Close ups of the Castle Esplanade Hoard. Reproduced by courtesy of Chester City Council/ Grosvenor Museum.

Moneyers names on reverse of coins

The Anglo-Saxon practice of putting the names of moneyers on the reverse of their coins has provided us with a valuable clue about the extent of the Scandinavian influence on Chester. Being a moneyer involved what we would describe as buying a franchise from the king to make a quantity of coins, so to be a moneyer you had to be a rich and influential man. 25% of the names on Chester coins are Scandinavian (a list is given in Chapter 12), with people such as *Raenulf* in the reign of Æthelstan (924-940) and *Þóraldr* (Thorald) under Æthelred (979-1016).

Jewellery: Broochs and ring-headed pins

Several ring-headed pins of a type used by the Vikings in Ireland have been discovered in Chester, and also at Meols; this reinforces the picture of very strong trade links through the Dee and the Irish Sea. Fragments of arm rings and brooches dated to 970-980AD in the Castle Esplanade Hoard from Chester resemble strongly jewellery discovered at Ballaquayle (Isle of Man). A Norse brooch discovered in Hunter Street, Chester, is identical to one discovered in Dublin and was almost certainly made from the same mould. The timberwork in cellared structures discovered in Lower Bridge Street, near St Olave's Church, is the same as structures excavated in Viking Dublin and York.

The names of streets and churches also bear out the impact of the Scandinavians. *Clippe Gate* (near Bridge gate) and *Wolf Gate*, (next to the present New Gate) derive from the names of the man *Klyppr* and woman *Úlfhildr* respectively. There is also Crook Street (from ON *krokkr,* or *Krókr*). St Bridget's Church and St Olave's Church, both in the southern part of the city, have been mentioned already. Finally there was a stonemason (or perhaps a school of stonemasons) based near the Church of St.John's producing high quality stonework in the Irish-Norse style and which is found in Chester and Wirral. He was clearly either of Scandinavian origin himself or he was producing work for Scandinavian clients. Irish-Norse stonework is considered later in this book, and also by W.G. Collingwood and J.D. Bu'lock (see Chapters 6 and 7 of P. Cavill, S.E.Harding and J. Jesch, *Wirral and its Viking Heritage*).

Resonances from the Chester Scandinavians

The mark of the Norsemen on the financial, administrative and legal arrangements of Chester and its shire remained at least until the 13th-

Century. One Norseman, *Gunnor,* held one third of the then important episcopal manor of Redcliff.   The twelve iudices of the city, mentioned in 1086 as chosen from the men of the king, bishop, and earl, and obliged to attend the Chester hundred court, resembled the lawmen of the Scandinavian boroughs. A powerful Scandinavian community at Handbridge, south of the city across the River Dee, was reflected in terms of its Domesday assessment, where the Scandinavian term *carucate* was used as a land measure rather than the English *hide.*

Chapter 7

VIKING WEST LANCASHIRE

The Viking Place-names of West Lancashire

Although the only ancient documents reporting the large-scale arrival and settlement of Scandinavians into the North-west of England refer explicitly to Wirral, the evidence from place-names is clear: the settlements extended from the River Dee all the way up to the North Lakes and Solway Firth. This was especially true of the coastal plain between the Rivers Mersey and Ribble, a region referred to until relatively recently as South-west Lancashire, but since the reallocation of county boundaries (Furness and Cartmel moving from Lancashire to Cumbria) an area which is referred to now as *West Lancashire*. This region is covered by the old Hundreds of West Derby and Leyland.

Eilert Ekwall[61] (1877-1964), Professor of English at the University of Lund, Sweden, was responsible for producing the seminal study on Lancashire Place Names in 1922[62]. Intriguingly he acknowledges in his foreword considerable help from W.G. Collingwood amongst others, and refers to the *Handbook of Lancashire Place Names* published shortly before in Liverpool by John Sephton[63]. By this time, scholars were well aware of the significance of the Norse movement into the North-west, after the re-discovery and publication of the *Three Fragments* describing the Wirral invasion by John O'Donovan in 1860. A more recent study building on the Ekwall work has been the short monograph by David Mills, published in 1976[64], although Lancastrians still await something comparable to the momentous work produced for Cheshire by John McNeal Dodgson. The latter study covered all names - including field names.

As with the whole of the North-west, contemporary historical accounts of the colonisation by Scandinavians is sparse. The Ingimund tradition for Wirral was proven by Wainwright[65] to be historical fact. According to tradition, the Scandinavian kingdom of Galloway in what is now South-west Scotland was set up in defiance of King Harald Hárfagri of Norway by one of the rebellious West Norwegian leaders Ketill Flatnose. When Hárfagri subsequently came to hunt him down in the Isle of Man he found no one there because they had cleared off to Scotland! That account may also have been relevant to the migrations into the Lake District and North and West Lancashire, reinforcing the Ingimund expulsions from Ireland in 902AD

[61] O. Arngart (1965) Eilert Ekwall, *English Studies* 46, 50-51.
[62] E. Ekwall (1922) *The Place-Names of Lancashire*, Manchester University Press.
[63] J. Sephton (1913) *Handbook of Place-Names*, Henry Young and Sons, Liverpool.
[64] D. Mills (1976) *The Place-Names of Lancashire* (London).
[65] F.T. Wainwright (1948) Ingimund's Invasion. *The English Historical Review*, 247, 145-167.

which would have primarily affected Wirral and South-west Lancashire.

North of the Ribble, Amounderness is named after the Scandinavian leader *Agmund*, and a 12th-Century account of the grant of Amounderness to the oversee of York by King Æthelstan (924-940) of Battle of Brunanburh fame says that he gained land from 'the pagans'. That account is strongly indicative of a Scandinavian presence in the 10th-Century.

There is however no record in the Anglo-Saxon Chronicles of the Danelaw extending into Lancashire. The chroniclers - pre-occupied with the military campaigns of the Danes from the East, completely missed this highly significant, although largely peaceful movement from the North and West. Besides the place-name evidence, archaeological evidence is significant, with major finds of buried treasure at Harkirke near Crosby and further North on the Ribble at Cuerdale. Also significant was the discovery of pieces of the Viking board game Hnefatafl, now beautifully restored and displayed in Warrington Museum.

Harkirke Archaeological finds

We have already referred to the impressive finds at Meols and Chester. But the northern shores of Mersey were also witness to a major find at a small piece of land called Harkirke (Ordnance Survey: SD325011). Although the coins have long since gone, fortunately the discoverer, William Blundell of Little Crosby Hall, produced a copperplate of 35 of the coins that were found. Despite the disappearance of the coins, the copperplate is now preserved in the Lancashire Record Office.

The story describing their discovery is intriguing and was recounted in 1992 by B.J.N. Edwards[66]. Blundell had planned to use a strip of land at Harkirke as a cemetery. On Sunday 7th April 1611 the first burial took place, but the following morning after the digging a 14 year old boy Thomas Ryse, walking Blundell's cattle, came across some silver coins on the sandy soil that had been dug up. He showed these to the other servants and then to Blundell. Ryse took him back to the site, along with Blundell's son Nicholas and an Edward Fenton. They were joined later by Blundell's brother Richard. More coins were found, eventually over 80, or "over fower score". Blundell describes, in an account now kept at the Lancashire Record Office (code: DDB1 24/12) how he produced an accurate drawing of the coins:

> After I had drawen these twenie ivee forms of sundrie Coynes
> afore placed, I fownde by more diligent revewe of the Coynes
> that there were dyvers and sundrie fashions of the money of

[66] B. J. N. Edwards (1992) The Vikings in North-west England: the Archaeological Evidence. In J. Graham-Campbell ed. *Viking Treasure from the North West*, Chapter 5, National Museums and Guides on Merseyside, Liverpool.

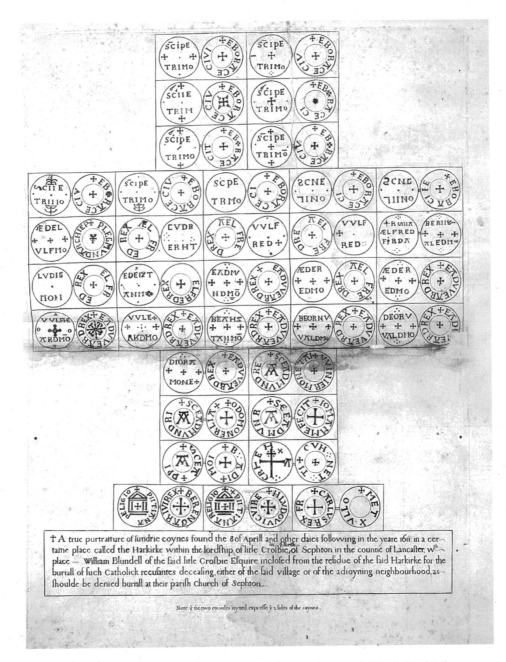

Copperplate print depicting coins from Harkirke, West Lancashire, found in 1611 (British Library, Harleian MS 1437, 128v-129r). The engraved plate was supposedly made in 1613, and is now in the Lancashire Record Office.

Hnefatafl or "Tablut" pieces from about the 10th-Century now at Warrington Museum. Courtesy of Angela Doyle and Keith Scott.

Sainte Peter, besides that forme which is here before first expressed. Formes of which Coynes I have here under drawen with other twoe of strange and to me unknowen Inscriptions upon there firste sides, which twoe are sett the lowest here under.

Blundell's grandson writing to his own son in 1686 said the total number of coins was 'about 300'. Unfortunately the ultimate fate of the coins was a mystery, although B.J.N. Edwards came up with two theories. The first is that, after being kept in Crosby Hall until 1642 they were sent to a safe place in Wrexham, and never seen again. The second is that a chalice and a pyx were made of some of the Harkirke silver. The pyx had on one side a crucifixion and the other carried the inscription

This was made of/ siluer found in/ the burial place/W.Bl.'

The chalice was stolen in the 19th-Century, and even the pyx was stolen in 1975. Fortunately it had been analysed by x-ray fluorescence spectroscopy in 1974 by the National Museum of Antiquities of Scotland which confirmed its antiquity. Blundell was a very religious man, and B.J.N. Edwards has suggested that he kept only 35 of the coins, and "made good use of the remainder as a pious offering". The Harkirke find was superseded by an even more spectacular find in 1840 on the South bank of the River Ribble at Cuerdale (see Chapter 8).

Hnefatafl pieces

Although West Lancashire hasn't yielded the same spectacular Viking age stonework as North Lancashire, the Lake District and Wirral pieces from the Old Norse board game *hnefatafl* or "Kings Tablut" have been found on the northern shores of the Mersey. This game dates back to before 400AD and is a forerunner of chess and *skák-tafl* ("check table") introduced later in the 11th/12th centuries. An original pair of hnefatafl pieces is currently at Warrington Museum and shown in the illustration. *Hnefa-tafl* means "headpiece table or board", where the *hnefi* has to break out of the centre of the board and avoid being surrounded by his opponent's pieces: a web site where you can play this game on-line is given at the end of the book. Describing the main *hnefi* piece the museum writes the following: "Jet figure with bevelled edges, ornamented with scratched lines and circles, possibly drawn with an instrument such as a compass". Of the other piece "Jet figure: cylindrical with bevelled top". In the illustation the drawing pin is included to give an idea of size.

Distribution of Place Names with Scandinavian Elements

Place names provide our main body of evidence for the mass migration of Scandinavians into West Lancashire. The evidence is particularly convincing for coastal regions north of the Ribble, and also for the coastal plain in West Lancashire, and largely among the sandhills and mossland. By contrast there is little evidence of major settlements on the higher ground to the east, with Anglezarke being the only major example, until the boundary with the former bastion of the Danelaw - Yorkshire - is approached.

Unlike Wirral, the Isle of Man and the North Lakes, there are very few place-names with *-by* in West and North Lancashire, the exceptions being the South-west, which probably relate to the Wirral group. The South-west Lancashire *-by* names, very common in the Danelaw, may be symptomatic of a substantial Danish presence reinforcing the Norse community (and this is backed by the Ingimund tradition for Wirral), but their scarcity in the rest of the region indicates that by contrast to the Norse, the Danish influence on most of West and North Lancashire was not major.

The most significant place-name in West Lancashire is probably Thingwall: this is just off the M62 motorway near Knotty Ash. Its existence is strongly indicative that the Scandinavians had a separate and major administrative unit independent of the English communities to the east of the county. There are also, in place-names, examples of what are known as *Scandinavian inflections*, such as in Litherland and Lathom. These suggest a knowledge of the grammatical system of advanced Old Norse among the population. Whatever, the evidence clearly points to a substantial Scandinavian colonisation of the coastal plain of West Lancashire in the 10th-Century, where the people, like the Wirral Scandinavians, moved into low quality lands which were either empty or only sparsely populated before their arrival.

West Lancashire place-names with definite Scandinavian origins and (facing page) their possible Viking forms.

Hestaskeið

Bekanshaugr

Lágrland

Norð-melr Þaraldrstún   Bróðratún

Krossnes   Holmr

Holmrskógr

Þaraldrskógr

Ólafrsargi

Birkidalr   Kjarr-kross   Burhskógr

Einulfsdalr   Skarbrekka Hlaðum

Birki-kjarr

Blæingrsskógr

Fornisby   Ormrskirkja   Griótbý

Skáli

Skjaldmarrsdalr   Leikrþveit

Altkjarr   Bikerstaðir

Litill-krossabýr   Lundr   Konungrskógr

Krossabýr   Reinn-ford

Sef-tún

Hlidarland   Eintré   Kirkjubý

Kirkju-dalr   Króksstaðir

Vestri Dýrabý

Hulm

Þingvöllr   Rá-bý

Lundr

Toki-stöð

Eikiberg

Place Names in West Lancashire with Scandinavian origins

A study of place-names provides the key evidence behind the mass migrations of Scandinavians into the area in the 10th-Century, and we consider here all the place-names in West Lancashire (excluding field, road or track names) with definite or probable Scandinavian origins. The list of names is based on the analyses provided by Ekwall (1922) and Mills (1976)[67]. The list does not include field-names. The Ordnance Survey coordinates are given to six figures (this corresponds to an accuracy of 100metres).

Aigburth, SJ387861. *Eikiberg* "Oaks hill", from ON *eiki* (oaks) and ON *berg* (hill). An early form (1250) includes Eikeberhe. Suburban town on a ridge, and now includes Mossley Hill.

Ainsdale, SD311122. *Einulfsdalr* "Einulf's valley" from ON *Einulfr* and ON *dalr* (or OE *dæl*). In the Domesday Book it is listed as Einulvesdel. Situated between sandhills and mossland.

Aintree, SJ380986. *Ein-tré* "Tree standing alone" from ON *ein* (one, alone) and *tré* (tree). An early form (1246) is *de Eyntre*. The tree would be a conspicuous feature in low lying ground, and may have marked a boundary.

Altcar, Great, SD325064 and **Little**, SD305068. "The carr or marshland beside the River Alt", from ON *kjarr* (marshland). Land, originally of low quality on the banks of the Alt.

Anglezarke, SD620160. *Ólafr-argi* "Olaf's shieling" after the ON personal name *Ólafr* (later Anlaf) and ON *argi*- a shieling, pasture. Early forms include Anlauesargh (1224). As with Arrowe in Wirral, and places like Grimsargh and Goosnargh north of the Ribble, the *argi* or *erg* was summer pastureland away from the main farmhouse, and would correspond to an ancient form of Scandinavian farming called transhumance, where the pastureland near the farmhouse was saved for winter fodder. This practice of farming is still followed in Norway, and also in Wirral at least until the Victorian period. Anglezarke is one of the few Scandinavian place-names in West Lancashire not in the coastal plain but on higher ground.

Argarmeols (lost, 1400 formerly near SD315145). *Erengrsmelr* "Erengr's sandhill" was destroyed by the sea at the end of the 14th-Century. The only surviving portion is now Birkdale. Early form is *Erengermeles* (Domesday).

Aynesargh (lost c1400, formerly SJ365955). Second element is ON *argi*, shieling: the significance of this is explained in the description for Anglezarke above. In Walton Parish.

Becconsall, SD447228. *Bekanshaugr* "Bekan's hill", from the ON personal name *Bekan*, and ON *haugr* (hill). Earliest known form is Bekanshou (1248). The personal name is originally Irish in origin and was adopted by the

Scandinavian settlers before the expulsion of 902AD. Appears to refer to a ridge falling to low land at the River Ribble.

Bescar, SD390135. "Birch marsh" from OE *birce* (birch) and ON *kjarr* (marshland). Early form includes Birchecar (1331). Because of the relative lateness of record of this name, the first element may originally have been ON *birki*.

Bickerstaffe, SD445044. Possibly from ON *stöð* (landing place) or *staðir* (homestead). Several suggestions have been made for the origin of the first element Bicker. These include ON *bikkja* (to overturn), although Ekwall thinks it is more likely to have been derived from an old English personal name.   An early form is *Bikerstad* (1190). Now a farming parish near Skelmersdale.

Birkdale, SD330156. *Birkidalr* "Birch-copse valley" or "Birch-tree valley", from ON *birki* (birch-copse) and ON *dalr* (valley). Birkdale was formerly part of Argarmeols (now gone). Early form includes Birkedale (1200). Since 1850 it has been an important commuter town on the Liverpool -Southport line, and the site of the famous golf-course.

Blainscough, SD572100. *Blæingrsskógr* "Blæing's wood" from the ON personal name *Blæingr* and ON *skógr* (wood). Early form: de Bleynescowe (1281). Near Standish.

Breck, Breck House, SJ360920, in Walton parish. From ON *brekka* "hill, slope". Early form del Brek (1323). One of many examples of *brekka* in Merseyside and West Lancashire. Breck Road is the start of the A580.

Bretherton, SD475205. North-west of Croston, on the River Douglas. E. Ekwall[68] considers Bretherton may derive from ON *Bróðratún* "the tun or farmstead of the brothers", rather than an OE equivalent. As Bretherton in 1190. It is possible that here, as in the Danelaw, the estate was handed over to a younger brother.

An old cross at Crosby.

Brettargh Holt, SJ410890. From ON *Bretar* "the Britons" and ON *argi* "shieling", the same element in Anglezarke and Arrowe Park. Early form: Bretarwe (12th-Century).

Burscough, SD445115. "The stronghold in or at the wood", from OE *burh* (stronghold) and ON *skógr* (wood). Early form includes Burscogh (1190).

Carr Cross, SD375140. From ON *kjarr* (marshland). Near Scarisbrick.

Crosby , Great and Little, SJ315990. *Krossabýr* "The cross village", or "The village with a cross or crosses" from ON *kross* and ON *býr*. Early forms include Crosebi (Domesday) and Crosseby (1212).

[68] E. Ekwall (1922) *The Place-Names of Lancashire*, p157

Croxteth Hall at Croxteth Park in West Lancashire (top), courtesy of Patrick Trollope, and Króksstaðir in Eyjafjörður near Akureyri, North Iceland (bottom), courtesy of Ragnar Th. Sigurðsson.

Crossens, SD373198. "The ness with the cross or crosses", from ON *kross* and ON *nes* (promontory). The hamlet is indeed on a promontory at the mouth of the River Ribble.

Croxteth, Croxteth Park, SJ405961. *Króksstaðir*, "Krokr's place or landing place" from ON personal name *Krókr* (or ODan *Krok*), and ON *staðir* (homestead) or ODan *stath* (place). Early form includes Crocstad (1257). Croxteth, as *Króksstaðir*, is another Mersey place-name in Iceland.

Cuerdley, SJ545875. On the Mersey, North-east of Widnes. Ekwall considers it possibly derives from ON *kofr* (chest) or *kufr* (rounded summit) and has a similar origin to Cuerdale near Preston. Early form is Kyuerlay (1246).

Cunscough, Cunscough Hall, SD410028. *Konungrskógr*, "The king's wood", from ON *konungr* or *kunungr* (king) and ON *skógr* (wood). Early forms include Conigscofh (1190).

Dalton, SD495083, **Dalton Lees**, SD502088. "Valley farmstead", from ON *dalr* and ON *tún* or OE *tun*. One of two Daltons in Lancashire.

Drummersdale, SD397130. "Log valley" or "valley with a lout" From ON *drummel* (log), or *drumbi* (a lout) and ON *dalr* or OE *dæl* (valley). Near Bescar and Scarisbrick.

Eggergarth (Halsall Parish) *Ekra-garðr* "small ploughed field enclosure" from ON *ekra* (small ploughed field) and ON *garðr* (enclosure). Early form Ekergert (1240). Eggergarth Road is now part of the main Maghull-Southport Road from SD365058.

Eller Beck, a tributary of the Douglas originates from the Old Norse *bekkr* (stream) and probably also *elri* (alders): "Alders stream", and a place-name on its banks is recorded as de Ellerbek in 1246.

Everton, SJ355925. The first element is possibly influenced by ON *efri* "upper", although it is most likely of English origin: David Mills[69] ascribes it to OE *eofor* "domestic pig". Ekwall says the following[70]

Everton: some possible Viking influence on its name? 'Efriton'.

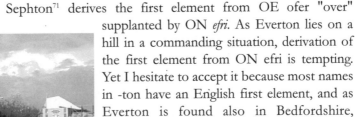

Sephton[71] derives the first element from OE ofer "over" supplanted by ON *efri*. As Everton lies on a hill in a commanding situation, derivation of the first element from ON efri is tempting. Yet I hesitate to accept it because most names in -ton have an English first element, and as Everton is found also in Bedfordshire, Nottinghamshire and Hampshire. I am inclined to derive it from OE personal name *Eofora*.

[69] D. Mills (1976) *The Place-Names of Lancashire*, p82.
[70] ditto, p115.
[71] John Sephton, see Chapter 2.

Vikings arriving at Formby. Part of the 2000 millenium "Formby Viking Festival". Photograph courtesy of Patrick Trollope.

Formby, SD295075. *Fornisbý* "Forni's village", from ON personal name *Forni* and ON *býr*, or ODan *bý*. An alternative is *Fornabý* "the old village" from ON *forn* (old). Early form includes Fornebei (Domesday). Ekwall points out that Fornaby is a very common Swedish name, and Fornebu was until recently the site of the main Oslo Airport.

Greetby (Greetby Hill), SD422084. *Grïótbý* or *Grïótabý* "Gravelly/stoney village" from ON *grïót* (stones, gravel) and ON or ODan *bý* (village). An alternative is *Grettirbý* "Grettir's village" from the ON personal name *Grettir*. Ekwall prefers the former interpretation, unless the earliest known form, *Grittebi* (1190), was miswritten. Another early form is de Greteby (1246). On the northern side of Ormskirk and now merged into it following expansion of the latter.

River Greeta (*Grïót-â*), from ON *â* (river).

Gunnolf's Moors, SD595213. From ON personal name *Gunnulfr*. Former name for eastern hilly part of Leyland, embracing Hoghton, Wheelton, Whittle-le-Woods. Early form: Gunnoluesmores (1212).

Harker, SD368086. From OE *hara* (hare) or *har* (grey) and ON *kjarr* (marshland). Early form Harekar (1225). Near Halsall.

Harkirke, SD325011. "Hoary Church" from OE *har* and ON *kirkja*. Early form Harkirke (1275). Site of a major archaeological find (see above).

Haydock, SJ565970. Second element "dock" from either ON *dökk* "hollow" or OE *docce*. First element is Celtic for barley: "Hollow where the barley is grown". Early forms include Hedoc (1169) and Haydok (1286).

Hesketh Bank SD445235, **Moss** SD435225 and **Sands** SD410260. *Hestaskeið* "Horse race-track", from ON *hestur* (horse) and ON *skeið* (race track, race course). Early form includes de Heskeyth (1293). The race course has been suggested by Ekwall to be on the level shore of Ribble (Hesketh Sands). Horse racing was a popular pastime of the Vikings and there are two other Viking "*hestaskeið*" on Wirral, one in Irby, the other in Thornton Hough parishes.

Holmes SD435190 and **Holmeswood** SD435168. "The islands", from ON *holmr* (islet, drier ground on a marshy area). Early form: Holmes juxta Maram de Tarlton, c1210.

Hopecarr SJ670980 *Hopkjarr* "a piece of dry land on a fen" from OE *hop* and ON *kjarr*. Now a Nature Trail on Pennington Brook (near the junction of the A580 with the A574).

Hoscar, SD470117. "Horse-carr" From ON *hross* or OE *hors* and ON *kjarr* (marshland). Early form, Horsecarr (1344).

Hulme SJ605910. From ODan *hulm* "island, water-meadow". Early form Hulm (1246). The place-name *Hulm* is characteristic of Danish, not Norse settlement. North of Warrington.

Kirkby, SJ420988. *Kirkju-bý* "Church village, from ON *kirkja* and ODan *bý* or ON *býr*. Early form includes Kyrkeby (1228). Identical name to the Kirkby in Wallasey. The present church is dedicated to the Anglo-Saxon St. Chad of the seventh-Century, so the Vikings may have renamed an existing earlier English settlement. There are a number of place-names in Iceland with the identical name

Kirkdale, SJ350935. *Kirkju-dalr* "Church valley" from ON *kirkja* and ON *dalr*. Early form includes Kierkedala (1201). The main Ormskirk-Liverpool

Top: Kirkby in West Lancashire seen from Boyes Brow. On their arrival the Vikings would have seen in the distance an earlier form of the old Saxon church of St. Chad's, and hence given the name Kirkby - Settlement at the Church. Bottom: Kirkjubær, near Hella, in Iceland, courtesy of Ragnar Th. Sigurðsson.

road cuts through the Kirkdale valley leading to Walton. The valley is the route that medieval parishioners may have taken to the church on Walton-on-the-Hill.

Laithwaite, SD565055. From ON *leikr* "play",and ON *þveit* "clearing". Early form Leiketheit (1200). One of the few "thwaites" in West Lancashire. Now part of the town of Wigan.

Lathom, SD458107. *Hlaðum* "at the barns" from ON *hlaða*. See the following chapter. Early forms include Lathum (1196).

Leyland, SD545228. "Fallow-land" from ON *lágr* (low) or OE *læge*, and ON, OE *land*. Early form Lailand (Domesday). The town indeed stands on low ground near the River Lostock.

Limbrick, SD680240. Possibly ON *lind-brekka* "lime-tree slope". In Standish Parish. One of the many *brekka* in Lancashire.

Litherland, SJ340980. *Hlíðarland* "Slope land", "Land on a slope", from ON *hlíðar* and ON *land*. Early form includes Liderlant (Domesday). Litherland is now a northern extension of Liverpool and covers the higher ground rising from the mouth of the River Mersey. As considered in further detail in the following chapter, the name has an inflectional form characteristic of an advanced form of Old Norse: its existence gives undisputed proof of a large and influential population of Scandinavians in the whole area.

Lunt, SD347020. From ON *lundr* (a grove or small wood). Early form: de Lund (1251).

Lunt's Heath, SD516882. From ON *lundr*. Early form: du Lund (1292). Near Cranshaw Hall, off the A5080.

Myckering Farm, SD046402. *Mykiar-eng* "Manured Meadow" from ON *mykr* (manure), ON *eng* (meadow). Near Aughton. Early form: Mykeringe (1581).

Meols Hall, West Lancashire.

North Meols SD360190. *Norð-melr* "The sand-hill in the north", from ON *norð* and ON *melr* "sandbank". Recorded as Normoles in 1194. The earliest known form, recorded in the Domesday Book, is in fact *Otegrimele* "Audgrim's sandbank" and Ekwall has suggested this has come from either the ON personal name *Oddgrimr*, or more likely *Audgrimr*. Also **Meols Hall** at SD366183. The North Meols parish occupied the sandy strip between the sea and Martin Mere, and its name mirrors South Meols which has not survived as a name, and Argarmeols, also now lost, but considered above. The Meols on Wirral was a significant

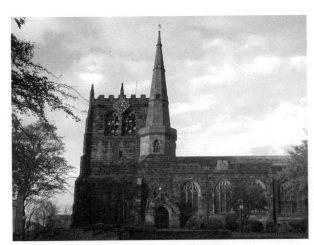

The site of Orm's church in Ormskirk. The present Church probably occupies the site of the original Viking church.

sea-port in Viking times, and there are corresponding place-names in Iceland.

Ormskirk, SD415085. *Ormrskirkja* "Orm's church" from ON personal name *Ormr* and ON *kirkja*. Early form includes Ormeskierk (1203). The original church was named after the founder, although it is a surprising coincidence that in 1203 another Orm was the landowner. The Scandinavian settlers may well have discovered an Anglo-Saxon church on their arrival. The present church lies on a hill surrounded by low land.

Rainford, SD480010. *Reinn-ford* "Ford at a boundary strip", from ON *reinn* "strip of land forming the boundary of a field or estate"[72] and OE *ford*, as suggested by David Mills. Harald Lindqvist had earlier suggested first element as ON *reyn* "rowan trees" but Eilert Ekwall considers it unlikely in the absence of surrounding Scandinavian names[73]. Early form: Raineford (1198)

Rainhill, SJ492915. Possibly from ON *reinn*. Early form Reynhull (1246). On a hill five miles south of Rainford.

Rainhill Stoops, SJ502903. Nearby Rainhill, with the Stoops, as recorded in 1786, in which ON *staup* (steep drop) has been added.

Ravensmeols, Raven Meal Hills, SD285055. *Hrafns-melr* "Hrafn's sandhill" from ON personal name *Hrafn* and ON *melr* (sandbank). On sandy ground near Formby, and the site of an old manor, now washed away by the sea. One of the many Meols on the West Lancashire and Wirral coastline.

Ridgate (Prescot parish). "The cleared road". From Middle English *rüdden* "to clear" and ON *gata* "street, road".

Roby, SJ432908. *Rá-bý* or *Ra-býr* from ON *rá* "boundary" and ODan *bý* (village, town) or ON *býr* (village, settlement). Similar to Wirral's Raby and probably represented the eastern boundary of the main West Lancashire Scandinavian settlement. Now marks the boundary of Childwall. Early forms include Raby (1238).

Roscoe Low, SD617133. *Rá-skógr* "Boundary wood". From ON *rá* (boundary) and ON *skógr* (wood). On a hill, 525 ft. Early form: Rascahae (1190). First element could be "Roe". In Standish parish.

Sarscow (in Eccleston parish). *Sæfarisskógr* "Sæfari's wood" from ON personal name *Sæfari* and ON *skógr* (wood). Early forms: Saferscohe and Sarescogh (1401).

Scarisbrick, SD380133. *Skarbrekka* "Skar's slope" from ODan or ON

[72] See E. Ekwall (1922) *The Place-Names of Lancashire*, p.107.
[73] ditto.

Scarisbrick Hall

personal name *Skar* and ON *brekka* (slope).   Early form includes de Skaresbrek (1232). The name may arise from the slight rise from two streams near what is now Scarisbrick Hall. Although the first element is more popular amongst Danish settlers, the second element is Norwegian.

Scarth Hill, SD428066. Hamlet situated on high ground to the south east of Ormskirk. From ON *skarð* (notch, cleft, hill or mountain pass). Early form Scarth (1190). The hill is South-east of Ormskirk and rises to about 100 metre. The Ormskirk-Rainford road runs across it.

Scholes, SD589058. In Wigan parish. From ON *skáli* "hut". Early form del Scoles (1332). *Skáli* is characteristic of Norse settlers rather than Danish

Scholes, SJ490934. In Prescot parish. From ON *skáli*. Early form Eschales (1190).

Scholes (formerly in Sefton parish, now lost). From ON *skáli* "hut". Early form Scoles (13th-Century).

Sefton, SD355014. *Sef-tún* "Sedge farmstead", or "Farmstead where rushes grow" from ON *sed* "sedge, rush" and OE *tun* or ON *tún* (farmstead), and describes the nature of the land near the River Alt where the mill and church stand. Early form includes Sefftun (1222).

Skelmersdale, SD470065. *Skelmersdalr* "Skelmers valley", after the personal name *Skelmer* (this name has been suggested by David Mills to have probably originated from ON *Skjaldmarr*) and ON *dalr* (valley). Listed as Skelmersdale in 1202.

Snubsnape SD532203. In Leyland parish. From ON *snape* "pasture" or OE *snæp*. Ekwall suggest the first element may be related to Old Icelandic *snubbottr* "stumpy". Early form: Snubsnape (1372).

Sollom, SD452188. From ON *Sól-hlein* "sunny slope" as suggested by Ekwall. Hamlet on the south slope of a ridge on the bank of the River Douglas near Tarleton. Mills suggests the compound form OE *sol* and ON

Scarth Hill courtesy of Patrick Trollope.

hegn "muddy enclosure". Early form de Solame (1372).

Tarbock, Tarbock Green, SJ465875. Although Ekwall considered the first element probably comes from OE *porn* (thorn), he also pointed out it could derive from the ON personal name *Thor, Þor,* or *Thori*. The second element is OE *broc* (brook) or ON *bekkr* (stream). Early forms include Thorboc (1243). The famous local comedian Jimmy Tarbuck bears the name.

Tarleton, SD450206. "Tharald's farmstead" from ON personal name *Þaraldr* and OE *tun* or ON *tún*. Listed as Tarleton in 1200.

Tarlscough (SD435142) *Þaraldrskógr* "Tharald's wood", from ON personal name *Þaraldr* and ON *skógr* (wood). Early form includes Tharlescogh (1190).

Thingwall, SJ410910. *Þingvöllr* "Assembly field", from ON *þing* (assembly, parliament) and ON *völlr* (field). Early form includes Thingwalle (1212). Meeting place of the Thing or parliament of the Scandinavian community for part of, or most, of West Lancashire. The Hall is in the Knotty Ash area, home of another famous Liverpool Comedian, Ken Dodd, and close to West Derby. Like Roby, it has an exact counterpart in Wirral where the Wirral Norse leader Ingimund held his Assembly or parliament. It is not known who led the West Lancashire Thing. It might possibly have been for a time the Irish Sea Norseman Ragnald. Eilert Ekwall says "the meeting place was obviously the round, gently sloping hill on which Thingwall Hall now stands".

Toxteth, SJ354883, Toxteth Park. *Tokisstöð* "Toki's landing place, from ODan or ON personal name *Tóki* and ON *stöð* (landing place) or ON *staðir* (homestead). Early form: Tokestath (1212). The name *Tóki* was most popular in East Scandinavia rather than Norway, so Tóki was probably a Dane rather than a Norseman. It is also interesting to speculate if this is the same Tóki who gave his name to Tokesford, an old crossing of Wallasey Pool in Wirral. If he was a Dane then he probably did come from Wirral.

Ulnes Walton, SD508198. North-east. of Croston, on both sides of the Lostock. First element from ON personal name *Úlfr. Walton* is OE for the farmstead of the Welshmen. Ulf de Walton lived around 1160.

Walton Breck, Warbreck, SJ360930. Second element is from *brekka* "hill, slope". Early form Brecksyde (1616).

West Derby, SJ400935. "The west settlement with the deer". Although on the eastern outskirts of Liverpool and outside the Danelaw, Ekwall considers the origins are most probably the same as Derby in Danelaw Derbyshire, and the first element is from the Danish *diur* "deer". Another suggested root which locals would understandably agree with has been ON *Dýrabý* "the splendid town" from ON *dýrr*. Listed in the Domesday Book as *Derbei*. With the Danelaw Derby, Ekwall says "it is realy quite plausible that the Northmen

Aerial photograph of the Mersey estuary with Toxteth in the foreground. Tóki's landing place (stöð) or staðir (homestead) was here. Courtesy of Phillip Parker.

Walton Breck Road (Old Norse - brekke) and Skerries (Old Norse - sker) adjoin Anfield Stadium, home of Liverpool FC..

may have given Derby its name because there was a deer-park in the place". If it was indeed named by Danes and not Norsemen this has resonances also for the interpretation of the many Wirral and South West Lancashire *bys*. Early form: Westderbi (1177).

F.T. Wainwright's contribution

We now consider one of the most significant essays written about the Scandinavians in West Lancashire, by the late historian Frederick Threlfall Wainwright (1917 -1961) a local man and former pupil of Prescot Grammar School (1930-35).   He was the scholar who not only proved beyond any reasonable doubt the essential features of the Ingimund tradition for Wirral, but was also responsible for putting Ekwall's momentous work on Lancashire Place-Names into its firm historical context. Despite its age (written in 1948) it is still regarded as the seminal contribution on the subject.

Chapter 8

THE SCANDINAVIANS IN WEST LANCASHIRE

FREDERICK THRELFALL WAINWRIGHT

Reprinted from
Transactions of the Lancashire and Cheshire Antiquarian Society, 58
(1945-6), 71-116.

This is part of a paper "The Scandinavians in Lancashire" in which F.T. Wainwright describes the place-name and personal name evidence for the Norse settlements of Lancashire and puts this in its historical context. Only those parts of his paper concerning West Lancashire are presented: parts concerning Amounderness, the Vale of Lune and Furness and Cartmel, areas also significantly settled by Vikings, have been silently omitted. The sub-headings are editorial.

Invasion of the Norsemen and settlement

During the early years of the tenth-Century hoards of Scandinavians settled in North-western England, and it has long been recognized that this immigration is distinct from the movement which had introduced a Danish population into eastern England before the end of the ninth-Century. The new settlers appeared along the coast which stretches from the Dee to beyond the Solway; they were Norwegians not Danes, and most of them had sailed not direct from the homeland but from Scandinavian colonies in Ireland and the Isle of Man. They arrived in small separate companies seeking lands to cultivate rather than monastries to plunder; it is highly unlikely that they were a "great army" organized for and intent upon military conquest. It is generally believed that they came as peaceful farmers not as hostile warriors, although it would be easy to overemphasize this aspect of the settlement, for Norsemen in this age would be prepared to meet violence with violence. But it is unlikely that, under the conditions which existed, they would deliberately stimulate resistance against themselves, and although local skirmishes may well have occurred there is no reason to imagine here military operations such as preceded the Danish settlement. Large-scale battles, mass slaughter, or even organised looting, could scarcely have escaped the notice of English chroniclers, and their unbroken silence is significant. On the other hand, the Norsemen definitely brought confusion to an area where conditions were already confused. Their presence alone would greatly aggravate the social and political insecurity of northern England and in particular of the area known as Lancashire. It is equally clear that they exercised an appreciable influence on the course of the Anglo-Scandinavian struggle for the possession of England, the chief historical theme of these years. And their influence did not end with the tenth-Century: they have permanently changed the racial and social structure of the area and they have left a mark on the development of Lancashire which persists even today. In short the Irish-Norse settlements in the North-west are no less significant than the Danish settlements in the East, and for Lancashire no other event is of greater historical importance.

The most surprising feature of this movement is its failure to achieve mention in contemporary annalistic literature. Neither the Anglo-Saxon Chronicle, our fullest record of the events of this period, nor any other chronicle compiled within this island contains the slightest indication of a Scandinavian settlement in North-west England. The sole reference occurs in an obscure Irish chronicle of doubtful authority and, even so, it concerns only a single expedition to the neighbourhood of Chester in Wirral[74]. Of the many other expeditions no record survives, and from a study of the chronicles one could never guess that Lancashire and the lands to the North received a Scandinavian population which in numbers and importance quite overshadowed the Norse colonists in Wirral. The above introductory paragraph, therefore, is based largely upon non-literary sources, a discussion of which forms the main subject of this essay.

Norwegian invaders
The central fact of the story, that the Scandinavians in North-west England were Norwegians and not Danes, was first clearly stated in 1856 by Robert Ferguson in his book, *The Northmen in Cumberland and Westmoreland*. Inspired by the pioneer work of J. J. A. Worsaae[75], Ferguson undertook a detailed examination of the two North-western counties and set out to prove his theory of "an immigration more particularly Norwegian proceeding from the western side of the island". His evidence and his arguments would not now be accepted, but his main conclusion remains substantially correct. The labours of scholars like J. C. H. R. Steenstrup, Alexander Bugge, W. G. Collingwood, and Harald Lindkvist, gave precision to these studies, and E. Ekwall has set them upon a solid foundation. Of Ekwall's works only two need to be mentioned here. His *Scandinavians and Celts in the North-west of England* is a definitive survey of Irish-Norse place-name formations, and his *Place-Names of Lancashire* is the inevitable starting-point for all investigations

[74] The Story of Ingimund's expedition to Wirral is printed on pp227-237 of *Annals of Ireland, Three Fragments*, edited by John O'Donovan, Irish Archaeological nd Celtic Society, 1860. A translation of the story is given above, in Chapter 3. For a discussion on the reliability of this account, see F.T. Wainwright, 'Ingimund's Invasion' (reprinted in P. Cavill, S.E. Harding and J. Jesch's book *Wirral and its Viking Heritage*, English Place-Name Society, 2000).

[75] *Minder om Danske og Nordmoendene i England, Skotland og Irland*, Copenhagen, 1851; published in English as *An Account of the Danes and Norweigians in England, Scotland and Ireland*, London 1852.

into the Scandinavian settlements of Lancashire and the source from which is drawn much of the evidence discussed below.

The chief features of the settlement have been surely sketched by Ekwall. He has shown that the occurrence of Norse test-words (e.g. *brekka, gil, skáli,* and *slakki*) appearing in Scarisbrick, Norbreck, Warbreck, Holgill, Lowgill, Thrushgill, Brinscall, Feniscowles, Scales, Ashlack, Ayneslack, Nettleslack, etc.) stamps the whole settlement as Norwegian[76]. He has illustrated the Irish affinities of these Norse settlers by stressing certain Irish words (especially ON *erg* or *argi*, MIr *Airge*, in Anglezarke, Arkholme, Goosnargh, Grimshargh, etc.) and certain Irish personal names (e.g. *Gusan* in Goosnargh, *Beccán* in Becconsall and Beacons Gill, etc.). He has also shown that inversion-compounds, so named because the second element defines the first in the Celtic manner, were due directly to Irish influence but were introduced into England by Scandinavians. Inversion compounds, numerous in Cumberland and Westmorland, are strangely rare in Lancashire, but examples may be found among the minor names, e.g. *Starhourauen, Scartherwlmer,* and *Rudswain,* all thirteenth-Century forms preserved in *The Chartulary of Cockersand Abbey.*

The above are names which are distinctively Norse or Irish-Norse. When one comes to count the names in *-by, -kirk, -holme, -scough*, etc., which formally may be either Danish or Norse in origin, one finds that over a hundred major place-names, i.e. names of townships and villages, in Lancashire are Scandinavian. The list could be trebled if places below the status of village were included, and it would run into thousands if the Scandinavian names of fields and other minor topographical features were added. A distribution map of the major place-names alone, however, indicates with some precision the areas of most intensive Norse settlement.

West Lancashire Place Names

South of the Ribble Scandinavian place-names are conspicuous in the low-lying coast plain between Liverpool, Southport and Preston, and here they are indeed numerous. They include: Aigburth, Thingwall, Toxteth, Roby, West Derby, Croxteth, Kirkdale, Aintree, Litherland, Kirkby, Crosby, Lunt, Altcar, Formby, Ormskirk, Skelmersdale, Lathom, Burscough, Greetby, Scarisbrick, Tarlscough, Ainsdale, Birkdale, North Meols, Ravenmeols, "Argarmeols", Crossens, Hesketh, Becconsall, Tarleton, and a few similar examples. The Scandinavian character of this area is beyond question. In all probability the Norse colonists were numerous enough to introduce their own way of life. Names like Litherland, preserving a pure Scandinavian genitive in *-ar (hlíðar,* genitive singular of ON *hlíð*), and Lathom (*hlaðum,*

---

[76] This has now been questioned, by scholars such as Gillian Fellows-Jensen, who favour a significant Danish influence in South-west Lancashire and particularly Wirral, with the large numbers of place-names with the element *-by*, more associated with Danes than Norwegians.

dative plural of ON *hlaða*) could have arisen only in a district where a Scandinavian language complete with inflections was spoken. And a name like Thingwall ("assembly or 'parliament' field(s)", ON *þingvöllr*) implies the existence of a Scandinavian community living under its own rules and customs.

In the area of Lancashire south of the River Ribble, major place-names are numerous only in the coastal districts. In the higher central and eastern districts they are comparatively rare although one or two distinctively Norse names occur, e.g. Brinscall (ON *skáli*) near Chorley, Anglezarke Moor (ON *argi*) near Rivington, Sholver (ON *argi*) near Oldham, and Scholes (ON *skáli*) near Wigan. But the intensity of Scandinavian settlement cannot be measured by the frequency of Scandinavian place-names alone. Other factors must be considered. Much depends upon the nature of the names: for example a name like Flixton (ODan *Flik*, OE *tun*) or Urmston (ODan *Urm*, OE *tun*), essentially an English formation, theoretically proves no more than the presence of a single Dane whereas a strict Scandinavian formation, especially if it is a grammatical compound, implies a strong Scandinavianized neighbourhood. The development of English place-names is often modified by the Scandinavians, and such Scandinavianized names reflect a powerful Scandinavian element in the surrounding population. Also to be taken into account is the fact that in the central and eastern parts of South Lancashire the Scandinavians would find English communities already in occupation of much of the available land, and Scandinavian influence upon the place-nomenclature would naturally be less obvious here than in an area where settlers and earlier place-names were few or non-existent. Thus it would be unwise to argue that Norse settlement in South Lancashire was confined to the low-lying marshes.

But the marked concentration of Scandinavian place-names suggest that in the main the Norsemen were content to occupy lands which English had rejected and left vacant. It has been shown that the earliest Anglian settlers in this area preferred the rising ground between 100 feet and 500 feet above sea-level and deliberately avoided the marshy coastlands[77]. The Norsemen settled most intensively in these low-lying lands, and it is highly probable that they found them scantily peopled and in some parts quite uninhabited when they took them over in the early years of the tenth-Century. The distribution of place-names therefore suggests that the Norse settlement was characterized not by dispossession but by a willingness to accept the less attractive districts which had been neglected by the English. Even in an area where the Scandinavians settled in their greatest numbers there is some slight evidence that the native population was not disturbed: Ekwall has stated that

[77] F.T. Wainwright (1941), The Anglian Settlement of Lancashire, *Transactions Historical Society of Lancashire and Cheshire* 93, pp1-45.

Halsall, which lies in the heart of the Scandinavianized area, "is almost purely English in its early place-nomenclature"[78]. The parish of Halsall embraces land which rises above the level of the surrounding country, and the area attracted some of the first Angles who settled in Lancashire as is indicated by the ancient folk-name Mellingas (Melling) and by the occurrence of two or three British place-name elements the survival of which is probably due to Anglo-Celtic racial contact during the earliest phase of the Anglian settlement[79].

Peaceful Settlers?

Place-names, it will have been noticed, throw some little light upon the conditions under which the settlement was carried through. The light is faint and uncertain, it is true, but the problems are at once important and obscure. Any evidence is valuable if it contributes to our understanding of what was happening in Lancashire at this date and if, in particular, it contributes to our knowledge of the relations between Englishmen and Norsemen. The older view is that the settlement was fairly peaceful in character[80], but this view has been challenged, and Ekwall describes it as "only a hypothesis" and one that cannot easily be accepted[81]. It may be useful, therefore, to bring together the scattered shreds of evidence. And, in the first place, it may be admitted that the old view is little more than an assumption arising from the fact that no known chronicle mentions organized settlement, or settlement at all, by Scandinavian immigrants in Lancashire. As such it is no more than an *argumentum a silentio*, but it is none the less powerful for that since it is almost inconceivable that an organized military conquest or a violent social upheaval, even in the remote North-west, should altogether escape the notice of both contemporary and later annalists. To this may be added the positive, if somewhat inconclusive evidence of place-names. It has been shown above that the distribution of Scandinavian place-names in south Lancashire suggests very strongly that the Norsemen were willing to occupy the poorer lands along the coast, lands which the earlier English settlers had deliberately avoided. If this is correct then the settlement can hardly have been preceded by a military conquest, for conquerors would not have chosen to live in neglected marshlands. There is no reason to believe that relations were cordial, but there is equally no reason, at least from the evidence of place-names, to suspect any violent hostility.

---

[78] *The Place-Names of Lancashire*, p238.

[79] On the so-called historical significance of the so-called 'British' place-names in Lancashire, see F.T. Wainwright (1941) The Anglian Settlement of Lancashire, *Historical Society of Lancashire and Cheshire* 93, p1-45.

[80] See for example, Robert Ferguson (1856) *The Northmen in Cumberland and Westmorland*, p16, and Harold Lindqvist (1912) *Middle English Place-Names of Scandinavian Origin*, p33.

[81] *Scandinavians and Celts*, p.3. See also *Place-Names of Lancashire*, p256.

Parallel with Ingimund in Wirral

The story of Ingimund's settlement in Wirral provides another clue to the nature of the Scandinavian settlement in Lancashire. The Irish tradition, which alone preserves the story of Ingimund, seems to have originated as a genuine contemporary record of events[82]. As it stands the story is at once too full and too fragmentary: too full for credence in its treatment of the Battle of Chester and too fragmentary in its concentration on Ingimund to the exclusion of all other Viking leaders whose expeditions afflicted Wirral, Lancashire and the far North. But as our sole annalistic record of Norse settlement in North-west England it is a highly important source . The story in brief is as follows: Ingimund, a Viking leader, sails from Ireland and, after a vain attempt against North Wales, settles with his followers near Chester. But this settlement occurs only after permission has been sought and obtained from Æthelflæd, Lady of the Mercian English, who was acting for her sick husband Ealdorman Æthelred. The struggle for possession of Chester came five or more years later, and it is quite clear that the settlement itself in c902 was fairly peaceful in character. These proceedings, the only recorded account of a Norse settlement in the North-west, may well have been paralleled in Lancashire. North of the Mersey the old Northumbrian kingdom had collapsed; such authority as remained seems to have been exercised by virtually independent ealdormen and ecclesiastics. Whether or not, under these circumstances, the Norsemen found it necessary or even possible to seek formal permission to settle is a question of no great importance. The point is that the sole surviving account of an Irish-Norse settlement is an account of a settlement which was in the main peaceful, and there is as yet no sufficient reason to doubt that the Norse settlements in Lancashire proceeded along similar lines.

Some conflict

It would be ridiculous, however, to believe that the Scandinavian settlement of Lancashire was unattended by any kind of violence. The story of Ingimund illustrates how armed conflict could develop from a peaceful settlement. In Lancashire too, there must have been many skirmishes, and it is suggested below that the arrival of the Norsemen accentuated the social disorder arising from the collapse of the central authority. But isolated skirmishes do not constitute a military conquest and the flight of a few individuals cannot be read as the mass displacement of a population. No considerable area in Lancashire is devoid of English place-names. In most of the county the English element is the dominant element, and even in the

---

[82] See Chapter 3 and F.T. Wainwright (1948) Ingimund's Invasion, *English Historical Review*, 43, 145-169, reproduced in P. Cavill, S.E. Harding and J. Jesch (2000) *Wirral and its Viking Heritage*, English Place-Name Society, 43-59.

coastlands of South Lancashire, where English settlers were comparatively few and Norse settlers comparatively numerous, English place-names are common (e.g., Allerton, Aughton, Bootle, Halsall, Hutton, Huyton, Liverpool, Longton, Lydiate, Rufford, Walton). This survival of English place-names proves a corresponding survival of English influence and, therefore, of an English population. There is no evidence of widespread molestation even in areas where the Scandinavians were most powerful.

Comparison with the Danish Wreak Valley in Leicestershire

In some parts of England, English place-names may have been swept away or buried beneath a heavy layer of Scandinavian nomenclature; it would be legitimate to assume, for example, that any settlers in the Wreak Valley were socially and politically overwhelmed by the Danes - so great is the number of Scandinavian place-names and so remarkable is the lack of English place-names. But the Wreak Valley has no parallel in Lancashire. Here the settlement was carried through not by an army organized for war but by isolated and independent bands of Norsemen without a common leader and without a common plan. Under these circumstances it is unlikely that the newcomers would deliberately introduce unnecessary violence into their relations with the earlier settlers. The nature of the Scandinavian immigration would go far to make it a peaceful movement, and at least theories of military conquest, mass slaughter, displacement, and dispossession, may be safely forgotten.

Intensity of Settlement

We have discussed briefly the origin of the Scandinavian immigrants, the distribution of their settlements, and the nature of their relations with the earlier inhabitants. Another important problem concerns the magnitude of this immigration, How many Scandinavian settlers arrived in what is now Lancashire? We shall never be able to answer this question with any precision; the most that can be achieved is a series of impressions, each throwing some light upon the force of the movement or upon the strength of the Scandinavian element in what quickly became an Anglo-Scandinavian population. The clearest impression comes not from major place-names, the names of towns and villages which were the main concern of Ekwall, but from minor names, the names of fields, field divisions, woods, roads, streams, trees, crosses, and the many other minor topographical features named in every village. Thousands of these names testify to the strength of the Scandinavian influence in Lancashire, and they go far towards filling the gaps left behind by the study of major place-names. Evidence of this kind requires careful handling, as will be seen, but there can be no doubt of its importance as contributing to an understanding of the force of the Scandinavian immigration.

Scandinavian and Scandinavianized minor names are not as a general rule direct evidence of Scandinavian settlement, for most of them arose centuries after the settlement had been carried through. But they do accurately reflect the language of the area, and if this language is strongly Scandinavianized we may safely assume a strong Scandinavian element in the local population[83]. Field-names and other minor names often provide positive evidence of Scandinavian influence in districts where the major place-names have been slightly affected. The vast parish of Whalley, which covers the whole of the eastern half of the hundred of Blackburn, is a case in point. A bleak fell and forest district, lying on the Yorkshire boundary and remote from the western coast, it does not seem an area likely to have attracted Scandinavian settlers. The older sites were small and unimportant, and only one place of any size has a Scandinavian name - Clitheroe, which probably contains ON *haugr*. But there are a number of significant "booths" (ON *búð*, ODan *boþ*): Barley Booth, Crawshaw Booth, Goldshaw Booth, Hay Booth, Wheatley Booth, Wheatley Carr Booth, etc. And other names also support the conclusion that there has been some Scandinavian settlement in the area. It is when we turn to an area of heavy Scandinavian settlement, however, that evidence of this kind becomes truly impressive.

Scandinavian minor names in West Lancashire

In the coastal plain between the River Ribble and the River Mersey, Scandinavian minor names are almost too numerous to be counted. The following list gives only a selection from a few medieval sources[84] (the prefix "c." means "approximately"):

1492	Norris	*Ayscogh* (Woolton) - ON *skógr*.
13th cent.	PNLa	*Bretarwe* (Brettargh, Woolton) - ON *argi*.
1317	Norris	*le Carr* (Speke) - ON *kiarr (kjarr)*.
1385	Norris	*Cheldwalgate* (Speke) - ON *gata*.
1460	Norris	*le Flatte* (Hale) - ON *flot*.
1436	Norris	*Halesnape* (Halewood) - ME *snape*.
1342	Norris	*le Holm* (Garston) - ON *holmr*.
1326	Norris	*le Kirkeway* (Garston) - ON *kirkja*.

[83] For a fuller discussion of the difficulties attending an attempt to interpret historically the Scandinavian settlement in minor names see F.T. Wainwright (1945-6) Field-names of Amounderness Hundred, *Transactions of the Historical Society of Lancashire and Cheshire* 97, 71-116.

[84] For abbreviations used in the following pages see note at end of the Chapter.

	1332	Norris	*le Mukelholme* (Garston) - ON *holmr.*
	1333	Norris	*Quyndale* (Speke) - ME *whin.*
	1292	Norris	*Qwyndalemor* (Garston) - ME *whin.*
	1357	Norris	*Ruscar milne* (Halewood) - ON *kiarr.*
c.	1275	Norris	*le Rutherakis, Rutthyerakes,* c. 1290
			Norris *le Rutherack, Rotherrakys,* c. 1300
			Norris *le rederrakys* (Garston) - ON *rák*
	1337	Norris	*le Sperth* (Garston) - ON *sporðr.*
	1350	Norris	*le Watergate* (Woolton) - ON *gata.*
c.	1400	Norris	*Wolletungate* (Speke) - ON *gata.*
c.	1200	CC	*Coltesnape* (Sutton) - ME *snape.*
c.	1265	CC	*Kirkegate* (Eccleston in Prescot) - ON *kirkja.*
c.	1277	PNLa	*Rudegate* (Ridgate, Whiston) - ON *gata.*
c.	1185	CC	*Eschales,* 1268 CC *Scales,* 1311 Norris *le Scoles* (Eccleston in Prescot)[85] - ON *skáli.*
	1491	Norris	*Akeforthe* (Huyton) - ON *eiki.*
c.	1245	Norris	*le Kar* (Huyton) - ON *kiarr.*
	1394	PNLa	*Aynesargh* (Kirkby) - ON *argi.*
	1323	LI	*Brek* (West Derby) - ON *brekka.*
	1334	Norris	*le Brekke* (Walton) - ON *brekka.*
	1332	Hoghton	*le Brekfeld* (Kirkdale) - ON *brekka.*
	1310	Norris	*le Houtterack* (Kirkdale) - ON *rák.*
c.	1454	Norris	*Ladebreke* (Walton) - ON *brekka.*
c.	1210	CC	*Scales* (West Derby) - ON *skáli.*
c.	1305	Norris	*le Sondrakes* (Walton) - ON *rák.*
c.	1344	Norris	*Quallebrekmore* (Walton) - ON *brekka.*
c.	13th cent. PNLa		*Scoles* (Ince Blundell) - ON *skáli.*
c.	1255	CC	*Akescof* (Scarisbrick) - ON *eikiskógr.*
	1331	PNLa	*Birchecar* (Scarisbrick) - ON *kiarr.*
c.	1190	LPC	*Brakenesthweit* (Ormskirk) - ON *þveit.*
	1340	CC	*Horsecarr* (Hoscar Moss, Lathom) - ON *kiarr.*
c.	1225	CC	*Naihalarthe,* 1251 CC *Nathelarghe,* 1451
		CC	*Natlargh,* 1461 CC *Natlergh,* 1537 CC *Natler* (Scarisbrick)[86] - ON *argi.*
c.	1190	LPC	*Scarth* (Scarth Hill, Lathom) - ON *skarð.*
c.	1225	CC	*Snape* (Snape, Scarisbrick) - ME *snape.*
	1303	PNLa	*Thoraldestub,* 1398 PNLa *Tharoldstube* (Scarisbrick) - ON *Þóraldr, Þaraldr.*[87]

---

[85] Compare *Scholes Fields, Scholes Hill, Scholes Meadow* in the Tithe Award Schedule (1840).
[86] See E. Ekwall (1918) *Scandinavians and Celts in the North-west of England,* p.80, for other forms. Ekwall suggests the first element may be the Irish name *Naile.*

[87] The personal name *Þaraldr* also appears in Tarlscough (Burscough).

c.	1180	PNLa	*Wik* (Wyke House, Scarisbrick) - ON *vík.*
c.	1210	CC	*alt flat* (Melling) - ON *flot.*
c.	1185	CC	*Cunig(g)escofh* (Cunscough, Melling)- ON *konungr, skógr.*
c.	1220	CC	*Ekergert* (Lydiate) - ON *garðr.*
c.	1200	CC	*Fulwat(h)schahe* (Melling) - ON *vað.*
c.	1275	CC	*Mellingscofer* (Melling) - ON *skógr.*
c.	1200	CC	*Murscoh* (Lydiate) - ON *skógr.*
c.	1275	CC	*Rudswain* (Melling) - ON *Sveinn.*
c.	1200	CC	*Ruthwait, Ruhwait(h)* (Melling) - ON *þveit.*
c.	1185	CC	*Thorp* (Melling) - ON *þorp*, ODan *thorp.*
c.	1200	CC	*Tunesnape* (Lydiate) - ME *snape.*
c.	1200	CC	*Alserhou* (Ainsdale) - ON *haugr.*
c.	1200	CC	*Birkedene* (Ainsdale) - ON *birki.*
c.	1215	CC	*Bleshoudale* (Ainsdale) - ON *haugr.*
c.	1200	CC	*Bradehou* (Ainsdale) - ON *haugr.*
c.	1240	CC	*Bradoukar* (Ainsdale) - ON *kiarr.*
c.	1200	CC	*le Crocland* (Ainsdale) - ON *krókr.*
c.	1215	CC	*Elreslete* (Ainsdale) - ON *slétta.*
c.	1200	CC	*Gilanrehou* (Ainsdale) - OIr *Gilleandrais*, ON *haugr.*
c.	1200	CC	*Grenihou* (Ainsdale) - ON *haugr.*
c.	1200	CC	*Hou* (Aisndale) - ON *haugr.*
c.	1225	CC	*Keshou, Kethou* (Ainsdale) - ON *haugr.*
c.	1200	CC	*Lathebot* (Ainsdale) - ON *hlaða.*
c.	1200	CC	*Malcanrehou, Melcanerhou, Melkanerhou, Melkenerhou* (Ainsdale) OIr *Maelchon*[88], ON *haugr.*
c.	1290	Hoghton	*le Northbretis* (Ravensmeols) - ON *brekka.*
c.	1200	CC	*Oddisherhe*, c. 1215 CC *Oddisharie* (Ainsdale) - ON *argi.*
c.	1200	CC	*Rauenesdalemeudws, Romesdale, Ramisdale* (Ainsdale) - ON *Hrafn.*
c.	1275	Hoghton	*Sandholm* (Ravensmeols) - ON *holmr.*
c.	1275	Norris	*le Scadelondis* (Formby) - ON *skáli.*
c.	1200	CC	*Scatherwlmer*, c. 1215 CC *Scartherwlmer* (Ainsdale) - ON *skarð*, OE *Wulfmær.*

---

[88] ditto.

c.	1200	CC	*Sciphou* (Ainsdale) - ON *haugr*.
c.	1200	CC	*Slidrihou* (Ainsdale) - ON *haugr*.
c.	1200	CC	*Sceitebuscart* (Ainsdale) - ON *skarð*.
		PNLa	*Stangerhau* (Ravensmeols) - ON *stangarhaugr*.
c.	1200	CC	*Stardale* (Ainsdale) - ON *storr*.
c.	1240	CC	*Starhourauen* (Ainsdale) - ON *storr*, *haugr, Hrafn*.
c.	1275	Hoghton	*Wattholmwra* (Ainsdale) - ON *holmr, vrá*.
c.	1185	CC	*Winscarthlithe*, c. 1200 CC *Winscartlithe* (Ainsdale) - ME *whin*, ON *skarð, hlíð*[89].
c.	1215	CC	*Witemeledale*, c. 1225 CC *Quitemeledale* (Ainsdale) - ON *melr*.
c.	1200	CC	*Wra* (Ainsdale) - ON *vrá*.
		PNLa	*Blowick* (North Meols) - ON *blá-vík*.
c.	1275	Hoghton	*le Meleacres* (North Meols) - ON *melr*.
c.	1250	Hoghton	*Threleholmes* (North Meols) - ON *holmr*.
c.	1230	CC	*Le Bradegate* (Hoole) - ON *gata*.
c.	1250	CC	*Burnildesgate* (Tarleton) - ON *Brynhildr*[90], *gata*.
c.	1240	CC	*Crocfeld* (Hoole) - ON *krókr*.
c.	1220	CC	*Crocland* (Hoole) - ON *krókr*.
c.	1200	CC	*Elremure* (Bretherton) - ON *elri, mýrr*.
c.	1210	CC	*Elremurekar* (Bretherton) - ON *kiarr*.
c.	1200	CC	*Holmes* (Holmes, Tarleton) - ON *holmr*.
c.	1240	CC	*Morbreces* (Bretherton) - ON *brekka*.
c.	1200	CC	*Siverthesarhe* (Bretherton) - ON *argi*, ON *Sigfroðr* (or OE *Sigefrið*).
c.	1177	LPC	*Torp*, 1190 ff. CC *Thorp* (Bretherton) - ON *þorp*, ODan *thorp*.
c.	1200	CC	*les Croke landes* (Hutton) - ON *krókr*.
c.	1549	LPD	*Crokinges* (Penwortham) - ON *krokr, eng*.
c.	1230	CC	*Harekar* (Hutton) - ON *kiarr*.
c.	1210	CC	*Holm* (Hutton) - ON *holmr*.
c.	1200	CC	*Lairclade* (Hutton) - ON *leirr*.
c.	1200	CC	*Leirburnesike, Layrburnesike, Lairburnesike* (Hutton) - ON *leirr*.
c.	1215	CC	*Rokar* (Hutton) - ON *kiarr*.
c.	1230	CC	*Ulvesdale, Ulvedene* (Hutton) - ON *Úlfr*.

[89] It is not possile to distingush between OE *hlíþ* and ON *hilð*, but in this case the combination with *whin* and *skarð* points to ON *hilð*. Also in Ainsdale occur *Grenelithe* and *Suthlithe*.

[90] See E. Ekwall (1922), *Place-Names of Lancashire*, p.251

c. 1200	CC	*Saferscoke* (Sarscow in Eccleston, Leyland) - ON *skógr*.
c. 1200	CC	*Scalecroft* (Clayton-le-Woods) - ON *skáli*.
c. 1372	PNLa	*Snubsnape* (Leyland) - ME *snape*.

These and other Scandinavian minor names abound all over the coastal plain of (south) West Lancashire. Especially interesting are names which preserve specifically Norse elements like *brekka*, *skáli*, *slakki* and *erg* (MIr *airge*), and Irish personal names like *Gilleandrais* (*Gilanrehou*), *Maelchon* (*Malcanrehou*), and *Naile* (*Naihalarthe*). Three possible examples of inversion-compounds have been noted above: *Rudswain* (Melling), *Scartherwlmer*, and *Starhourauen* (Ainsdale). The high proportion of Irish-Norse "tests" and the corresponding rarity of Danish "tests"[91] confirm the conclusion, already drawn from major place-names, that the Scandinavian settlers in this area were not Danes but Norwegians from Ireland. As evidence of the force of the Scandinavian immigration, however, minor names are more impressive than major names. Their number and their variety leave us in no doubt as to the extent to which West Lancashire has been Scandinavianized. They are especially numerous around the modern town of Southport - note the examples in Ainsdale - and there certainly was a very powerful Scandinavian settlement in this district. For a long time the language spoken here must have been at least as much Scandinavian as English, for minor names prove that for centuries people used not only Scandinavian words but also Scandinavian grammatical inflexions. In the face of such evidence we must think of the Scandinavian settlement as arising from a mass-migration.

A Scandinavian Language spoken in Lancashire

To appreciate fully the vitality of the Scandinavian language in Lancashire it is not sufficient merely to note the number and variety of the Scandinavian words embedded in minor names. Scandinavian inflections have been noted in Amounderness (genitive singular of ON *Agmundr*), Arkholme (dative plural of ON *argi*), Lathom (dative plural of ON *hlaða*), Litherland (genitive singular of ON *hlíð*), Osmotherley (genitive singular of ON *Asmundr*), Sawrey (nominative plural of ON *saurr*), etc. Amongst examples from minor names we have:

[91] The lost *Thorp* in Melling and the lost *Thorp* in Bretherton may possibly suggest Danish influence. At least it is unlikely that we should find an uncompounded OE *þorp, þrop*, in Scandinavian England, and we should look rather to ON *þorp*, ODan *thorp*. The Scandinavian *thorp* cannot be regarded as a safe Danish 'test word', but it is true to say that in England it was commonly used by the Danes and seldom used by the Norwegians. The rarity of *thorpe* in North-west England, indeed, has been considered a sign that Danish influence here was slight.

Hartebeck (gen. sing. of ON *hiortr* or *Hiotr)*[92]
Melcanerhou[93] (gen. sing. of OIr *Maelchon*)
Roalderiddinc[94] (gen. sing. of ON *Hróaldr*)
Scarthewlmer[95] (nom. Plur. Of ON *skarð*)
Stangerhou[96] (gen. sing. of ON *stong*)
Stancoleriding[97] (gen. sing. of ON *Steinkollr*)

Such names form perhaps the most convincing answer to the question "Was the Scandinavian language spoken in Lancashire?". They prove that at least in some districts the language was to a great extent Scandinavian not only in vocabulary but also in grammatical construction. There is good reason to believe that field-names, when their meanings become obscure, either fall out of use or are distorted to a degree unparalleled in major place-names, the latter being more firmly established over a wider area. If this be true then it would appear that Lancashire men of the thirteenth-Century understood the significance of, for example, a Scandinavian genitival inflection. How many Norsemen would be required to Scandinavianize so thoroughly the language of Lancashire is a matter of opinion, but we may dismiss any theory which would restrict their numbers or their influence.

A straightforward conclusion about language

The main conclusion is straightforward. Field names, ancient and modern combine to prove beyond all dispute that the Scandinavians introduced their language into Lancashire as a vital force which remains powerful even today. Field-names of the 12th and 13th-Centuries show that the Scandinavian language, complete with its inflectional forms, was once understood and spoken in Lancashire. Modern field-names and dialect words - the latter deserve fuller treatment than is possible here - show that the speech of Lancashire men is still highly Scandinavianized. In this sense, therefore, minor names provide the most impressive proof of the force and intensity of the Scandinavian settlements of the tenth-Century.

Personal Names

The evidence of personal names points clearly, if less emphatically, to the same conclusion. In Lancashire during the 12th and 13th centuries occur such names as: Hagemund (ON *Agmundr*), Arkel (ON *Arnkell*), Oschil (ON *Áskell*), Assolf (ON *Ásúlfr*), Auti, Outi (ON *Auði*), Outhkel (ON *Auðkell*), Bernolf, Bernulf (perhaps ON *Biornúlfr* rather than OE *Beornwulf*), Brian

[92] E. Ekwall (1922) *Place-Names of Lancashire*, p.181.
[93] See above.
[94] c. 1250 Hoghton - in Lea near Preston
[95] E. Ekwall (1918) *Scandinavians and Celts in the North-West of England* p.46
[96] See above.
[97] c. 1255 Hoghton - in Hothersall

(ON *Brján*, OIr *Brian*), Colman (OIr *Colmán*), Dolfin (ON *Dólgfinnr*), *Gamel(l)*, Gamul (ON *Gamall*), Gillemichel, Gilmichel (*Gael. Gillemicel*), Gille (ON *Gilli* OIr *Gilla*), Grimcil (ON *Grímkell*), Grym (ON *Grímr*), Gunild (ON *Gunnhildr*), Gunne (ON *Gunni*), Gunware (ON *Gunnvor*, ODan *Gunnor*), Award (ON *Hávarðr*), Liolff, Liulf, Lyelf (ON *Hlífólfr*), Rainkill, Ranechil, Ranikel, Rauenkel, Ravanchil (ON *Hrafnkell*), Roald (ON *Hróaldr*), Ingerith (ON *Ingiríðr*, ODan *Ingrith*), Chetel, Ketel (ON *Ketill*), Laysing, Leising, Leysing (ON *Leysingr*), Magnus (ON *Magnús*), Ormer (ON *Ormarr* rather than OE *Ordmær*), Orm (ON *Ormr*), Patrick (OIr *Patraicc*), Sefare (ON *Sæfari*), Sigherith, Sygerith (ON *Sigríðr*, ODan *Sigrith*), Siward (ODan *Sigwarth* or OE *Sigeward*), Steinfin (ON *Steinfinnr*), Steinchil (ON *Steinkell*, ODan *Stenkil*), Steyn (ON *Steinn*, ODan *Sten*), Stainulf, Staynulf, Steinolf, Steinulf, Stenulf (ON *Steinólfr*, ODan *Stenulf*), Sunneva (ON *Sunnifa*), Suein, Swain, Swayn, Swein (ON *Sveinn*, ODan *Sven*), Thorold (ON *Þóraldr*), Turbern (ON *Þorbiorn*), Thorfin, Thorphin, Torgin (ON *Þorfinnr*), Turgis (ON *Þorgils*), Thore (ON *Þórir*), Torolf, (ON *Þórólfr*), Thurstan, Turstan (ON *Þorsteinn*), Ulf (ON *Úlfr*), Waltheof, Walthef (ON *Valþiófr*)[98].

A few Scandinavian personal names, e.g. Thurstan, survive into modern times, but by the middle of the 4th-Century most of them, and most of the English formation too, had been displaced by continental names which rapidly increased in popularity after the Norman Conquest. At an earlier time, however, as the above examples show, there was a prominent Scandinavian element in the personal nomenclature of Lancashire.

Among the examples listed above will be noticed further indications that the Scandinavian settlers were Irish-Norsemen. There are names of Irish origin (e.g. Brian, Colman, Gille and Gillemichel); there are names which so far have been noted only in West Scandinavian (i.e. Old Norse, not Old Danish or Old Swedish) sources, e.g. *Dólgfinnr*, *Hlífólfr*, *Sunnifa*, *Þorfinnr*, and *Valþiófr*. And a number of other names appear in forms which are Norwegian rather than Danish, e.g. Gunware, Ingerith, Swayn, Steyn, Steinchil, Stainulf, etc.[99]

Customs and Institutions: wapentakes, byrlaw, drengs and "things"

The Scandinavians introduced not only their language and their personal names but also their customs and their institutions. The ramifications of Scandinavian influence in Lancashire will become apparent only when the social and economic structure of the area has been thoroughly investigated,

[98]   These names are taken from such sources as the Domesday Book, CC, Hoghton, LAR, LI, LPC and Norris. They all occur before 1300, but the list is by no means exhaustive, of course, even for the sources quoted here.

[99]   Gunware (ON *Gunnvor*) is distinctivley Old Norse, for the normal Old Danish form is *Gunnor*, with loss of *v*. In the form Ingerith (ON *Ingiríðr*) there is no syncope of medial *i* as there is in ODan *Ingrith*. Swayn, Steyn, Steinchil, Stainulf etc. clearly preserve the OWSc dipthong, but this is not at all a safe test of OWSc origin, for the normal OESc monophthongization (e.g. in ODan *Sven, Sten, Stenkil* and *Stenulf*) is not uniformly operative in England.

but the outlines of the picture may be drawn from evidence which lies near the surface. The Scandinavian word "wapentake" almost permanently ousted the English word "hundred", we find clear traces of the "byrlaw" as an administrative unit, and in early records there are many references to "drengs" (ON *drengr*) a social class which gives its name to a particular kind of tenure. "Ploughlands" and "oxgangs" displaced "hides" and "yardlands" as the normal units of land-division, and the Scandinavian ora of sixteen silver pennies was at least sometimes used in the reckoning of money and values. We have seen from place-names that "things" (ON *þing*), popular assemblies, were not unknown in Lancashire, and elements like *afnám, eng, argi, flot, inntaka, rein*, etc. which are common in minor names[100], suggest that the main features of the rural economy were highly Scandinavianized. In short, the picture in the Middle Ages is one of a society which may accurately be called Anglo-Scandinavian.

Danish Invaders

Evidence from various sources, then, combines to show that the Scandinavian settlement of Lancashire assumed the force of a mass-migration. At every point it has been emphasized that the new colonists were Irish-Norwegians not Danes. This emphasis is necessary if one is to understand the story of the Scandinavians in Lancashire, but it would be unwise to deny the presence of at least a few Danes among the Norwegian hosts. Our knowledge of Viking expeditions forbids an assumption of racial homogeneity, and we know that the "Great Army" of Danes attracted Norwegian adventurers. It is highly probable, therefore, that some Danes accompanied the Norse emigrants from Ireland[101]. To them we may perhaps attribute the occasional and isolated traces of Danish influence such as the occurrence of the Old Danish *thorp*.[102] The rarity of these traces, however, and the corresponding frequency of Norse "tests" prove the overwhelming dominance of the Norse element in the new Scandinavian population.

The Danish contribution to the story of the Scandinavian settlement in Lancashire does not end with the possibility of a few wanderers incorporated into the Norwegian hosts. The Danes played an independent part in the story, but their contribution should be kepy separate from the main theme. Ekwall has drawn attention to a Danish colony in the neighbourhood of Manchester and to further indications of Danish influence in the Lune valley[103]. But for Lancashire history the thin Danish overlap from the East

---

[100]   See F.T. Wainwright (1945-6) Field-names of Amounderness Hundred, *Transactions of the Historical Society of Lancashire and Cheshire* 97, 71-116.

[101]   There were certainly Danes among the Norsemen of Wirral: see Chapter 3,4 and F.T. Wainwright (1942) North-west Mercia, 871-924, *Transactions of the Historical Society of Lancashire and Cheshire*, 94, 3-55, reproduced in P. Cavill, S.E. Harding and J. Jesch (2000) *Wirral and its Viking Heritage*, English Place-Name Society.

[102]   For examples, see above.
[103]   E. Ekwall (1922) *Place-Names of Lancashire* pp245, 247.

fades into insignificance beside the heavy Norse immigration from the West.[104]

Irish Invaders

Another problem, interesting to raise but impossible to solve, is whether or not there were many native Irish among the Norse settlers. The existence of Irish elements in the place-name nomenclature of Lancashire has been sufficiently proven, but it is not at once clear whether these should be attributed to the presence of Irishmen among the Norsemen or merely to the effects of the Norsemens sojourn in Ireland. It is reasonable to assume that the Norsemen brought over some Irish women as wives, and it is very likely that a few Irish adventurers had thrown in their lot with the "Fair Strangers"[105], but there is no reason to believe that there was in the population here an Irish element which retained its own identity. If any such groups of Irishmen, unassimilated by the Norsemen, had existed, one might have expected to find at least a few genuine Irish place-name formations. There are none. Ekwall has shown that those place-names which reveal Irish influence were introduced by Scandinavians and not by Irishmen[106]. Names like Ireby and Ireleth may be held to commemorate "the men from Ireland", but this description could be applied to Norsemen as well as to Irishmen. We may accept it as likely that some Irishmen accompanied Scandinavians to Lancashire, but we must attribute traces of Irish influence in Lancashire place-names to associations which the Norsemen themselves had formed before they left Ireland.

Most of the Viking settlers arrived early in the 10th-Century

The date of the Norse immigration is a question which has often been discussed. Ferguson believed that the Norwegian settlements in Cumberland took place between A.D. 945 and 1000[107]. Lindkvist saw the movement as "a gradual process" covering the greater part of the 10th-Century and extending into the eleventh[108]. Ekwall concluded that "it took place in a fairly late period of the Viking age, very likely from about 900", a view to which most scholars would now subscribe[109]. We know from Irish chronicles, and in particular from the trustworthy *Annals of Ulster*, that in 902 there arose a crisis which involved the expulsion of great numbers of Norsemen from Ireland. It seems likely that this crisis lies behind the whole Scandinavian

---

104 But see Chapter 4. Modern scholars are of the opinion the Danish influence in Wirral and probably South-west Lancashire was significant.

105 i.e. *Gall-Ghaidhill* who are described in a passage preserved in the *Three Fragments*, p. 128, as 'Scoti and foster-children to the Northmen'. The Irish attitude to these renegades is illustrated by another passage (*Three Fragments* p.138): 'they were a people who had renounced their baptism, and they were usually called Northmen, for they had the customs of the Northmen, and had been fostered by them, and though the original Northmen were bad to the churches, these were by far worse, in whatever part of Erin they used to be'. There was certainly an Irish element among the Norsemen of Wirral: see Chapter 4.

106 *Scandinavians and Celts in the North-west of England*, pp.48-55.
107 *The Northmen in Cumberland and Westmorland*, p11.
108 *Middle-English Place-names of Scandinavian Origin* p.xxxiii.
109 *The Place Names of Lancashire* p.255.

colonization of North-western England. Secondly, Ingimund's settlement in Wirral, the only literary parallel to the Norse settlements in Lancashire, is explicitly linked with the crisis of 902. Thus the literary evidence, such as it is, points to the first decade of the 10th-Century.

Confirmation comes from a study of the military arrangements of Edward and Æthelflæd. By 907 the Norsemen in Wirral had become a menace so great that Æthelflæd was compelled to strengthen Chester and to install a garrison there[110], a move which failed to prevent the outbreak of armed conflict but which probably explains the successful maintenance of English authority in the area. Further north the growing power of the Norsemen was consolidated by the arrival of Ragnald in about 914 and by his establishment as king at York in 919. Long before the death of Æthelflæd in 918 the confused political scene in northern England was dominated by the Norsemen, and the fact that the rivers of the north-west would form their natural lines of communication with Ireland itself implies that the western coast was securely in their hands. Æthelflæd was fully conscious of the crisis that was developing, and her fortresses at Eddisbury, built early in the summer of 914, and at Runcorn, built late in 915, probably in December, were directed primarily against the menace that lay in the North-west. Again we are driven to place the immigration early in the 10th-Century, for by the middle of the second decade, apparently Æthelflæd had recognized the danger as acute.

Another clue to the date of the immigration is supplied by Athelstan's grant to York. This proves that the name Amounderness was current before 930 and that Agmund, the Scandinavian leader thus commemorated, was alive before that date. We can scarcely avoid the conclusion that Norse settlement in this area began soon after 900 and had gone far by 930.

Were Lake District Settlements later than in West Lancashire and Wirral ?

Place-names do not readily allow close chronological conclusions, and they are of little value in this problem. But Ekwall[111] has suggested that the comparative lack of inversion-compounds in Lancashire[112] may indicate that the settlements here are earlier than those of Cumberland and Westmorland. The Norse immigration into Cumberland and Westmorland may well have

---

[110] On the significance of the restoration of Chester, which is recorded without comment in manuscripts B and C of the *Anglo-Saxon Chronicles*, see F.T. Wainwright (1942) North-West Mercia, 871-924, *Transactions of the Historical Society of Lancashire and Cheshire*, 94, 3-55, reproduced in P. Cavill, S.E. Harding and J. Jesch (2000) *Wirral and its Viking Heritage*, English Place-Name Society, 19-42.

[111] *Scandinavian and Celts in the North-West of England*, pp.102-103. The suggestion is that inversion-compounds, common in Cumberland and Westmorland, 'point to far stronger (Goidelic) influence than loanwords'. This could be explained by a longer association with the Irish, and we might conclude 'that the districts in which inversion-compounds are common were colonised comparitively late'.

[112] This applies also to Wirral.

been a later or a longer process, and we ought to link the Norse settlements in Lancashire, in date at least, with the Norse settlements in Wirral. All the scattered scraps of evidence suggest that the movement began and reached its climax between 900 and 910. We are not bound to believe that all settlement ceased after the first great impetus had subsided. The remote districts would be colonized gradually through the centuries, but by expansion from the older centres of settlement rather than by further immigration from over the sea.

Scandinavian settlement proven beyond question

However, in spite of the unbroken silence of chroniclers it is possible to sketch with some confidence the outlines of the Norse settlement of Lancashire. The fact of its occurrence is beyond question, and fairly safe conclusions may be drawn with regard to its date, its nature, its intensity and its development.

The Norsemen caused considerable confusion

Conditions in North-western England during the early 10th-Century are obscure in the extreme. The arrival of the Norsemen must have caused considerable confusion for, even if they did not introduce the more violent excesses of military conquest, their numbers alone would be sufficient to disorganize life in the area. By A.D. 900, however, the Northumbrian state had been shattered, and the Norsemen merely emphasized the political confusion which had existed for at least a generation. The central government of Northumbria, long declining in effectiveness, had collapsed in 867 when the Danes had captured York. Halfdan's settlement of 876 was concentrated in the valleys of the Yorkshire Ouse and its tributaries; west of the Pennines a few English nobles and clergy maintained a precarious independence[113] and no doubt assumed responsibility for law and order. Until the end of Alfred's reign, it seems, the lands between the Pennines and the western sea offered an asylum to harassed Englishmen from the east. This period of uneasy quiet ended with the turn of the Century. Before 915 conditions were such that nobles and high ecclesiastics were moving eastwards across the Pennines, and we hear no more of native magnates. The ordinary Englishman perhaps felt the impact of the Norsemen less severely, but it was certainly a time of confusion.

---

[113] Some light is thrown upon conditions in Northern England by the *Historia de Sancto Cuthberto* (*Symeonis Monachi Opera Omnia*, 1, 208-210 Rolls Series).

The Cuerdale Hoard. Courtesy of David Flowers, National Museums and Art Galleries, Liverpool.

Treasure hoards at Cuerdale and Harkirke, Crosby

This impression is confirmed by two great Lancashire hoards, one found at Cuerdale in 1840 and the other at Harkirke (Crosby) in 1611. It has been suggested that the Cuerdale Hoard was buried by the defeated Danish army retreating from Tetenhall in 910; this may or may not be so, but both hoards belong to the early part of the 10th-Century, and the fact that it was thought necessary to bury money and valuables in such quantities is an indication that the times were troubled.

Key role for the North-west Scandinavians

The fortification of Chester seems to have been directed primarily against the Norsemen in Wirral, but Eddisbury and Runcorn[114] seem to have been built after Ragnald's arrival in Northern England gave an increased importance to the Norsemen who controlled the western coast and the direct route to Dublin.

It may be stated with some confidence that the hoards of Norsemen in Northern England and the alarm which they inspired there provide the key to an understanding of otherwise inexplicable developments. It might not be too much to say that the history of England in the early 10th-Century turns largely upon the Norsemen, upon what action they took and, above all, upon what action they might have taken.

The influence of the Norsemen persists even today

Finally it should be remembered that the influence of the Norsemen was not limited to conditions and events of the 10th-Century. We have seen how the new settlers left their mark on the racial complex, the social structure, the place-names, the language, and the art-forms of Lancashire and the north-west. Their influence long outlasted the 10th-Century. It was a dominant factor in the history of Lancashire throughout the Middle Ages and it persists even today. As a mere episode the Norse immigration must be considered outstanding. But it was not a mere episode. It was an event of permanent historical importance.

---

[114] And perhaps a fortress built early in 915 at *Weardbyrig*, a place not yet satisfactorily identified.

Final Note

In many instances above place-names are used as evidence without any apparent attempt to supply early forms or even derivations. In every such instance all relevant details will be found in Ekwall's *The Place-Names of Lancashire*. To give this general reference seems the only way to avoid unnecessarily choking the text with details which, though essential, are readily accessible elsewhere. In every case, however, where names quoted do not appear in *The Place-Names of Lancashire* sufficient details of date and source are appended. The following is a list of abbreviations used in the quotation of forms of names.

CC	*The Chartulary of Cockersand Abbey*, edited by William Farrer, Chetham Society, New Series vols. 38, 39, 40, 43, 56, 57, 64 (1898-1909).
Hoghton	*De Hoghton Deeds and Papers*, edited by J. H. Lumby, Record Society of Lancashire and Cheshire, vo. 88 (1936).
LAR	*Lancashire Assize Rolls*, edited by John Parker, Record Society of Lancashire and Cheshire, vols. 47, 49 (1903-1905).
LI	*Lancashire Inquests, Extents, and Feudal Aids*, edited by William Farrer, Record Society of Lancashire and Cheshire, vols. 48, 54, 70 (1903-1915).
LPC	*Lancashire Pipe Rolls and Early Charters*, edited by William Farrer, Liverpool (1902).
LPD	*Pleadings and Depositions in the Duchy Court of Lancaster*, edited by Henry Fishwick, Record Society of Lancashire and Cheshire, vols 32, 35, 40 (1896-1899).
Norris	*The Norris Deeds*, edited by J. H. Lumby, Record Society of Lancashire and Cheshire, vol. 93 (1939).
PNLa	E. Ekwall, *The Place-Names of Lancashire*, Manchester, 1922.

By this means and by the introduction of undisguised lists at certain points I have tried to preserve the readability of this essay. The general reference to Ekwall's work also serves to throw the reader back upon what is, after all, the basis of Lancashire place-name studies.

Chapter 9

THE HAMMER AND THE CROSS: MERSEY PAGANISM AND CHRISTIANITY

The highly respected Mersey Northernist and scholar William Gershom Collingwood, (1854 - 1932) wrote the following in 1928.

> It is the popular belief that wherever the Norse came they destroyed the churches. But by the time of their settlement - here about 900 - they had become Christianized to some extent.

The first exposure of the British Isles to the Viking visitors from Scandinavia were the raids on Lindesfarne and other coastal Monasteries in the 8th-Century, and this has forever coloured peoples' impressions of what they were all like. However, by the beginning of the tenth-Century many had been living adjacent to - and in some cases mixed with - Christian Celtic communities in Ireland.

Scandinavian refugees from Ireland as they approached the Mersey coastline in c902AD would have seen the wooden predecessor of the present church of St. Hilary in the distance on the Wallasey 'brekka'.

Pagans or Christians?

It is true that most people associate the Vikings with destruction when in reality many used violence only when they had to. They were also constantly referred to by English writers as "Heathen". The Scandinavian population in Wirral, West Lancashire and Chester - especially those who had come from Ireland - had in reality been Christianized "to some extent" before their arrival. It is therefore not surprising that they brought with them at least two churches dedicated to a Gaelic Saint and constructed an array of monuments and carvings dating from the middle of the tenth-Century onward. With Norse place-names and other hints of similar origin also involved, we can hardly doubt that these were the chapels of Christian 'Vikings' who had brought their religion with them from Ireland.

Arno Hill in Wirral

This hill or mound, just off Storeton Road in Oxton, Wirral is named after the Old Norse personal name *Árni* or *Erni,* and in the following quotation from the *Cheshire Sheaf,* the 1909 writer (A.H. Arkle of Oxton) is speculating on its relation with a similar place near Whitby in Yorkshire. *Árni* is assumed to be buried here.

FROM CHESHIRE SHEAF, VOL. 7, DECEMBER 1909, PAGES 101-102, EXTRACT FROM ARTICLE 1437

I have seen no reply to my enquiry respecting the reason for this name which is applied to the small hill at the south end of the Oxton ridge. I therefore venture a suggestion which has occurred to me through reading a paragraph in Young's "History of Whitby". It seems that there is an "Arno Cross" on the North Yorkshire Moors near Rosedale, and the author referred to suggests that this is a corruption of Arne Houe or Howe as it stands on a Howe, Arne being a family name. Now it may appear at first sight that there is no connection with the "Arno" in Oxton, but on looking further into the matter and trying to imagine how the place looked before it was quarried and before any houses had been built, one cannot be struck by the fact that the hill must have presented an appearance exactly corresponding to that of a Howe or pointed little Hill. From this point there is now a very beautiful and extensive view, but in old times the view must have taken a still wider area of many miles in extent and therefore is just the place for the burial of some ancient Chieftain .... *Oxton. A.H. Arkle.*

The Arno. Arni's haug, Oxton, Wirral

Arno Hill represents an example of a likely pagan Viking burial mound. Many of these have been found in Scandinavia. Some of the most interesting are at Borre in Vestfold, South-east Norway (not far from the Oslo Torp airport). Vestfold was the kingdom of Harald Harfagre, the 9th-Century king who united Norway and has

Anundshög, Västerås, Sweden. The main mound is the left. Another smaller mound can be seen in the distance. Courtesy of Bernhard Kauntz.

'Viking Funeral' Painting of 1893 by Frank Dicksee. Courtesy of Manchester City Art Galleries.

been considered largely responsible for the subsequent exodus of peoples out of Norway - the Viking Age. Two of his forefathers were considered to be buried here[115] - a *King Eystein Fart* considered to be his great-great grandfather, who drowned after being knocked into the sea by the sail-yard of a passing ship, and his son *Hálfdan*. Although these mounds had been disturbed by vandalism, they were used as symbols of Norwegian nationalism in the 19th-Century as Norway strove for its full independence from Sweden. It is here that kings from the Royal dynasty known as the *Ynglings*[116] were presumed buried, and supposedly going back to the fertility god/king *Yngvi-Frey*.

Burial mounds were deemed appropriate for people of high esteem in a Scandinavian community. Whereas Oxton's *Árni* or *Erni* could not claim to be of the *Yngvi* line he certainly must have been someone of prominence in early 10th-Century Wirral. Another Viking burial mound with parallels to *The Arno* is at *Anundshög*, the largest of a group of mounds to the east of the city of Västerås in Sweden, just a short distance off the highway. It was built in the 11th-Century in honour of *Anund*, and, like The Arno, rises as high as the trees beneath it.

Another possible site for a burial mound has been considered in Heswall, and this was the topic of some interesting discussion concerning a field named Harrow Hay. This is listed as *Harrowe Hay* in (1293) which according to John McNeal Dodgson could be from *Haerri-haugr* "The higher hill enclosure" from ON *haerri* (higher) and ON *haugr* (hillock, burial mound) or from similar Anglo-Saxon roots *herra* and *hoh*. The old English *hearg* "heathen shrine" has also been suggested in an article by Prudence Vipond[117]

115 Magnus Magnusson (2000) *The Vikings*, Tempus, Stroud, p33-34.
116 The *Yngling Saga*. In Snorri Sturluson's *Heimskringla* (Translated by Samuel Laing), Everyman, Dutton, New York, 1961
117 'Harrow Fields in Heswall-cum-Oldfield?' *Journal of the English Place-Name Society*, 25, pages 9-10.

leading Margaret Gelling to re-examine her earlier view that the western limits of such shrines was Staffordshire[118].

There is no evidence however of the other type of pagan burial attributed to Vikings: a burning ship as witnessed in the famous Kirk Douglas film "The Vikings" and also pictured in the spectacular 19th-Century painting by Frank Dicksee[119].

Thursdays and Fridays

Yngvi-Frey of the Ynglings has been considered to have given his name to Friday or its various forms in the northern world (although it actually comes from the Norse goddess *Frigg*). The god who gave his name to Thursdays is considered as more important in Mersey folklore, particularly as he is allerged to have left his hammer called "Mjöllnir" in or near Thorstein's farmstead in Thurstaston. Whilst we can offer no guarantee of the accuracy of this particular piece of folklore, the stone is still used as the site for modern day pagan marriages and is the place at which the Morris Men herald the summer at daybreak on May 1st every year - see page 176 of *Ingimund's Saga*.

Transition Period

The religious situation during the early settlement period would probably have been similar to that in Iceland up to the period when Christianity was officially adopted - through compromise and consensus - by the *Alþingi* at Thingvellir in the year 1000: before then Christianity made converts whilst warily coexisting with the old pagan beliefs, as related in the *Kristni saga*. One would imagine this to be the position in the Wirral at least in the earlier part of the 10th-Century. This would be a society where the Christian priests and the corresponding pagan *goði* or (plural) *goðar* would excercise mutual toleration until the Christian faith became completely adopted.

Scandinavian Churches

There are many place-names in the area which bear evidence of Christian activity. In West Lancashire there is *Ormskirk* - where Orm presumably had his church. There is also *Kirkby* - the settlement by or at the church, *Kirkdale* - church valley, *Harkirke* in Crosby - which we have seen was the site of an accidental discovery of treasure. There are also two places now lost: a *le Kirkeway*, recorded in 1326 in Garston and a *Kirkegate*, recorded in 1256 in

---

[118] 'Paganism and Christianity in Wirral?' *Journal of the English Place-Name Society*, 25, page 11.
[119] D.W. Wilson (1992) *Vikings and Gods in European Art*, Moesgård Museum, Denmark.

Two views of St. Olave's Church in Chester. The current church is on the site of the original Scandinavian church. St. Olave was first canonized in the 11th-Century and it is thought the first building originated then.

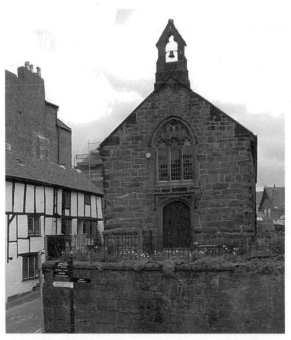

Eccleston, Prescot. In Wirral there are several place-names denoting Christian activity, and in the Scandinavian enclave of South Chester there were formerly two Viking churches. One was dedicated to St. Bridget of Ireland (450-525 AD), but has now gone. The other on Lower Bridge Street is dedicated to Ólaf the Saint, or King Ólaf Haraldsson (995-1030AD): the current church, used by the evangelical Cheshire Revival movement and its charismatic priest, Reverend Graham Dalton is positively thriving.

St. Olave's Church Chester.

King Ólaf the Saint - Ólaf Haraldsson - was responsible for making Norway a Christian country. His predecessor Ólaf Tryggvason - whose statue stands proud in modern day Trondheim - is credited with starting the process, but it was Ólaf the Saint who secured, after many years struggle, the christianization of the whole of Norway, including the inner regions which were clinging on to the old beliefs in Thór, Óðinn and Valhalla. He is credited with the saying 'let the sword pave the way for the cross'. This he achieved by 1024, where at a Thing on the island of Moster, Christianity was accepted as the official faith in Norway. His power in Norway diminished with the growing power of King Canute in Denmark who had secured England and had by 1028AD effectively taken control of Norway too, with Earl Hákon as his overlord. Ólaf died in battle on 29th July 1030. Shortly after his death, Ólaf was officially declared a Saint in Trondheim and his Christian Law was soon accepted by all in Norway. The 29th July is marked in the Norwegian calendar as *Olsok*, Ólaf's vigil.

St. Bridget's at West Kirby

Although the Church dedicated to the Gaelic St. Bridget in Chester has long since gone, another church dedicated to her - and also founded by the Vikings - is in West Kirby, and, like St. Olave's in Chester, is thriving. St. Bridget (St. Brigid) is, with St. Patrick, joint Patron Saint of Ireland. Bridget was one of the most remarkable women of her times, and demonstrated extraordinary spirituality, charity, and compassion for those in distress. Legend also attributed many miracles to her. Her death on February 1st 525AD is marked by a feast day in Ireland. Besides Ireland, Wirral and formerly Chester, there are many churches elsewhere dedicated to her, including London (St. Bride's, Fleet Street), Cumbria, the Hebrides and even Germany.

St. Bridget's West Kirby. Believed to have been founded by the Norsemen after their arrival from Ireland and named after the Irish Patron Saint. The original church was probably wooden. Photograph courtesy of Revd. Roger Clarke.

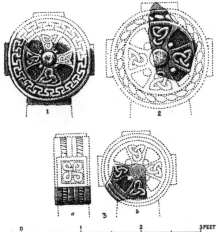

Norse Crosses at West Kirby. Drawings from W.G. Collingwood. In these sketches from 1928, Collingwood has used dotted line projections to estimate the original complete form.

1: Cross-head (red sandstone) apparently found at Hilbre in 1852. Now in the Grosvenor museum, Chester; 2: Fragment of cross head (red sandstone), in the museum at West Kirby

3: Another fragment (red sandstone) in the museum at West Kirby (a) side view (b) front view; 4: Cross-shaft (found 1893, red-sandstone), in the museum at West Kirby. 11th-Century, thought to be from the time of King Canute. Two adjacent sides shown; 5: Another red-sandstone cross-shaft in West Kirby from the same time. All four sides shown.

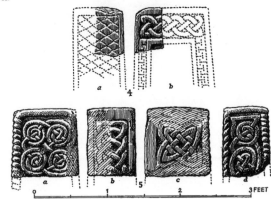

Scandinavian stonework in West Kirby and Hilbre

It was in this part of Merseyside that a number of stone crosses from the Scandinavian period could be found together with the famous Hogback tombstone. Much of the material was discovered during the 1869-1870 restoration of St. Bridgets. Collingwood, in his 1928 paper "Early monuments of West Kirby" reprinted as Chapter 7 in Wirral and its Viking Heritage, wrote the following about the stonework:

> From the absence of any stones of the tenth-Century we may infer that the St. Bridget's of the Norse was rather a poor church in rude surroundings. Stone monuments are not made until there is well-being and until circumstances permit the

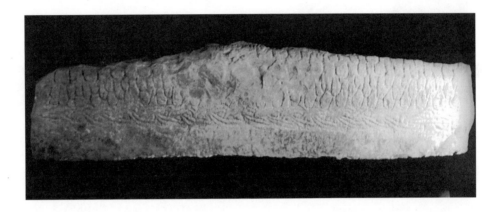

Hogback tombstone at St. Bridget's Church, West Kirby. Top left: Photograph of the front, taken in 1999 after restoration by the Merseyside Conservation Centre of the front. Bottom left: drawing by W.G. Collingwood of the front, as published in 1928: dotted line projections illustrate the likely form of the once intact stone. Above: 1999 photograph of the back.

Norse Tombstone slabs (from about 1100AD). Left: found 1864 at Hilbre; Top right: rusticated slab fragment; Bottom right: slab at West Kirby. 1928 sketches at West Kirby museum by W.G. Collingwood.

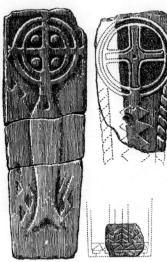

Norse Tombstone slabs (from about 1100AD). Left: found 1864 at Hilbre; Top right: rusticated slab fragment; Bottom right: slab at West Kirby. 1928 sketches at West Kirby museum by W.G. Collingwood.

Restored ring-headed church cross, Bromborough. This cross was re-erected at St. Barnabas's church 1958, on St. Barnabas's Day. Courtesy of David Randall.

growth of artistic taste. This did not come about at West Kirby until King Knút's (Canute) time, and then perhaps the demand was created by the supply. There was someone at Chester who was making fine crosses; his fame reached West Kirby and people there wished to be in fashion. They sent for him and he made them examples of his best work.

So the crosses in the illustration on page 133 probably date from King Canute's time in the mid-11th-Century (four to five generations after Ingimund).

The hogback or "recumbent" Norse tombstone is also believed to have been produced during this period. Collingwood in his article gives a full description of the tombstone and its relation to others of the period. The stone from which it was produced was originally thought to have come from Storeton, like the stonework in Neston considered below, though the source that subsequently appeared to be favoured by geologists is the sandstone from the Upper Coal Measures near Ruabon and Cefn. If it had indeed come from outside the area this adds further testimony to the importance of the person whose grave it once stood by. The tombstone now resides inside St. Bridgets church after being beautifully restored in 1999 by the Merseyside Conservation Centre.

Some fifty or so years later (c.1100AD) after the production of the crosses there was a renewed desire for tombstones and, according to Collingwood, this time the West Kirby people had among them a 'smith' who could make the kind of thing which then satisfied their Norse cousins in Galloway and elsewhere. To this smith is attributed the tombstone slabs at Hilbre and another slab at West Kirby. To the same smith has also been attributed the first stone church form of St. Bridgets from which fragments of architectural detail still remain in the existing church. Detailed descriptions of all the monuments mentioned here and the other Scandinavian monuments found on Wirral given by both Collingwood and J.D. Bu'Lock are reprinted in *Wirral and its Viking Heritage.*

Another ring headed cross has been restored at Bromborough[120]. But it is at Neston where a recent penetrating analysis of some ancient stonework there has led to some important conclusions about the origins of the Scandinavian settlers.

Scandinavian stonework at Neston

In the parish church of St Mary and St. Helen at Neston resides more impressive Scandinavian stonework, or fragments of crosses. Thought originally to be Saxon, the style, like that of the West Kirby crosses is clearly Viking, as shown by the painstaking work of Dr. Roger White and the late John D. Bu'Lock. Bu'Lock's 1958 article was reprinted in Chapter 6 of *Wirral and its Viking Heritage*, as we have already mentioned, and that article drew attention to the pieces at Neston. This was greatly reinforced by three articles from Roger White, who is now at the Ironbridge Institute, Shropshire: two as research notes which appeared in 1985[121] the other a full research paper[122] which appeared in 1986. White assigns the sculpturing of the stones to the period between 930AD to about 1020AD, coinciding with the construction of similar stonework and crosses in the Isle of Man. He suggests that, besides being Viking in style, they were also probably made by a Viking craftsman.

Discovery of the Neston Stonework

In 1874 much of the old Norman church was pulled down and rebuilt. Four standing crosses of the circle-headed type were found in the foundations, and these were described in an article the following year by H.E. Smith[123], and the assumption was subsequently made that the stones were Saxon. Another fragment was noted in the belfry acting as a lintel, with half as much embedded in the wall itself. Fortunately this was not structural, and so some 110 years later, White was able to obtain permission to remove it, as part of a commission from the Neston Civic Society and the Parkgate and District Society to display and describe the stonework. In his 1986 paper, White described the five fragments in detail, assessed to be made largely of Storeton-type red sandstone. We summarize his findings here:

Neston Cross Fragment 1: Face A has a standing figure of a priest with arms upraised. Face B is a narrow panel of ring chain interlace. Face C consists of more ring-chain interlace. Face D a line pattern between cable borders.

[120] D. Randall (2003) *The Search for Old Wirral.* Countyvise Ltd, Birkenhead.
[121] R.H. White (1985) Norse period crosses at Neston, *Liverpool University Archaeological Newsletter* 1, 14-15 and (1985) *Liverpool University Archaeological Newsletter* 3, 1-2.

[122] R.H. White (1986) Viking period sculpture at Neston, Chester, *Journal of the Chester Archaeological Society*, 69, 45-58.
[123] H.E. Smith (1875) Archaeology in the Merseyside District and Liverpool, *Trans. Historic. Society of Lancashire and Cheshire*, 3rd series, 3, 85-108.

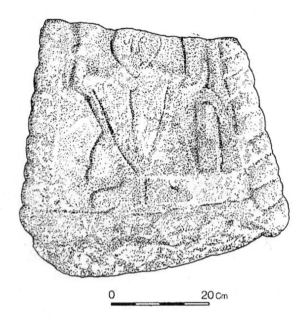

Neston Cross Fragment 1, side A.

Neston Cross Fragment 2: Face A has a figure of an Angel placed horizontally, and has wings and a pleated 'skirt' at the waist. Face B is as cross fragment 1. Face C shows two men fighting with knives. They are dressed in broad 'kilts' presumably jerkins or tunics. Face D is as cross fragment 1.

Neston Cross Fragment 3: Face A: six strand plaitwork forming the foot of the cross. Face B is unclear. Face C has a small fragment of interlace similar to cross frament 1. Face D: as cross fragment 1.

Neston Cross Fragment 4: Face A has a cabled arc, forming part of the outer ring of the circle head. Face B has the remains of a design as cross fragment 1. Face C is similar to Face A. Face D has the beginnings of a line pattern but is damaged.

Neston Cross Fragment 5: Face A has a hunting scene involving a stag, a dog and a man with a spear. Above the scene are the 2 lower halves of a man and a woman (on the left). The woman has her arm around the man wearing a characteristic short 'kilt'. White points out that behind the woman is a long vertical bar consisting of a tassel with a knot above and the beginning of plaitwork: Roger White presumes this is the woman's pigtail. Face B: as cross fragment 1. Face C: is divided into two unequal panels by a bar, which represents ground level for the upper panel. Upper panel shows two men jousting or fighting on horses. The lower panel shows one animal chasing another animal. Face D: as cross fragment 1.

White has attempted some image reconstruction or piecing together of the fragments and made some interesting comparsions with elsewhere in the Viking world:

1. The Priest of Fragment 1, side A: Similar figures are seen on stonework in Winwick (Lancashire), Brompton and Nunburnholme (Yorks) and Hexham.
2. The angel on Fragment 2, side A: This has close affinities with the angel depicted on the crucifixion cross slab from Kirk

Neston Cross Fragments 2 and 5, after suggested reconstruction of R. White. Left:: Face A; Right: Face C. Reproduced, permission of R. White

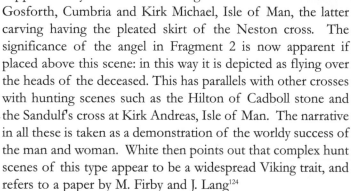

Michael, Isle of Man. By placing this fragment above Fragment 5, the puzzling feature of the horizontal angel can be accounted for by producing a complete narrative.

3. Fragment 5, side A, with Fragment 2 placed above. The spearman and hound are very familiar in Dark Age sculpture and the scene is close to the market cross at Kells and the stone at Hilton of Cadboll, Highland. The man and woman above this were probably those commemorated by the cross, which is similar to the huntsman scene on the cross at St. Mary Bishophill Junior, York. The indication of a pigtail on the woman is supported by those on Viking women at Gosforth, Cumbria and Kirk Michael, Isle of Man, the latter carving having the pleated skirt of the Neston cross. The significance of the angel in Fragment 2 is now apparent if placed above this scene: in this way it is depicted as flying over the heads of the deceased. This has parallels with other crosses with hunting scenes such as the Hilton of Cadboll stone and the Sandulf's cross at Kirk Andreas, Isle of Man. The narrative in all these is taken as a demonstration of the worldy success of the man and woman. White then points out that complex hunt scenes of this type appear to be a widespread Viking trait, and refers to a paper by M. Firby and J. Lang[124]

4. Fragment 5, side C, with Fragment 2 placed above. Christian interpretations have previously been given for the jousting and animals chasing, with the men fighting above (for example, parallels with Cain and Abel). However White considers a secular interpretation more likely, given the interpretation of Manx stones of the same date, namely such scenes commemorating episodes from the life of the deceased. The Christian element to the cross is the angel on side A, and the carving of the priest on Fragment 1.

White concludes that the existence of the Neston cross reinforces the view that Viking sculpture tends to commemorate the wealth, status and worldy deeds of the deceased, and contrasts the use of sculpture by the Anglo-Saxons more as a religious tool. Or put another way - these crosses are not for religious instruction but to celebrate the lives and activities of the

---

[124] M. Firby and J. Lang (1981) The pre-Conquest Sculpture at Stonegrave, *Yorkshire Archaeological Journal*, 53, 17-29.

deceased. Even the priest is seen in a secular rather than religious role: accompanied by the tools of his trade and indicating his important role in the community, with the chalice and mandiple easily understood as symbols of power to the recently converted Wirral Vikings. The cross is clearly Viking in origin, not Anglo-Saxon.

Significance of the Neston Stonework: Wirral and the Isle of Man

White's penetratring analysis makes it quite clear the community in Wirral had strong links with the rest of the Viking world, particularly the Isle of Man. This would appear to strongly reinforce the view expressed by G. Fellows- Jensen that many of the settlers came from here. It was a stepping stone for Norsemen from Ireland and also Danes coming in an anti-clockwise migration from the Danelaw, via Cumbria and the Isle of Man.

Chapter 10

THE THINGS OF WIRRAL AND WEST LANCASHIRE

The Danish historian J.J. Worsaae, one of the great 19th-Century writers on Vikings wrote the following in 1852:

> The name of the village of Thingwall in Cheshire affords a remarkable memorial of the assizes, or Thing, which the Northmen generally held in conjunction with their sacrifices to the gods.

and then went on to write:

> It lies, in conjunction with several other villages with Scandinavian names, on the small tongue of land that projects between the mouths of the rivers Dee and Mersey. At that time, they generally chose for the holding of the *thing*, or assizes, a place in some degree safe from surprise. The chief ancient thing place for Iceland was called, like this Thingwall, namely Thingvalla, originally *þingvöllr*, *þingvellir* of the *thing-fields*, from wall, ODan, *vold*, a bank or rampart.

The local administration that Worsaae is referring to in his 1852 book *"The Danes and Norwegians in England, Scotland and Ireland"* is the Thing at Thingwall in Wirral (ON *Þingvöllr*, from *þing*=assembly and *völlr*=field, "Assembly Field"), recognised as the centre of Scandinavian Wirral. Before he wrote this - which would have been eight years before O'Donovan published in Ireland his discovery of the *Three Fragments* - historians were completely unaware of the significance of the Scandinavian settlements that had taken place in the North-west of England during the 10th-Century, and completely in the dark concerning the extensive Norwegian contribution to this movement. Worsaae too, would have been unaware of the consequences of the expulsions of the Norsemen from Ireland in 902AD, but what his book did do was to make English historians realise for the first time that Scandinavians came into England from Norway as well as Denmark.

The Things - like the one at Thingwall, in Wirral, one at Thingwall Hall, Knotty Ash in South-west Lancashire and Tynwald in the Isle of Man - provided the means of government throughout the Scandinavian world. The corresponding place in Iceland, *Þingvellir* (*vellir*=fields, the plural of *völlr*) was used from 930AD until relatively recently. Although the place of government in Iceland has moved from there the government is still known as the *Althing* (Old Norse *Alþingi* - the "All Thing") and the government in Norway at Oslo is still referred to as "*Storting*" (from Old Norse *stór-þing* "the Great Thing" - *stór* has been considered as the same element in Wirral's Storeton).

Cross Hill, Thingwall. Site of the Wirral Thing. The view is from the Reservoir side of Barnston Road.

The Wirral Thing

The precise location of the Wirral Thing referred to in Worsaae's classic work is believed to have been at Cross Hill, across the Barnston Road (A551) from the Reservoir, and a site which would have provided a reasonable elevation for a speaker to make himself heard. The site would have been right at the centre of the large Scandinavian colony. Aliki Pantos, writing in the *Journal of the English Place Name Society*, has recently said the following[125]:

> The existence of hills or mounds at a Scandinavian meeting-site would be in keeping with the evidence from Scandinavia and elsewhere in Britain. In Scandinavia it was the norm for assembly sites to have a *thingbrekka*, an 'assembly-hill' from which announcements were made; that this was also the case at Scandinavian sites in Britain is demonstrated by Tynwald Hill on the Isle of Man. The possibility of there being one or more mounds in this area might then support the identification of Cross Hill as the meeting-place of Norse Wirral.

The antiquity of the Wirral Thing would have dated from not long after Ingimund's arrival in 902AD or thereabouts, and if so, would have pre-dated the Iceland *Alþingi* by some 30 years and also Isle of Man's *Tynwald*, dated as 975AD, by some 70 years.

---

[125] (1998), vol. 31, pp91-112.

As we have already noted earlier, the Scandinavian settlers had established soon after their arrival a community with a clearly defined bounary, its own leader (*Ingimund*), its own language (Norse), a trading port (Meols) and place of assembly or government (the Thing). Although officially in the North - west corner of English Mercia, the political situation was so confused in the 10th-Century - at least in the first decades - that the Scandinavian community was politically independent and answerable to nobody else: neither the English, the Welsh, the Dublin Norse, the Isle of Man, Iceland, and not even

Norway, so at least initially it would have had complete autonomy, i.e. it formed in effect a North Wirral national Parliament! The planning and execution of attacks on Chester was a demonstration of this autonomy. From 920AD with the Mercian leader Edward the Elder (who had effectively taken over from Æthelflæd) apparently purchasing some land in the area from Scandinavian overlords, its powers may have been put more in check with Mercian authority, and its official role, at least for a period, may have been reduced to that of a local government but still serving a population generally hostile to Mercia.

The Cross Hill Thing may have represented not only the main Wirral settlement but also the outliers such as at Helsby, Whitby, South Chester and the Talacre area across the Dee.

Thingwall Hall, Liverpool, site of the South-west Lancashire Thing

The South-west Lancashire Thing

Across the Mersey, the community of West Lancashire Scandinavians had their own Assembly or Thing at another Thingwall, now Thingwall Hall and the site of a leisure complex. Back in Viking times its function was somewhat different.

The Hall is in the Knotty Ash district of Liverpool, home of another famous Liverpool Comedian, Ken Dodd, and close to West Derby, significantly the centre of the old hundred of West Derby which formed the greater part of

West Lancashire. This indicates it probably represented the meeting place for the whole of the Scandinavian community for West Lancashire, or at least the West Derby Hundred. Like the Wirral Thing it would have had complete autonomy, at least for the formative years of its lifetime.

A Chester Thing?

J.J.A. Worsaae writes in 1852[126]:

> In the towns occupied by the Danes, as in the five burghs - or, if Chester and York be included, in the "seven cities" - there was certainly a Danish Thing, as well as in the rural districts.

Since estimates are that by Domesday 25% of the city was Scandinavian, and most of that concentrated in the southern sector, it is not unimaginable they had their own Thing. Or more probably, since they were an outlier of the Wirral colony, they were absorbed into the Cross Hill gatherings.

Function of the Thing

The purpose of a Thing was to assemble representative people from the community to decide on matters of adminstration, policy (including military) and law. Popular codes of law used by the Norsemen were the "Grey-Goose code" (*Grágás*) originating from the Trondheim area from King Magnus the Good, son of Ólaf the Saint. It is thus possible that the Wirral and West Lancashire Things had a similar legal code to Grey-Goose, a code which was also used by the Icelanders. Also important was the "Bjarkø law": this was a special law governing commercial and mercantile affairs and was at one time accepted as a kind of international law. International trade through Scandinavian Wirral's port at Meols might thus also have been regulated by the Thing.

Throughout the Viking world there were two types of Thing - the district or *Fylkis-thing* which was equivalent to local government with limited powers and answerable to higher authorities, and the central or *Lögthing* (or "Logthing") which had far reaching powers at national or regional level. The *Althing* "All-thing" at Thingvellir, Iceland, and the Storting at Oslo are both examples of a Lögthing or Central Thing.

The Lögthings were so powerful they would even influence the choice of monarch or leader: succession to the throne or leadership depended on a combination of hereditary and elective principles: the king had not only to

---

[126] on page 159 of his 1852 book.

Thingvellir in Iceland.
Meeting place of the
 Icelandic Althing.
Picture taken at
Almannagja. Besides its
extreme historical importance,
it is also of considerable
geological interest: The cliffs
are volcanic lava. On one side
is Europe and the other is
America: this place is the only
place in the world
where you can see continental
plates drifting apart.
Picture courtesy of
Ragnar Th. Sigurðsson.

be a member of the royal dynasty but also had to be accepted by the people at the Things.   Ingimund himself would have been chosen following this process during a meeting of a Thing in Dublin or back home in Norway, and the Wirral Thing would have decided on his successor(s). Lögthings also dealt with disputes between leaders of different regions: the district Fylkis-things were not equipped to do this. The Wirral and West Lancashire Things, like the others, would have scheduled meetings once or twice yearly, and also when emergencies arose.

Hustings, Hustings!

General elections and the United Kingdom is exposed to 'Hustings'. The modern term Husting is indeed now used in connection with meetings or gatherings concerning a major election. In Victorian times it was used to describe tribunals in the city of London. The origins are Scandinavian, deriving from the *hus-thing* or "House thing". J.JA. Worsnaee[127] writing about London in 1852 says....

> The most striking and remarkable memorial of the early power of the Danes and other Northmen in London is this - that the highest tribunal in the city has retained to our days its pure old northern name "Husting". Hustings or Husthings are also especially mentioned in the Sagas as having been held in the North, particularly by kings, jarls and other individuals. The Husthing in London was originally established in order to protect and guard the laws and liberties of the city and the customs of the courts of judicature; and the principle magistrates were judges.

[127] p.19 of his 1852 book.

The Thingwalls of the British Isles. Courtesy of Gillian Fellows-Jensen.
1: Tingwall, Shetlands; 2. Tingwall, Orkneys; 3. Tiongal, Isle of Lewis 4. Tinwhil, Isle of Sky; 5.
Dingwall, Cromarty Firth; 6. Tinwald, Dumfriesshire; 7. Dingbell Hill, Nortumberland; 8. Thingwala,
Whitby; 9. Tynwald Hill, Isle of Man; 10. Thingwall Hall, Liverpool; 11. Thingwall, Wirral.

Things in the British Isles

J.J.A. Worsnaee wrote on p158 of his 1852 book the following about the Things in the British Isles, adding an interesting comment about the Danelaw districts of Yorkshire and Lincolnshire:

> The Danes and the Norwegians in North England settled their disputes and arranged their public affairs at the Things, according to Scandinavian custom. The present village of Thingwall (or the Thing-fields) in Cheshire[128] was a place of meeting of the Thing, and not only bore the same name as the old chief Thing place in Iceland, but also the old Scandinavian Thing places, "Dingwall" in the north of Scotland; "Tingwall" in the Shetland Isles; and "Tynewald" or "Tingwall" in the Isle of Man. There were incontestably in the Danish parts of England certain larger or common Thing-meetings for the several districts, which were superior to the Things of separate ones; and it may even be a question whether traces of them are to be found in the division into Ridings, at present used only in Yorkshire, but which formerly prevailed also in Lincolnshire.

Thingwall in Wirral and Thingwall Hall of West Lancashire are two of ten or eleven place-names in the British Isles which are known to have derived from these ancient Thingwalls or meeting places. The others are *Tingwall* in the Shetlands, *Tingwall* in the Orkneys, *Tiongal* in the Isle of Lewis, *Dingwall* in north-east Scotland, *Tinwald* in the Solway area of the Scottish borders, *Dingbell Hill* in Northumbria[129], *Thingwala* in Whitby, and *Tynwald* in the Isle of Man - which still meets every 5th July. These were reviewed in an exhaustive study by Professor Gillian Fellows-Jensen[130], and in comparison with those in Scandinavia. She says the following about the others:

Tingwall, Shetlands. The 'Law-Ting' met in a small holm (island) within a lake, and hence it became known as the Law-Ting Holm, reached by a causeway or stepping stones, known as the Lawtainy.

Tingwall, Orkney. There are no records of meetings here, so it may have been a local or district Thing, although its site is central.

Tiongal, Isle of Lewis. In the heart of the Norse settlement, although may of only had local significance. The lower land on the nearby coast would have been suitable for grazing the horses of the delegates.

---

[128] Wirral
[129] Only possibly.
[130] G. Fellows-Jensen (1996) Tingwall: The significance of the name. In D. J. Waugh and B. Smith editors, *Shetlands Northern Links. Language and History*, Scottish Society for Northern Studies.

Tinwhil, Isle of Skye. We are unsure of the precise location, although Ordnance Survey coordinates NG415583, where Glen Hinnisdal broadens out has been suggested. There are no records of meetings, but it was easily accessible.

Dingwall, Ross-shire. Its survival as the name of an administrative centre suggests that it continued as an assembly place long after the Norse were absorbed into the local Gaelic population.

Tinwald, Dumfriesshire.   It lies close to the River Nith, marking the western boundary of Scandinavian place-names.

Dingbell Hill, Northumberland. Little evidence for Scandinavian place-names in the whole area, but might have marked the easternmost penetration of Scandinavians from Cumberland. The name however may be coincidental and have nothing to do with Scandinavians and their Thing-sites.

Thingwalla, Whitby. Now lost, but it is thought this Thing was a meeting place for Norse settlers in Eskdale or perhaps the whole of Cleveland. The area is rich in Scandinavian place-names.

Tynwald Hill, Isle of Man. The most well-known of the thing-places, and stands on a bronze-age burial mound, and probably an assembly place long before the Vikings arrived. The Manx parliament, although in Douglas (the "Tynwald Chamber") does have one meeting a year on the old midsummer day of 5th July, and is a highly popular tourist attraction.

Thing-haug names
There are also another group of names in northern and eastern England which preserve the place-name Thing but in conjunction with *haugr* (mound). Examples are *Thingoe* in Suffolk, *Thinghou* in Lincolnshire and *Thinghou* in Norfolk, as well as *Fingay Hill* in the North Riding of Yorkshire. It is significant that these names appear in areas of marked Danish settlement, and there are no such examples in areas such as Southern and South-western England which have little evidence of Scandinavian settlement.

Things in Scandinavia

The following were examples of Logthings in Norway, as recorded in Snorri Sturluson's *Heimskringla* "Orb of the World". 1. The *Eyrathing* or *Örething* (at Niðaros, Trondheim the old Norwegian capital): this later moved to the Frosta Thing. 2. The *Frosta Thing* (Trondheimsfjord): the Frosta Thing's laws were established by Hákon the Good, Harald Hárfagri's son. 3. The *Eidsiva Thing (Heiðsævisþing)* at Hamar, Heiðsævi - Lake Mjøsen: this Thing later moved further south to Eidsvöll. The *Eidsiva Thing Laws* - Heiðsævislög - were established by Hálfdan the Black, father of Harald Hárfagri: the Eidsiva Thing was also visited by Harald Hárfagri. 4. The *Gula Thing* (western Norway): the Gula Thing's laws were also established by King Hákon the Good. 5. The *Borgar-Thing* (Borg, Sarpsborg) - 50 miles south of Oslo on the east side of Oslofjord.

The following were some of the many district or Fylkis-things in Norway, as recorded in *Heimskringla*: Arnaness Thing, Kefsisey Thing (Lofoten Islands), Hrafnista Thing (now Ramstad in Namdal) and the Unarheimr Thing. In Denmark there was the *Viborg Thing* (Viborg is an ancient town in north Jutland) and in the Faroe Islands there was the *Løgthing*.

Gillian Fellows-Jensen has pointed out that *Thing-haugr* names seem to be most common in Denmark although there is a Tinghaugen in Vestfold, Norway, the area where Harald Hárfagri came from. In Denmark the name *Tingsted* also appears in Falster and Bornholm, and comes from *Þing-staðr* "Assembly Place"

Besides the regular meetings and emergency meetings of the Things, they were also held on special occasions such as the "Gangdagaþing", a Thing held in the precession days of the Ascension week, two weeks before Whitsuntide. Snorri in his *Heimskringla* records two such, one at *Hamarsfjörður* (1st June, 1139AD) and one at *Unarheimr* (now Onareim on the island of Tysnes, Sunnhordland).

Lifetime of the Wirral and West Lancashire Things

The lifetime and power of the two known Mersey Things, are difficult to assess. The Wirral and West Lancashire Things apparently had some degree of autonomy for at least a significant part of the 10th-Century - and at times virtual complete authority. The powers would wax or wane depending on what was going on in the global English-Scandinavian struggle for supremacy. Clearly from the stories of the attacks on Chester, in the formative years the Wirral Thing was autonomous in its authority, even though nominally the area was still part of English Mercia under Æthelflæd's jurisdiction It is clear she allowed the Wirral Norse to rule themselves, and only tried to check their activities when they developed designs on Chester. Across the Mersey, West Lancashire was part of the Kingdom of Northumbria with its centre at York: this was switching hands between the Danes and the English and then in 919AD the Norsemen Ragnald seized control.

Ragnald and Edward the Elder

Of Ragnald, N.J. Higham[131] has suggested that, following the expulsions from Dublin in 902AD, this Irish-sea Viking, who was to become a powerful figure in the history of 10th-Century England, settled in the River Ribble area in parallel to Ingimund's activities in Wirral. He stayed in Ribble until 913-914AD when he successfully launched a campaign against the then hostile Isle of Man: his power base then switched to there. From there he seized control of York in 919AD establishing Northumbria (including Lancashire, which was then "South-west Northumbria") as a Norse Kingdom. The same year his cousin Sithric had also re-established the Viking power base of Dublin. However the area affecting both Things had become confused. The English King Edward the Elder, who had taken control of Mercia from Æthelflæd might possibly have purchased the area south of the Ribble, including Wirral, from Scandinavian lords in 920. Higham says the following:

> If so, that transfer would have been facilitated by the governmental confusion which had resulted from Scandinavian immigration on both sides of the Mersey estuary, and the consequent decline of the lower Mersey as a boundary....
> In Domesday book, Lancashire below the Ribble was organised in hundreds and hidated - like Mercia but unlike any other part of Northumbria....
> The hundredal courts presumably provided safe lodgings for Edward's men when travelling between Mercia and Ribble, in the midst of a population who resented Edwards' authority and identified themselves with Northumbrian and Scandinavian separatism.

Officially the area was "English" although the people and customs were not. For the next years the Things may have become vehicles for official - or un official - local or regional government as the big power players of Sithric, Edward and Ragnald sorted their business out on a higher platform.

---

[131] N. J. Higham (1992) Northumbria, Mercia and the Irish Sea Norse, 893-926. In J. Graham-Campbell ed. *Viking Treasure from the North West,* Chapter 3, National Museums and Guides on Merseyside, Liverpool.

King Canute and the Normans

The Battle of Brunanburh in 937AD, considered in the forthcoming chapter, would have, at least for a while, compromised the freedom of the Scandinavian communities of the North-west. The powers of the two Mersey Things would have been suppressed, although all warring factions would presumably have cleared off shortly after the battle. It is not known how rapidly the Things would have recovered after this, although the period of rule by the Scandinavian Kings in England in the early decades of the 11th-Century would have provided the optimum environment for them to thrive as local government institutions. Even after the Northern Conquest, the West Lancashire Thing, situated at the centre of the West Derby hundred, would probably have played an important part in the government of that region. The Wirral Thing - or resonances from its pre-conquest structure, also appeared to have played an important role in the post-conquest administration of North Wirral which essentially formed the 'Caldy Hundred'. What gives us a clue about this is that the baronial arrangement of North Wirral after 1066 was quite different here compared with elsewhere. It was for the most part split into four compact parcels and given to four of the most powerful Norman barons of Cheshire[132]; this was in contrast with the rest of Wirral where the Domesday holdings were dispersed. John McNeal Dodgson says the following[133]

> The North Wirral situation represented a Norman adaptation of an administrative pattern that already existed when the Norman Earls took over the shire. It looks as though the Norse enclave in Wirral was so politically distinctive that it justified a special feudal administration.
>
> The Norse element must have remained dominant for some time, at least long enough to impress its consciousness of identity upon the pattern of regional government over and above the parochial level, as the distribution of place-names in Wirral indicates. The place Thingwall is in the Norse northern end of the peninsula, and can only be the organization of a Norse organization. In Domesday Book what is now the Hundred of Wirral was known as the hundred of Wilaveston which met at Willaston. Half-way between Thingwall and Willaston is Raby 'the farmstead at the boundary-mark'. It looks as though the Norse colony had a defined boundary within within which it owned its own jurisdiction. This special

---

[132] See J. N. McN. Dodgson, in P. Cavill, S.E. Harding and J. Jesch (2000) *Wirral and its Viking Heritage*, Chapter 5. (See also N.J. Higham (1993) *The Origins of Cheshire*. Manchester University Press, Manchester, U.K.).

[133] ditto, page 65.

jurisdiction is commemorated in the feudal arrangement of North Wirral in post-Conquest times.

It is apparent that the Wirral Thing at least in some form or other was active at the time of the Conquest, although the hundredal organisation may have by then marginalized it somewhat.

A closer view of Cross Hill, Thingwall. Here the Wirral Norse leader Ingimund is reported as having said the following, in connection with a confrontation with the English over lands at Chester (translation into Icelandic courtesy of Eyrún Hafsteinsdóttir and Jón Baldvinsson): "Förum first bónarveg að þeim, og ef við náum þeim ekki með góðu, þá skulum við taka þá með valdi" "Let us beseech and implore them first, and if we do not get them willingly in this way let us contest them by force".

Emergency Meetings of the Things

There would have been at least two occasions of emergency for the fledgling community on Merseyside. The first would have been in 907AD, if the Ingimund tradition is to be believed. The Ingimund story reports how, some five years after the settlements started, the colonists became discontent with the poor quality of much of the land they had been allocated, and so Ingimund "came to the leaders of the Norsemen and the Danes; he made a great complaint in their presence, and he said that they were not well off without good lands and that it was right for them to seize Chester and to possess it with its wealth and its lands". "Let us beseech and implore them first, and if we do not get them willingly in this way let us contest them by force". This meeting is most likely to have taken place at Cross Hill.

Almost two generations on, in 937AD, if the great weight of evidence is to be believed, a much larger crisis appeared to arise for both local Things and their energetic, but largely peaceful Scandinavian or Anglo-Scandinavian communities on both sides of the Mersey.

Chapter 11

937A.D. THE BATTLE OF BRUNANBURH

The respected historian John McNeal Dodgson, wrote in an article in the *Saga-Book of the Viking Society* (vol 14, part 4, 1957) the following

> In no other locality does the context of geography, politics and place-names accord so well with the few facts we possess concerning the contest.

Wirral probably marks the location of one of the most significant battles in the history between the Norwegian Vikings, their Celtic allies and the English. This occurred about two generations after the arrival of Ingimund and the first settlers: Brunanburh, 937AD.

Despite its significance, there has in the past been considerable uncertainty as to where Brunanburh was, with claims ranging from the Humber, Burnswalk in Dumfrieshire and Blackburn and Burnley in Lancashire. However, the great bulk of the historical and philological opinion is now in favour of Wirral, particularly because of the philological connection of Brunanburh with Bromborough. The first to put the case for Bromborough forward seriously in a paper of 1907[134] was Francis Tudbury, the Oxford trained antiquarian, encouraged by the Icelandic scholar Eiríkur Magnússon. Eiríkur had encouraged Tudsbury in his Wirral theory, as Andrew Wawn, writing in *Wirral and its Viking Heritage*[135] recalls:

> The Icelander's improbable reconstruction of oral tradition involved Egil Skallagrímsson having survived the 937AD battle, returning to Iceland and reporting the events to his daughter. Eventualy a twelfth-Century Icelander, perhaps a descendant of Egil and certainly familiar with such oral sources, sought to compose a saga about the great Viking poet; he visited Britain in search of supplementary sources, which he allegedly found in some early medieval chronicle.

Whereas such oral tradition is open to question, the evidence provided by John McNeal Dodgson most certainly was not[136], and two works in particular provide convincing arguments: the 1957 paper referred to above, published

---

[134] F.W.T. Tudbury (1907) Brunanburh AD 937 (London and Chester)
[135] P. Cavill, S.E. Harding and J. Jesch (2000) *Wirral and its Viking Heritage*, Chapter 9, English Place-Name Society, Nottingham
[136] building on a paper by A.H. Smith (1937) The Site of Brunanburh, *London Medieval Studies* I. i, 56-9, who had suggested Bromborough on onomastic grounds.

John McNeal Dodgson
(1928-1990)

in the Saga book of the Viking Society[137] and Part IV of his mammoth treatise *The Place Names of Cheshire*[138]. The significance of the battle and its possible background have been considered more recently by N.J. Higham, of the University of Manchester, who convincingly argues that this area of English Mercia was particularly targeted by Scandinavians in the early tenth-Century because of its vulnerability.

Essentially, whereas the rest of what is now England was taken - by the English to the South and West, by the Danes to the East, and the Celts in Wales and Scotland, the North-west of England was very insecure and "up for grabs": a natural place for any strong, organized raiding army to strike.

The Wirral and Lancashire colonies by then would have been well established following nearly 35 years of continuous settlement and vigorous, occasionally armed, expansion towards the wealthier English districts of the south and east. Outliers had been established from the Wirral enclave into South Chester and the Helsby area, and also across the shores of both the Mersey and Dee. Across the Dee, for example, Talacre is Norse. Across the Mersey the colony of West Lancashire Scandinavians would also have been well established. It is therefore proper to suppose that by 937AD there would have existed on either shore of both the Mersey and Dee estuaries centering on the Wirral a strong and active community of Norse settlers who would be very sympathetic to any military Norse expedition coming in or out by either estuary.

One such occurrence did apparently happen and is recorded in four sources: the Anglo-Saxon Chronicle, a mid-10th Century Latin poem quoted by the Norman writer William of Malmesbury, a further separate 12th-Century account by him and another 12th-Century account by a John or "Florence" of Worcester. The Icelandic saga *Egil's Saga*, written (it is thought) by Snorri Sturluson in the early 13th-Century, also records a battle which is named *Vínheiði við Vínuskógar* but is widely regarded as being one and the same as *Brunanburh*. Vínheiði við Vínuskógar literally means "Wen Heath by Wen Woods"[139]. Wen has been shown to have no geographic relevance, but the site along the ridge of high ground running from Bromborough to Oxton fits the bill: the heathland is Bebington Heath. The woods would be Storeton Hill.

The battle involved the Norseman Ólaf Guthfrithsson, referred to in the Anglo-Saxon Chronicles as "Anlaf", aided by Constantin II, king of the Scots, against an English force led by Æthelstan and his brother Edmund. After the battle, Ólaf and his defeated forces returned by ship to Dublin across what the writers refer to as *Dingesmere*.

[137] Volume 14, p303-16.
[138] pages 238-240.
[139] see, e.g., Bernard Scudder (translator) Egil's Saga, in *The Sagas of the Icelanders. A Selection*, 3-184, Penguin, 2000. A description of the battle, and Egil's involvement in it, is given on pages 81-92.

Egil Skallagrímsson: fought at Bromborough?

Background to Brunanburh

By the end of the second decade of the 10th-Century, the Dublin Viking Kingdom had recovered from the expulsions of 902AD, and in 934AD Ólaf Guthfrithsson had become its leader. He was not a friend of the English King Æthelstan, who was nephew of Æthelflæd, son of Edward the Elder and grandson of Alfred the Great. The problem arose in 926 when Edward's sister, married Sigtrygg, Norse ruler of the kingdom of Northumbria at York. Sigtrygg unfortunately died soon after, in 927A. His son by a former wife Ólaf Sigtryggson supported by the Norse King of Dublin, Guthfrith, treid to claim his inheritance of Northumbria by taking control of York. Æthelstan immediately responded by attacking the city, destroying the defences and expelling both Ólaf Sigtryggson and Guthfrith. 934AD Guthfriths son Ólaf succeeded to the throne of Dublin and was ready for revenge, something which played an important part of Viking life (as was seen repeatedly in the Icelandic Sagas). Another powerful leader ready for revenge against Æthelstan was King Constantan II of the Scots, whose lands had been ravaged by Æthelstan in 934AD. Ólaf and Æthelstan, together with King Owain the Bold of the Strathclyde Britons then formed a formidable alliance. Their aim: to bring down Æthelstan. The alliance of Celts and Norsemen swept into England and confronted their common enemy at a place called Brunanburh. Until recently, no-one has been quite sure where Brunanburh was, but, thanks to the painstaking work of scholars such as John McNeal Dodgson, Nicholas Higham and others, all the evidence now seems to point to one place: Bromborough, on Wirral.

The poem

The Anglo-Saxon poem, in its translated version from William of Malmesbury reads as follows[140], with Ólaf described as Anlaf.

> King Athelstan, the lord of warriors,
> Patron of heroes, and his brother too,
> Prince Edmund, won themselves eternal glory

[140] see, for example, A. Campbell (1938) *The Battle of Brunanburh*, London. See also R.A. Hamer (1970) *Choice of Anglo-Saxon Verse, Selected, with an Introduction and a Parallel verse translation*, Faber & Faber.

In battle with the edges of their swords
Round Brunanburh; they broke the wall of shields,
The sons of Edward with their well-forged swords
Slashed at the linden-shields; such was their nature
From boyhood that in battle they had often
Fought for their land, its treasures and its homes,
Against all enemies. Their foes fell dead,
The Scottish soldiers and their pirate host
Were doomed to perish; and with blood of men
The field was darkened from the time the sun
Rose at the break of day, the glorious star,
God the eternal Lord's bright candle passed
Across the land, until this noble creature
Sank to its resting-place. There many men
Lay slain by spears, and northern warriors
Shot down despite their shields, and Scotsmen too,
Weary, with battle sated. The West Saxons
Throughout the whole long passing of the day
Pressed on in troops behind the hostile people,
Hewed fiercely from the rear the fleeing host
With well-ground swords. The Mercians refused
Hard battle-play to none among the fighters
Who came with Anlaf over rolling seas,
Bringing invasion to this land by ship,
Destined to die in battle. Five young kings
Lay dead upon the battlefield, by swords
Sent to their final sleep; and likewise seven
Of Anlaf's earls, and countless of his host,
Both Scots and seamen.
There the Norsemen's chief
Was put to flight, and driven by dire need
With a small retinue to seek his ship.
The ship pressed out to sea, the king departed
Onto the yellow flood and saved his life.
Likewise the wise old Constantinus came,
The veteran, to his northern native land
By flight; he had no reason to exult
In that encounter; for he lost there friends
And was deprived of kinsmen in the strife
Upon that battlefield, and left his son

Destroyed by wounds on that grim place of slaughter,
The young man in the fight. The grey-haired man
Had little cause to boast about that battle,
The sly old soldier, any more than Anlaf;
They could not with their remnant laugh and claim
That they were better in warlike deeds
When banners met upon the battlefield,
Spears clashed and heroes greeted one another,
Weapons contended, when they played at war
With Edward's sons upon the place of carnage.
The Norsemen left them in their well-nailed ships,
The sad survivors of the darts, on *Dingesmere*
Over the deep sea back they went to Dublin,
To Ireland they returned with shameful hearts.
The brothers also both went home together,
The king and prince returned to their own country,
The land of Wessex, triumphing in war.
They left behind corpses for the dark
Black-coated raven, horny beaked to enjoy,
And for the eagle, white-backed and dun-coated,
The greedy war-hawk, and that grey wild beast
The forest wolf. Nor has there on this island
Been ever yet a greater number slain,
Killed by the edges of the sword before
This time, as books make known to us, and old
And learned scholars, after hither came
The Angles and the Saxons from the east
Over the broad sea sought the land of Britain,
Proud warmakers. Victorious warriors,
Conquered the Welsh, and so obtained this land.

The closing statement refreshes memories of the Saxon conquest of what became England from the Britons (Welsh).

Dodgson's identification of Brunanburh with Bromborough

Although none of the four English sources - nor *Egil's Saga* - pinpoints the location of Brunanburh, scholars like J. McNeal Dodgson appear to have little doubt the location was Bromborough: the interested reader is referred to the chapter in *Wirral and its Viking Heritage* and also the arguments presented in *The Place Names of Cheshire Part IV*, page 238-239.

15th-Century map of Wirral, showing Brunburgh. Courtesy of Paul Cavill.

Several reasons have been given - the battle must have taken place not far from the sea with the escape across *Dingesmere*. The existence of the strong Norse community on Wirral and on the opposite shore of the Mersey would have provided the ideal beachhead for Norse and Norse-Irish armies coming in and getting away again, and the regular phonological development of Brunanburh would have given Bromborough. Dodgson also addresses the three possible arguments against the identification of Brunanburh as Bromborough: 1. the battlefield is referred to in the five sources by various names; 2. John of Worcester places the landing of the Norsemen in Humber; 3. the lack of evidence about the identity of *Dingesmere*.

Dodgson's rebuttal of the first argument against. Of the other places proposed for the battle, only Burnswark in Dumfrieshire is synonymous with any of the other names in the sources - *Bruneswerce* - but this *werc* form is no more than a paraphrase of Brunanburh. The ON name *Vínheiði við Vínuskógar* in *Egil's Saga* was shown by A. Campbell in his book to be irrelevant to geography. Dodgson also points out that although the alternative names Brunandune, Brunefeld and Brunfort, which have as first element the OE pers.n. *Bruna*, do not appear among Wirral place-names, analagous ones do, at Brimstage and Brimston, in Bromborough parish itself.

Dodgson's rebuttal to the second possible argument against. He points out that even if this were true, the point of re-embarkation need not be near that of landing. The local historian Ann Anderson has dismissed the Humber as a sensible landing site for Anlaf's force coming from Dublin (see below). Nicholas N.J. Higham considers that John of Worcester, whose account was not contemporary, had got confused with Harald Hardrada's invasion of 1066.

Dodgson's rebuttal to the third possible argument against. He points out that since Dingesmere is a poetical "nonce word" and cannot be identified with anywhere, it is as likely to be the Dee as anywhere else. If it were discovered that this was a name for the Dee or the Irish Sea, then Bromborough's claim could be emphasised further.

Ann Anderson's identification of Brunanburh with Bromborough

The local historian Ann Anderson (1882 - 1969) writes the following from her privately published book on the *The Story of Bromborough* which elegantly complements Dodgson's seminal work. Her account, written in 1964, is as follows:

THE BATTLE OF BRUNANBURH (ANN ANDERSON)

Now we have a provocative subject: the site of the Battle of Brunanburh in AD 937. Bromborough is one of the forty claimants for the site. The rival sites include places as far apart as Burnswalk in Dumfrieshire, Musbury between Axminster and Colyton, Bamber Bridge in Lancashire (in which locality the famous Cuerdale hoard of Saxon coins was found), Burnard near Barton-on-Humber and Blackburn. This 'Waterloo' of the tenth-Century decided the fate of England: whether she was to be ruled by a Saxon or a Norse king. It was such a battle as had never been seen in Britain. When at last the Saxon king drew off his victorious forces, five kings, seven earls, and thousands of men lay dead on the field.

How did this conflict arise? *Cherchez la femme.* Yes, the trouble really started over a woman. Somewhere about the year AD915, Athelstan, the West Saxon king, gave his sister in marriage to Sithric, the Norse king of Northumbria who, on his marriage, embraced the Christian religion. Finding it, however, not so convenient as his old faith - which had allowed him to murder and pillage to his heart's content - he repented of his conversion, and got rid of his wife and his religion together. Athelstan, to avenge the honour of his sister, marched an army into Northumbria. To complicate matters, Sithric died suddenly, so Athelstan vented his wrath on Sithric's sons, Anlaf and Godfrid, whom he turned away and annexed Northumbria to his own kingdom. Anlaf fled to Dublin and Godfrid took to a mode of life always congenial to his race, namely piracy.

Anlaf, however, determined to win back his father's kingdom, formed a league with Constantine II, king of Scotland, his father-in-law, and with the Welsh and Norsemen in Northumbria and East Anglia. He also received strong contingents of warriors from the region of the Baltic, and as his own Irish forces were large, it was altogether a formidable army that Athelstan had to encounter. Now for the question: where did the battle take place?

The story is given in poetic form incorporated into the Anglo-Saxon Chronicle. The poem does not give the least indication of the locality of the engagement. The first point to note is that Anlaf came over with his forces from Ireland, and it seems hard to understand why he should have gone pleasure cruising round the Pentland Firth to land in the Humber or somewhere on the east coast when he had estuaries like the Mersey, Dee and Ribble opposite his door.

Wirral was a Scandinavian stronghold and he would be likely to make for a landing-place where he had friends. Let us visualize the scene. Anlaf, with his Hiberno-Norse forces, sailed from Dublin. The Scots, probably from Clyde or Galloway, joined them off the Isle of Man[141], the common rendezvous. The united forces cruised along the coast of Wales to pick up their Welsh allies. Their passage up the Dee would be barred by Chester or Shotwick castle, undoubtedly a Saxon fort.

Wirral held friends, so what more likely than that he should land, perhaps at Wallasey, perhaps at Bromborough Pool, an ideal creek for the landing of such boats as those of Anlaf. Thence they would march into Mercia, avoiding Chester on the one hand and Shotwick on the other, and await events. Commanders in those days, landing on enemy territory, never liked to move far from base until they had won their footing, and Anlaf could hardly be nearer to his base at Dublin than in Wirral. Meanwhile, knowing well the storm was brewing, Athelstan had gathered together the whole of his available forces, and had encamped, if the tradition of William of Malmesbury is reliable, in the Midlands, ready to strike in whatever direction his enemy landed. If our contention is correct that Anlaf's landing place was Bromborough Pool, then Athelstan would move his men as quickly as possible to attack, for it as desirable that an invader should be intercepted before he had ravaged the country around. It was Analf's game to stay on the defensive just as it was Athelstan's to attack. The late Mr. Godfrey Matthews believed that the ridge of high land at Spital just above the dam, and continuing to Bidston would make an admirable defensive position for Anlaf's army; and if Brunanburh is Bromborough, there is little doubt that it was on the ridge from Spital to Higher Bebington that the battle was fought. The name 'Red Hill' or 'Bloody Hill' in that neighbourhood, supports that claim.

The Chronicle account implies that the Northmen were on the defensive:

       Edward's children the shield-wall cleft
After the terrible defeat:

---

[141] N. Higham suggests the rendezvous point may have been the River Ribble, near Preston.

> There put to flight was
> The Northmen's chieftain
> By need driven
> To the ships' prow
> With a little band.

These lines suggest a hurried flight to their ships and a quick embarkation.   With ships anchored in the Pool at Bromborough Pool the distance would have been short. Summarizing Bromborough's claim:

(a) Given the existence of a Brunanburh there was but one Brunanburh in England in 937, just as there is but one Bromborough today

(b) The Dee and Mersey whose estuaries are divided by the Wirral Peninsula have, from time immemorial, been the favourite place of embarkation to, and debarkation from, Ireland.

(c) In the map entitled *Die Britischen Inseln* (1880) Brunanburh is placed on the 'Meresige' about the present position of Bromborough

The Saga Book of the Viking Society, vol. XIV, part 4, sums up the position thus:

> Bromborough in Wirral would appear to be the most eligible place for the battle-field. In no other locality does the context of geography, politics, and place-names accord so well with the few facts we possess concerning the context.

Although there are some factual inaccuracies in Ann's account (she mixes up Ólaf Sigtrygson with Ólaf Guthfrithson and the date of Sithric's (Sigtrygg) wedding is 926 and not 915) her arguments complement Dodgson's well.

Battle lines

As pointed out in the above passage by Ann Anderson, the battle would have extended over a wide area and along the ridge from Spital & Higher Bebington: the Wirral has two approximately parallel ridges of high ground running through it, principally sandstone based. Along the west side it forms the hills at Heswall, Thurstaston and Caldy. Along the Eastern side it runs from Spital through to Higher Bebington/ Storeton, and then through to Oxton (including Arno Hill), Bidston and Wallasey (including the Breck): It

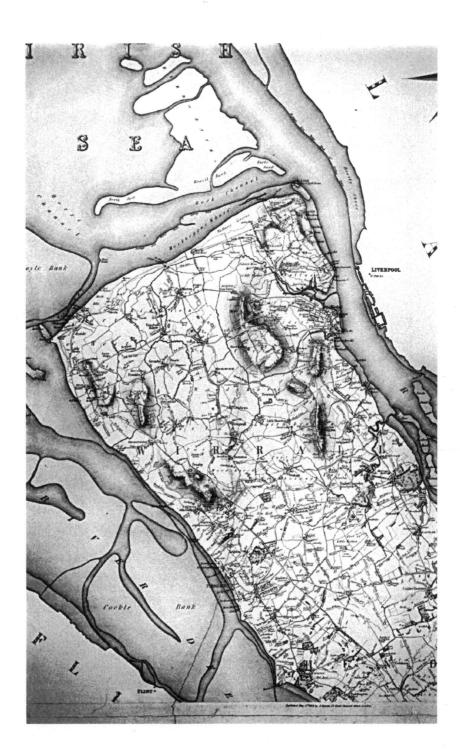

1831 map by A. Bryant of the Wirral (exluding the southernmost regions) showing the ridges of high ground running along the western and eastern sides.   Courtesy of Chester & Cheshire Archives & Local Studies.

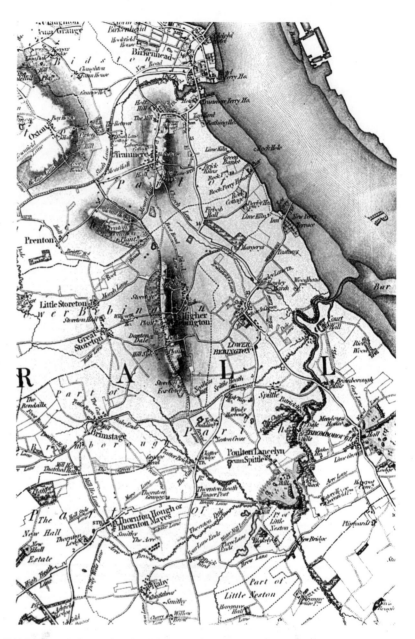

Part of the 1831 Bryant map showing the ridge of high ground in the Storeton/Bebington area running up to Tranmere Pool and Oxton. Courtesy of Chester & Cheshire Archives & Local Studies.

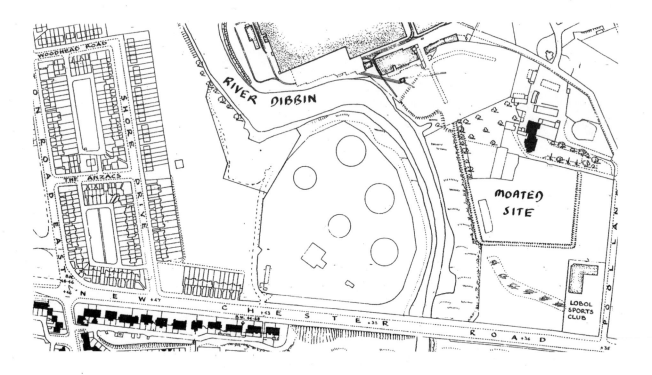

Site of the original manor court (at SJ345842) where a ditched moat still remains. An earlier moated site is believed to have played an important site of the battle of Brunanburh which would have taken place over a wide area. Courtesy of Gavin Hunter, Unilever Research, Port Sunlight.

Old photograph of the Court House Farm before its demolition in 1969. From a 1948 publication "The Hardwares of Cheshire" by Roberta Glasgow, Courtesy of Gavin Hunter.

is the southern area of this ridge, at least up to Storeton Hill, which could have represented a battle line, with presumably *Ólaf* *and Constantine's* army towards the west and north.

A prominent area of the battle was formerly believed to have been Wargraves presumably because of the unusual name. More recently the highly ditched/moated site of what used to be Bromborough Court House (off Poole Lane) - presumably the site also of *Bruna's* stronghold - has been considered as being a principal area in the battle. The remaining moat/ditch (as marked on Ordnance Survey maps) does not appear to be the original, as reported for example by the local archaeologist Gill Chitty: a Viking iron ring of small diameter similar to one in bronze found at Meols has been found there, discovered by a Mrs Edwards when she was living at Court House Farm: it was her son who suggested the ring was possibly medieval.

Red Hill Road, Soldiers Hill and Battlefields
In Ann Anderson's passage, according to local tradition a 'Red Hill' or 'Bloody Hill' along the ridge the Storeton/Bebington boundary may have been appropriately named with reference to the battle. Further research amongst the locals has revealed an interesting collection of folklore on the matter. The local historian, Allan Alsbury, author of Fir-Bob Land[142] has made the following observations:

> 1. Local records reveal no mention of a Red Hill but Red Hill Road running down from the ridge (now Mount Road) towards Storeton village: it runs parallel to - and then turns north to join - "Rest Hill Road".
> 2. Various older residents of both Storeton and Higher Bebington (of families that have lived there for several

142 Countyvise Ltd, Birkenhead.

generations) make one or more of the following points:
● Red Hill, or Red Hill Road was so named from 'the blood that ran down it'.
● the short, inclined length of road between the small roundabout at Storeton leading to the junction with Rest Hill and Red Hill Roads, is known as "Soldiers' Hill" (Area A on the illustration following).
● lands at the side of Rest Hill Road (not precisely defined as to location) as it rises towards Mount Road ridge are known as "Battlefields" (Area B on the illustration)
3. A newspaper contribution, undated but almost certainly about 1955-60, with no by-line although in the style of a frequent contributor of local history snippets of that time who generally signed as *C.R.R.* read as follows "One of the local fairy stories to which the writer was entertained as a boy was that Kings Road had been named after King Alfred who was thought to have fought the battle of Brunanburh in the locality. This was, of course, not true, King being a private though prominent individual of a much later date. It was also said that King's Road had not been impoved since King Alfred's time, and this could well be true".

The latter story is clearly folklore: King Alfred would have had to have risen from the grave to fight at Brunanburh - he'd been dead by almost 40 years! Nonetheless this, and the other two points do however indicate a great deal of lingering folklore pointing to a conflict. The illustration gives a view from the field to the south of Red Hill Road looking up to what is now known as Prospect Hill (just above the letter B of Bracken Lane on the sketch map overleaf). The location of "Battlefields" (Area B on the map) is to the far left.

Part of the ridge of high ground between Storeton and Bebington parishes, seen from Red Hill Road in the foreground. Behind the pylon on the eastern side of Mount Road is what is now Prospect Hill. Does the answer to Brunanburh lie below these fields? Does the pylon mark the thick of the battle?

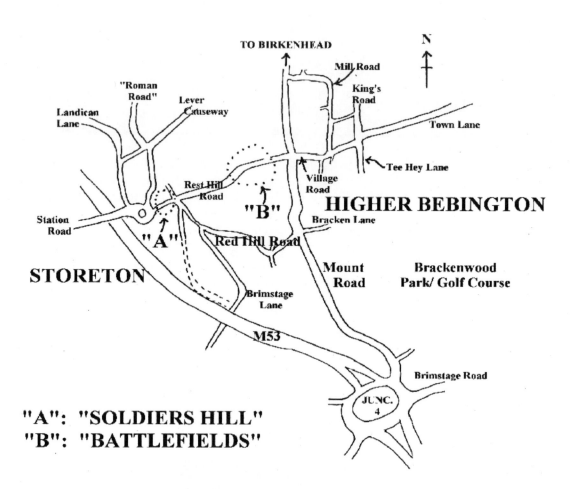

"A": "SOLDIERS HILL"
"B": "BATTLEFIELDS"

NOT TO SCALE

Sketch map of the boundary region between Storeton and Higher Bebington showing Red Hill Road, "Soldiers Hill" and "Battlefields". Based on a sketch provided by Allan Alsbury.

Dingesmere

The name *Dingesmere* appearing in the poem as the waters across which what was left of Ólaf Guthfrithsson's raiding army returned to Dublin no longer exists (if it ever did). It could either have been the Dee estuary or what is now the Mockbeggar Wharf stretching along from the Viking trading port of Meols along the North Wirral coast into the Irish Sea. The Mersey estuary also cannot be ruled out with either Wallasey Pool or, as Ann Anderson has suggested, Bromborough Pool as possible docking sites.

Local folklore about the Dee and Mersey

There is one more piece of local folklore which may provide a sting in the tail when assigning Dingesmere to the Dee Estuary. We have already seen in Chapter 5 how the path of the Dee had an important bearing on the success or failure of the Merseyside community in skirmishes with the Welsh. Another piece of folklore is that since Brunanburh the Vikings would always navigate the Dee rather than down the Mersey, since they thought the latter as cursed. Dingesmere?

Assembly point may have been the Ribble

N.J. Higham[143] has suggested the River Ribble may have been where the combined Norse and Scots fleets and armies met up before moving to Bromborough. Besides Merseyside, Scandinavians had been settling since the first decade of the 10th-Century in large numbers along the coastal plain in West Lancashire, Amounderness, the Lakes and the Solway, and the River Ribble area was no exception. As considered in the previous Chapter, following the expulsions form Dublin in 902AD, the Norse leader Ragnald may have been developing the River Ribble area and in particular Preston as his Scandinavian power base in parallel to Ingimund's activities in Wirral. Ragnald would have used this platform for taking control of York in 919AD establishing Northumbria (including Lancashire, which was then "south west Northumbria") as a Norse Kingdom. By 937AD the Ribble would have provided a safe anchorge point for the invading fleets of Irish-sea Norse and Scots. Ólaf could have marshalled the combined force here before moving down to meet the English head on at Bromborough. This is a plausible suggestion. The point of escape could still however been the Dee - or Mersey.

---

[143] N.J. Higham (1992) Northumbria, Mercia and the Irish Sea Norse, 893-926. In J. Graham-Campbell ed. *Viking Treasure from the North West*, Chapter 3, National Museums and Guides on Merseyside, Liverpool.

N.J. Higham's 1997 contribution to our understanding of Brunanburh
In 1997 a special volume was produced in commemoration of John McNeal Dodgson. This was edited by A.R. Rumble and A.D. Miller and titled *Names, Places and People. An Onomastic Miscellany for John McNeal Dodgson*.[144] In this volume Higham produced another seminal paper on Brunaburh[145], reinforcing Dodgson's arguments for its identification with Bromborough with new evidence and insights. Higham, who must now be regarded as the new authority on Brunanburh, also reviewed and analysed a 1980 paper by M. Woods[146] who had attempted to put forward an alternative site, namely *Brinsworth*, a hill on Ryknild Street, between the rivers Rother and Don. Woods had argued that this important battle-site should be sought "between the upper Trent and the Aire ... a heavily fortified zone where the wars of the second quarter of the tenth-Century were waged". By a careful re-examination of the events leading up to Brunanburh, Higham was able to show the case for Brinsworth was essentially untenable. Some of the key points of Higham's penetrating analysis are as follows:

- A recurring feature of such a reexamination is the importance of the Mersey in the conflicts between the several Scandinavian leaderships successively based at York, and the rulers of Mercia
- There is no literary evidence of any corresponding military investment by Mercian or West Saxon rulers in the Mercian Danelaw north of Nottingham.
- The argument that the region between the upper Trent and the Aire was a battle ground for armies from English Mercia and Wessex and the 'Northern Army' in the decades up to Brunanburh is at best unproven and at worst, implausible. "Arguments in favour of Brinsworth or any other site in this vicinity not named *Brunanburh*, *Brunandune* or *Weondune* must be set aside".

Higham also reviews the strategy of Ólaf in 937AD since it was this strategy which conditioned the locality in which the battle was fought. Local leaders at York might have sympathized with Ólaf, but the lack of coins from York bearing his name, and so proclaiming his cause, makes it unlikely he had taken up the reins of government there before invading Mercia. Further, the comparatively full descriptions of the fighting at Brunanburh make no mention of the 'Northern Army' - the Danes of York - whilst making clear distinctions between the Norse, Scots, Strathclyde Welsh, Mercians and West Saxons. These are just some of the arguments given to indicate there was

---

[144] and published by Paul Watkins, Stamford, U.K.
[145] *The Context of Brunanburh*, pages 144-156.
[146] M. Woods (1980) Brunanburh Revisited, *Saga-Book of the Viking Society*, XX (1978-80), 200-17 esp. 211.

little reason for Ólaf undertaking his Brunanburh campaign from York. In an earlier work, Higham, writing in *The Origins of Cheshire*[147], had also written the following:

> That the battle was fought on its banks (The Mersey) finds support in the *Annals of Clonmacnoise* which notes that the battle occurred 'on the plaines of othlynn'. The Annals are now only extant in a seventeenth-century translation, but this would seem to be a clumsy rendering of 'the plain oð (up to) the Lyme', a term which places the battle west of the Pennines.

Reconstruction of the possible events immediately surrounding Brunanburh

Higham has provided a possible reconstruction of what happened to Ólaf's forces shortly before and immediately after the Battle. It is a possibility that his forces did not immediately engage the English but went on a route of plundering deep into Mercia with the intention then to return to the Mersey with their spoils and then to prepare to take on Æthelstan. William of Malmesbury's account emphasized how after an initial delay Æthelstan immediately proceeded northwards. On hearing of the unexpected approach Ólaf's forces may have abandoned their plunderings and tried to reach the safety of the territories of Northumbria but were cut off from crossing the Mersey where their fleet may have been anchored (at the Ribble) by a faster moving Æthelstan. Being forced to head towards Wirral they turned when they realised they could escape no further. After being defeated what was left of the forces retreated again, heading for the far end of the peninsula at Meols:

> "the only beach-head site in the vicinity likely to have offered even a small number of vessels by which to effect an escape from the mounted English soldiers still harrying them. The few ships there would have been sufficient to rescue the High Command but could offer little succour to the rank and file"

Although rather speculative, this might offer the most plausible explanation yet as to what might have happened, and as to how the leaders were able to escape whereas many others perished.

Higham concluded the paper with a statement saying there is good reason to concur with Dodgson in his placement of Brunanburh on the west banks

---

[147] N.J. Higham (1993) *The Origins of Cheshire*, Manchester University Press, p.125.

of the Mersey. "In a confused day's fighting, spread perhaps over an extended field of battle, the armies of Kings Anlaf (Ólaf) and Constantine were routed by an enemy who had cut off their only realistic lines of retreat, via fords further upriver along the Mersey".

King Edgar refreshes Celtic memories of Brunanburh

Finally there is one more outstanding piece of evidence in support of a Wirral site for *Brunanburh*, recalled in *Wirral and its Viking Heritage*[148]. John of Worcester again, the 12th-Century historian, records the later tenth-Century king, Edgar, sailing on the River Dee with some 'colleagues' in the year of his coronation, 973AD.

> Edgar the peaceable king of the English, was blessed, crowned with the utmost honour and glory, and anointed king in his thirtieth year at Pentecost, 11 May, in the first indiction, by the blessed bishops Dunstan and Oswald, and by the other bishops of the whole of England in the city of Bath. Then, after an interval, he sailed round the north coast of Wales with a large fleet, and came to the city of Chester. Eight underkings, namely Kenneth, king of the Scots, Malcolm, king of the Cumbrians, Maccus, king of many islands, and five others, Dufnal, Siferth, Hywel, Iacob, and Iuchil, went to meet him, as he had commanded, and swore that they would be loyal to, and co-operate with, him by land and sea. With them on a certain day, he boarded a skiff; having set them to the oars, and having taken the helm himself, he skilfully steered it through the course of the Dee, and with a crowd of ealdormen and nobles following in a similar boat, sailed from the palace to the monastery of St. John the Baptist, where, when he had prayed, he returned with the same pomp to the palace. As he was entering it he is reported to have declared to his nobles at length that each of his successors would be able to boast that he was king of the English, and would enjoy the pomp of such honour with so many kings at his command.[149]

This indicates the importance of the Dee and the adjacent territories in the unification of England following *Brunanburh*. The significance of Edgar's actions here is that he is re-enacting Æthelstan's taking submission from the Celtic kings at Eamont bridge, Westmorland, in 926AD, reinforced by

[148] P. Cavill, S.E. Harding and J. Jesch (2000) *Wirral and its Viking Heritage*, Chapter 10, English Place-Name Society, Nottingham.
[149] R.R. Darlington and P. McGurk eds. (1995) *The Chronicle of John of Worcester*, 3 vols (Oxford), II, 423-25.

military power at *Brunbanburh* in 937AD. John of Worcester locates *Brunanburh* on the Humber in his Chronicle, and he does not therefore see that Edgar is asserting his authority over the kings and the waterways of those areas which have most recently fomented rebellion against the English crown. Edgar is refreshing Celtic memories of the English victory at *Brunanburh*.

Archaeological search

There have as yet been no significant archaeological finds to connect Brunanburh with a particular site in Wirral. Part of the problem is that the depth of the topsoil along the ridge of high ground from Bromborough to Oxton is only a few inches in places, a depth which would have retained nothing over the centuries. It could be a case of "looking for a needle in a haystack". But perhaps the surrounding deeper ground, possibly on the banks of the River Dibbin holds some secrets? Perhaps also the old fields that once bore the names of Dead Mans Wood (Dedemonnes Greue in 1323) and Lathegestfeld have a story to tell. Or possibly the Viking Grave-Group from the Meols finds has some connection. And what can we reasonably hope to expect to find? A mass grave? Or perhaps some arrowe-heads? At the moment it is pure speculation, but it is a topic that has now interested Norway's leading archaeologists such as Professor Christian Keller and Professor Arne Emil Christensen of the University of Oslo and the Olso Viking Ship Museum. Clearly a systematic study is called for.

The author discussing Brunanburh over a cup of tea with Arne Emil Christensen in the back garden of the Vikingskiphuset, Bigdoy, Oslo.

Chapter 12
VIKING PEOPLE AFTER BRUNANBURH

Whatever happened at Brunanburh, it appears that the local population, even on the Wirral side of the Mersey, remained relatively unmolested from the incoming - and outgoing - Dublin Viking, Scots and English armies. It is reasonable however to assume a fair number of the young Scandinavians would have thrown in their lot with their cousins from Dublin, and possibility one of the young kings who, the Chronicler says, was killed in the fighting, may have been a son or grandson of the great Ingimund himself. The impact on the local community on Merseyside was not terminal. We know this because by Domesday, Scandinavians, or at least men bearing Scandinavian names, were in control of most of the manors in Wirral and also 25% of the moneyers in Chester bore Scandinavian or Hiberno-Norse names.   Appearing in the list of pre-Domesday moneyers (see also below) and also in the list of the many Norse landowners in the Wirral and surrounds we find for example the following Scandinavians or Irish-Scandinavians:

> Arngrímr (recorded in Domesday Book as Haregrim, Aregrim), Árni (Erne, Erni) - possible the same Árni of The Arno in Oxton) , Arnkell (as Archil) , Ásgautr (as Ansgot, or Osgot - of Hargrave Hall), Beollán (Belam), Björnúlfr (Bernulf), Brunn (Brun), Frani (Fran), Gamall (Gamel), Grímkell (Grinchel), Grímr (Grim), Gunningr (Gunninc), Gunnarr (Gunner), Gunnvör (Gunnor), Guðleikr (Gotlac), Hákon (Hacon, Hacun), Hókun, Hálfdan (Halden, Alden), Hásteinn (Hasten), Hrafn (Rauen), Hrafnkell (Rauechel, Rauenchel, Rauecate), Hrafnsvartr (Rauesuar, Rausue), Hundingr (Hundingr, Hundin), Hundólfr (Hundulf), Karl, Karli (Carle), Ketill (Chetel), Kolbeinn (Colben), Loðinn (Loten), Morfari (Morfar), Ormr (Orme), Ragnaldr (Ragenal), Sigríðr (Segrid), Steinkell (Steinchetel), Steinn (Stein), Steinólfr (Stenulf), Tóki (Tochi), Úlfkell (Ulchel, Ulchetel), Úlfr (Ulf), Vetriðr (Wintrelet), Þjoðólfr (Dedol, Dedou), Þórðr (Toret, Toreth)

To this list we can add the following list of Scandinavian moneyers also recorded before and after Domesday:

[150] J.D. Bu'Lock (1972) Pre-Conquest Cheshire, 383-1066 (in *History of Cheshire* III), Chester.

Fargrímr (as Fargrim), Kolbeinn (recorded in Domesday as Colben), Kolbrandr (Coalbrand), Krókr (Croc), Húskarl (Huscarl), Svartkollr (Sweartcol), Svertingr (Swertinc), Sveinn (Swegen), Þóraldr (Thorald), Þormòðr (Thurmod), Hrafnsvartr (Ravenswart), Hundólfr (Unnulf), Raenulfr (Raenulf), Sunnúlfr (Sunoulf), Þorbjörn (Thurbern).

The following moneyers bearing names of Irish origin are also recorded, about which the historian F.T. Wainwright says the following: "there can be no doubt that the Norsemen who introduced these names had long lived in Ireland; perhaps also the Scandinavian hoards which settled in Wirral included many native Irish adventurers, as indeed is suggested by the *Three Fragments*"

Mældomen and Mælsuthan (10th-Century)
Macthusan (11th-Century - during the reign of King Canute)
Gillichrist (11th-Century-King Harald I and King Hardacanute)
Gillemor (12th-Century - Henry I).

Wainwright also noted that Scandinavian personal names continued in existence long after the Norman conquest. Although no collection is available, one frequently meets Scandinavian names in medieval documents. In the Chester Cartulary are found names of men like Anketill, Anschetill, Asschetill (ON *Áskell, Ásketill*), John Gamel (ON *Gamall*), Rauen (ON *Hrafn*), Orm (ON *Ormr*), Osgot (ON *Ásgautr*), Steinolf (ON *Steinólfr*), Sweinn (ON *Sveinn*) and Toki (ON *Tóki*), and the women's names Gunwara (ON *Gunnvör*) and Gutha (ON *Gyða*). All these names belong to the 12th and 13th centuries and they show that the Scandinavian influence on personal nomenclature was neither slight nor transient. One may also suppose that if Scandinavian names were still in use in the 13th-Century then some form of a Scandinavian language was still being spoken by the locals.

To this list of recorded Scandinavians we can add those whose names have been forever embedded in Wirral and West Lancashire place-names. The roster of Vikings on Wirral includes the following:

Árni (Arno Hill, The Arno in Oxton Parish), Grímr (Grymisgreue in Woodbank), Gunnhildr (Gonnille Pool in Tranmere), Fiðill (Fiddlestone in Burton Parish), Franki (Frankby) Ingríðr (Ingriessiche - Ingríðr's stream in Capenhurst), Karli (Calthorpe in Bidston), Ketill (Kettle Well

Garden in Wallasey and Ketilspol - Riveacre park in Hooton), Þóraldr (Mollington-Torrold, now Mollington), Ragnaldr (Rawnuesfeld in Whitby), Ragnhildr (Raynilde's Pool in Tranmere), Sigríðr (Sigriðr's Halfland in Wallasey), Steinkell (Steyncolesdale in Thurstaston), Sylla (Syllaby), Tóki (Toki's ford in Wallasey), Úfaldi (Ufilys brow in Saughall Massie), Úfaldi (Vfeldesgrene in Claughton - probably now Birkenhead Park), Þorsteinn, (Thorstein's farmstead, Thurstaston).

We can at last attempt to connect these "place-name" people with the lists of landowners and moneyers above. Surprisingly it seems that neither Þorsteinn who gives his name to Thurstaston, nor Úfaldi of Birkenhead Park are recorded as landowners or moneyers although the following stand out: Árni of Oxton, Karli of Bidston, Ketill of Wallasey and/or Hooton, Ragnaldr of Whitby, Steinkell of Thurstaston, Tóki of Wallasey, Grímr of Woodbank, Þóraldr of Mollington and Sigríðr of Wallasey.

Ufaldi's Green: Now Birkenhead Park

This list is extended across the Mersey into West Lancashire with Einulf (Ainsdale), Ólafr (Anglezarke), Erengr (Argarrmeols), Bekan (Becconsall), Blæingr (Blainscough), Krókr (Croxteth), Forni (Fomby), Gunnulfr (Gunnolf's Moors), Oddgrimr (North Meols), Ormr (Ormskirk), Hrafn (Ravensmeols), Sæfari (Sarscow), Skar (Skarisbrick), Skjaldmarr (Skelmersdale), Tharaldr (Tarleton), Tóki (Toxteth) and Úlfr (Ulnes Walton).

Sigríðr: lady of Wallasey

In 1280 Robert of Wallasey, a descendant of a Norman baron wrote the following:

> I, Robert son of Robert of Wallasey …. assign a half a selion which is called Seurydzis alfland.

The particular "half selion" or "alfland" (halfland) which he is kindly passing on to someone else once belonged to the Scandinavian lady Sigríðr (and

Original manuscript (from 1280) identifying Sigríðr (as Seurydzis) as well as the le Schepe Rake, le Rake and le Skere in Wallasey. This transcript is now in the John Rylands Library, Manchester (catalogue number: JRC1482)

whom he refers to as "Seurydzis"). This valuable charter, written in Latin is one of many that have been beautifully preserved in the John Rylands Library of the University of Manchester.

The translation, from the Latin, of this Charter up to the sentence with "Kirkby", the old Viking name for Wallasey Village is as follows[151]:

> Let it be known to all people both present and future that I, Robert son of Robert of Wallasey have given, granted and by this present my charter have confirmed to Phillip de Beynville (Benfield) and his heirs or assigns one bovate of land with appurtenances out of my demesne in the vill of *Kirkby* in Wallasey, namely that bovate which Thomas the Welshman held in the same vill of the gift of the lady Alina, and also twelve selions of land with the third part of one selion which extends to Hole siche ('Hole ditch') between the selion of Luke of Bidston and the selion of Alexander Samson, that is to say those selions with the third part of the said selion which William Welsh of Hooton held of me to farm in the same vill, and two selions and a half of which one is called the *Sheep Rake* ('the sheep path') and the other the Blodgreveland ('Bloodgrieve's land) extending as far as *the Rake* and the half selion which is called *Seurydzis Alfland* (Sæfrith's or Sigriðr's halfland) and one selion of land with calf lying between the church land and the land of William Samson with a certain fishery on Hoylake lying between the fishery formerly Alexander Samson's and *le sker* (the skerry -Fort Perch Rock). To be had and held of me and my heirs or assigns to himself and his heirs or assigns freely, quietly, well, peacefully and by inheritance with all liberties, rights of common and easements of the aforesaid vill of *Kirkby* universally pertaining.

Names in the above passage of Viking origin are highlighted by italics. The full translation is given in *Wirral and its Viking Heritage*. Not only does this Charter identify Sigríðr or Sæfrith as Seurydzis and her "Halfland", but it also identifies a skerry, ON *sker* (the site of Alexander Samson's Fishery), the lane called le Rake (possibly from ON *rák*) and a field called the *Sheep Rake*. And one old Merseyside name appears twice - that of the Samson or Sampson family.

Although the land named after her survived, it is likely that *Sigríðr* had long since gone by the time the 1280 Charter was written. It is however reassuring that at some stage between the Viking colonisation and the writing

<hr/>

[151] Translation and comments (in brackets) by Paul Cavill.

of the Charter she was a landowner, thus supporting the view that women played a prominent role in the pre-Norman administration of Merseyside, possibly even in the Things themselves.

Gunnhildr, Ragnhildr and other Women in the Mersey Norse Society

Other names of women appearing in the above lists include Ingríðr of Capenhurst near Chester and Gunnhildr and Ragnhildr of Tranmere. The appearance is a clear demonstration that in the Scandinavian community on 10th-Century Merseyside women played a significant role. This lasted until the Norman conquest of England in 1066 after which women's rights enjoyed in both the Scandinavian and English communities were suppressed. The appearance of the Tranmere women is particularly intriguing since the Chairman of Tranmere FC at the time of the 1100th anniversary of the 902AD settlements was also a woman (Ms. Lorraine Rogers). Three Icelandic sagas in particular bring out the importance of women in Scandinavian society: *Laxdæla Saga*, *Njál's Saga*, and *Eirík's Saga* (The Saga of Eirík the Red). The latter refers extensively to the Icelandic woman Guðríðr Þorbjarnardóttir ("Guðríðr, daughter of Þorbjörn") a Christian convert who was famous as a pioneer in the New World, a pilgrim to Rome and a virtuous mum! Kristín Bragadóttir and Patrick J. Stevens writing in *Stefnumót við Íslenska Sagnahefð* (Living and Reliving the Icelandic Sagas):

> The women of the North played a fairly traditional role in society, as the rigours of childbearing and domestic life defined their lives. Nonetheless, Germanic law generally accorded Nordic women certain rights that most (other) European women did not enjoy. Pre-Christian Icelandic women could seek divorce as well as refuse betrothal. Icelandic women had property rights; both the wife and mistress of Snorri Sturluson were women of considerable wealth.

The interested reader is referred to the seminal work on the subject by Judith Jesch[152]. The places commemorating *Gunnhildr, Ragnhildr, Ingríðr* and *Sigríðr* and many of the menfolk of their communities on both sides of the Mersey were vibrant in the Middle Ages. But what of the language of these people? How much of the Scandinavian tongue persisted though the centuries following the settlements and then the Norman conquest, penetrating into the dialect of the area? We can get a further idea that this was considerable from an old 14th-Century poem.

---

[152] J. Jesch (1991) *Women in the Viking Age*, Boydell Press.

Chapter 13
SIR GAWAIN AND THE GREEN KNIGHT: NORSE DIALECT IN 14TH-CENTURY CHESHIRE

Sir Gawain and the Green Knight, as depicted on the front cover of the children's book by Selina Hastings. Courtesy of Walker Books, London.

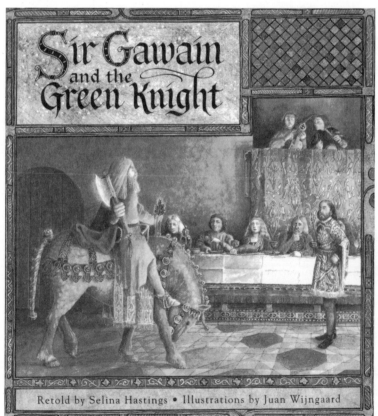

Retold by Selina Hastings • Illustrations by Juan Wijngaard

Sir Gawain and the Green Knight is a famous poem written in the 14th-Century. It tells of how a mysterious Green Knight arrives at the Court of Arthur and asks if anyone is brave enough to take part in a duel. Arthur regards the rules of the contest proposed by the Knight as foolish: the challenger is to take the first blow but the Green Knight must be allowed to take the second strike one year on. Sir Gawain volunteers himself and accepts the conditions. With the first blow the Green Knight loses his head but picks it up and rides away, but not before reminding Gawain of the condition he has agreed to, and to meet him at a place known as the Green Chapel in one year and a day. At the appropriate time Gawain keeps his word and goes in search of the Green Chapel. The journey is long, arduous and dangerous and he eventually stops at a castle where a Sir Bercilak or *Bertilak* welcomes him to stay. He passes a test of faith - in the form of Bercilak's wife who tries to seduce him - and then Bercilak points him in the direction of the Green Chapel, which happens to be not far away. The Green Knight is found, Gawain offers himself for receiving the second strike, but it is only a glancing blow: the Green Man spares Gawain for being a man of his word, then reveals himself to be Sir Bercilak. Gawain then returns to Camelot[153].

The interesting part of the story from a Merseyside and Cheshire

---

[153] There are many books on the Green Knight and its translation. See for example W.R.J. Barron, editor (1998) *Sir Gawain and the Green Knight*, Manchester University Press. A children's version is by Selina Hastings (1991) *Sir Gawain and the Green Knight*, Walker Books Ltd., London.

perspective is not just because it involves Sir Gawain travelling through Wirral looking for the Green Knight but also because the scribe of the poem and the poet himself/herself were apparently local: from somewhere in Cheshire or nearby. Unwittingly, the scribe or the poet of the Sir Gawain poem has thus provided an opportunity for us to gauge the type of language that was perhaps being spoken in daily life in the area: the language of the poem is generally in the dialect of (probably) Cheshire and is pervaded by a large number of Scandinavian dialect words - many unusual ones: surprising when it was written some 400 years after the settlements.

Scandinavian dialect words

Although the poem is about Arthurian Britain it has been said that approximately 10% of the words appearing are Old Norse, and many not of the type that had been assimilated into regular English speech (e.g., egg, window etc.)[154] - they were probably Scandinavian dialect words of Cheshire and the North-west. Some are still used today, such as *karp* ("carp on, to boast"). The vocabulary is quite different from the conventional Middle English of for example Chaucer and his Canterbury Tales.

The following are these dialect words (given in the dialect form with the original Norse in brackets) appearing in the poem, courtesy of Professor Nils-Lennart Johannesson, University of Stockholm, Department of English.[155] This is probably the closest clue we can get as to the type of English spoken in medieval Cheshire, Chester and Merseyside, and supplements information from those rentals and other official documents that were not written in Latin: as we shall see later, these include the remarkable case of the -doghters and -ssons who were living on Wirral at or about the same time as the Sir Gawain and Green Knight poet was alive.

asṫyt: at once, straight away [OE *(e)alswä* + ON *títt* 'often']
ay: always, ever [ON *ei*]
blande: mixture **inblande;** mingled, together [OE *bland*, ON *i blana*]
bole: tree-trunk [ON *bolr*]
bonk: bank, hill, slope [ON *banki*, OIcel *bakki*]
boþe: both [OE *bä*, ON *báþi.*]
boun: ready; dressed [ON *búinn*]
busk: get ready; dress [ON *búask*]
cayreõ: rides [ON *keyra*]
costes: condition, plight [OE *cost* influenced by ON *kostr*]
cros: cross [ON *kross*]

[154] A good web page is Dr. Scott Kleinman's (Assistant Professor of English, California State University, Northridge, USA) :*The Language of the Green Knight*: http://www.csum.edu/~sk36711/www2/eng1443/gawainvocab.htm

[155] http://www.hf.ntnu.no/engelsk/staff/johannesson/!oe/texts/imed/07imed/07gls.htm

derf: stout [ON *djarfr*]

dreped: killed [ON *drepa*]

dryõe: enduring [ON *drjúgr*]

felle: mountain [ON *fjall, fell*]

fro: from [ON *frá*]

garysoun: treasure [OF *garisoun*, sense inflection by ON *gersumi*]

gate: road, **gates** pl. [ON *gata*]

gayn: advantage, a good thing [ON *gegn*]

gaynly: fitly, rightly [ON *gegn* + ME *-ly*]

gef: gave [ON *gefa, gaf*]

glent: glance [ON *glenta* 'to glance']

õeõe (after): cry (for) [ON *geyja*]

õette: grant [ON *játta*]

hendelayk: courtliness [ON *-leikr*]

karp: talk [ON *karpa* 'boast']

kest: to cast [ON *kasta*]

laykeõ: plays, amuses himself [ON *leika*]

lemed: shone [ON *ljóma*]

lygeõ: to lie (lay) [ON *liggja*]

meekly: meekly [ON *mjúkliga*]

menskful: gracious; term of address lady [ON *mennskr* 'human' + OE *-ful*]

menskly: graciously [ON *mennskr* 'human' + ME *-ly*]

myre: mire, swamp [ON *mýrr*]

raged: ragged [ON *röggvaðr*]

rapes: to hasten, hurry [ON *hrapa*]

renk: man, knight [OE rinc; ON *renk-, rekkr*]

renneõ: runs [ON *renna;* cf. OE *iernan*]

same, samen: together [ON *saman*]

semly: seemly [ON *símligr*]

sere: separate; several [ON *sér*]

skere: pure [ON *skærr*]

skyl: reason [ON *skil*]

sleõly: warily [ON *slægr* + ME *-ly*]

stor: strong, severe [ON *stórr*]

tok: took, **tan** *pp.* [ON *taka, tók, tekinn*]

tore: hard, difficult [ON *tórr*]

trayst: certain, sure [ON *treistr, treista* 'trust']

tyl: until [ON *til*]

þay:. they [ON *þeir*]

þer, þere: there, where [OE, WS *þār*]

vmbe-teõe: to be surrounded [OE *ymbe*, ON *umb* + OE *tëon, tëah*]

vn-slyõe: unwary [OE *un-* + ON *slægr*]

wale: to choose, **waled** [ON *velja, valdi*]

warþe: ford [OE *waroþ* 'shore', with sense inflection by ON *vað* 'ford']

welcum: welcome, **to my cors** welcome to my company [ON *velkominn*; OE *welcuma*]

won, wone: dwelling [ON *ván*]

won, wone: (2nd meaning): course of action; multitude [ON *ván* 'hope']

pl: plural; pp: past participle.

Cheshire and the Scribe of the Poem

A further clue as to the local origins of the author of the Greene Knight poem comes from his (or her) awareness of the isolation and sparsely populated nature of Wirral during pre-Viking times. The relevant part of the poem appears in line 691-708[156]

691   now ridez þis renk þurȝ þe ryalme of logres
692   sir gauan on godez halue þaȝ hym no gomen þoȝt
693   oft leudlez alone he lengez on nyȝtez
694   þer he fonde noȝt hym byfore þe fare þat he lyked
695   hade he no fere bot his fole bi frythez and dounez
696   ne no gome bot god bi gate wyth to karp
697   til þat he neȝed ful noghe into þe norþe walez
698   alle þe iles of anglesay on lyft half he haldez
699   and farez ouer þe fordez by þe forlondez
700   ouer at þe holy hede til he hade eft bonk
701   in þe wyldrenesse of wyrale wonde þer bot lyte
702   þat auþer god oþer gome wyth goud hert louied
703   and ay he frayned as he ferde at frekez þat he met
704   if þay hade herde any karp of a knyȝt grene
705   in any grounde þeraboute of þe grene clapel
706   and al nykked hym wyth nay þat neuer in her lyue
707   þay seȝe neuer no segge þat watz of suche hwez
708   of grene

Translation: "Now passed Sir Gawain on God's behalf through the realms of Logres, though no game he thought it; and often alone he lingered at nighttime when he sought in vain for the way that he longed for. No companion had he save his horse,

---

[156] Translation by Ernest J.B. Kirtlan (1912) (Charles H. Kelly, London.)

nor no one but God to whom he might call by the way. And now he was nearing the north parts of Wales, with the Isle of Anglesey on the left. He fared over the fords along by the forelands. At the Holyhead Hill he had the heights behind him in the wilderness of Wirral. Few dwelt there that loved either God or man with a good heart. And ever as he fared he would ask any that he met if they had ever heard speak of the Green Knight in any part thereabouts, or of the Green Chapel. All denied with a nay that ever in their lives they had known such a knight of such a hue, of green."

Only a man or woman reasonably local to the area - and a learned one too - would be aware of the deserted state of Wirral in Arthurian times. A thorough analysis of the poem and its relation to Cheshire and Lancashire can be found for example in M. J. Bennett's book, *Community, Class and Careerism: Cheshire and Lancashire Society in the Age of "Sir Gawain and the Green Knight"* (Cambridge University Press, 1983).

G. Mathew suggests a South-west Lancashire origin of the poem

In 1968 G. Mathew, in his book *The Court of Richard II* (London) made the suggestion that the previously unidentified poet of Sir Gawain & the Green Knight was connected with Sir John Stanley of Storeton Hall, Wirral, Cheshire, and then of Lathom in West Lancashire.

Sir John Stanley (1350[157] -1414) was second son of Sir William Stanley of Storeton. Sir John would have been brought up in Storeton where his father was Master Forester. The Storeton Stanley family owned manors in Staffordshire, and the family held land at Storeton before 1300. Sir John de Stanleigh - Sir John Stanley - married in 1385 Isabel, daughter and heiress of Sir Thomas Lathom, of Lancashire, moved to Lathom and became ancestor of the Stanley family of Lathom and Knowsley. There is also a nice connection in that the Stanleys of Alderley, are also descended from him: this included John Stanley, Icelandophile friend of Anna Seward and Walter Scott (see Chapter 2 above). The Stanleys also became the Earls of Derby: the founder of Leasowe Castle was the 5th Earl. Sir John was clearly a local Wirral and West Lancashire man, with family connections with North Staffordshire.

Mathew's reasoning for suggesting that Sir John Stanley was the Patron of the Poet was as follows:

1. the dialect of the poem suggests it was written in or near South west Lancashire

---

[157] Dates range from 1340 - 1362.

2. the poem ended with the statement typical of the King's Court: Hony Soyt qui mal pence "shame on those who think any bad in what I have written", suggesting it was written for a Knight of the Garter.

3. The only Knight of the Garter in or near South-west Lancashire was Sir John Stanley.

Edward Wilson[158] added that if the Storeton family of Storeton were connected with the poem then lines 701, 702 which translated say:

> *In the wilderness of Wirral… Few dwelt there that loved either God or man with a good heart.*

Storeton Hall Farm. The site of the 14th-Century home of the Stanley family who some have connected with the Sir Gawain and the Green Knight poem.

could be interpreted as the Stanleys simply showing their contempt for the outlaws infesting Wirral in the 14th-Century, or their discontent at the loss of privileges and income of the master-foresters in 1376…or it was perhaps simply an expression of some wry local humour?

158 E. Wilson (1979) Sir Gawain and the Green Knight and the Stanley Family of Stanley, Storeton and Hooton, *The Review of English Studies*, 30, 308-316

Samuel and McIntosh's analysis suggest the scribe of the poem is from South-east Cheshire

Using the technique of *Dialect Mapping*, in 1963 A. McIntosh[159] had established that the scribe or the poet came from Cheshire, and was able to pinpoint this to the South-eastern part of the county, bordering Staffordshire. His mapping was then demonstrated in a Linguistic Atlas he produced in 1986 with M.L. Samuels and others[160] using techniques developed earlier for modern dialects.

The significance of the Scandinavian elements in the poem in relation to the dialect of the North-west Midlands and further north has been considered in some detail by T. Turville Petre in his book *The Alliterative Revival*[61]. One academic[162], has even gone as far as suggesting that Stanley wrote the poem on the grounds that the Stanley family had connections with South-east Cheshire and the Staffordshire border, that Sir John was accused of murder until pardoned from execution - possibly mirroring the experience of Sir Gawain awaiting the second blow from the Green Knight - and finally because the language of the poem was similar to a letter that Stanley wrote in 1405 to Henry IV. The suggestion was also made that the crossing point of Sir Gawain from North Wales to Wirral was from Holywell to Gayton, and even that Storeton Hall was the fictitious Castle of Sir Bercilak. Although the connection with Stanley is open to question, what is beyond dispute is that Sir Gawain and the Green Knight was written in the dialect of (probably) Cheshire and it shows us how extensive the Norse influence at that time still was for the whole region.

More Scandinavian dialect words

To the list of dialect words from the poem we can of course add many others such as those coming from the practice of naming fields and roads right up to the Victorian period. This includes the rakes, the slacks, the klints, the skerry's, the flats and the arrowes.

The poet and the scribe have long since gone. Most of the dialect words have also long since gone with them. *Ingimund, Gunnhildr, Ragnhildr, Ingríðr* and *Sigríðr* and all the other Scandinavians of the earlier Chapters have also long since gone and even the places named after many have long fallen out of use. But, forty or so generations on from the period of the settlements, is there any evidence for the descendants of these people and the other Scandinavians that once farmed the *argis* and fished the *skers* around the Mersey shores? Modern genetic methods, combined with surname, place-name and other tools may provide some clues.

[159] A. McIntosh (1963) A New Approach to Middle-English Dialectology, *English Studies*, 44, 1-11 (see page 5).

[160] A. McIntosh, M.L. Samuels and others (1986) *A Linguistic Atlas of Late Medieval English*, 4 vols. (Aberdeen, 1986).

[161] T. Turville-Petre (1977) *The Alliterative Revival*, D.S. Brewer Ltd., Cambridge. Pages 75-77.

[162] A.G. Breeze: A letter of Sir John Stanley (d. 1414) and Sir Gawain and the Green Knight. 14th International Conference of the Spanish Society for Medieval English Language and Literature, Las Palmas de Gran Canaria (3-5 October 2002) Also: http://www.ithaca.edu/faculty/twomey/sggk/Breeze-authorship.html

Chapter 14
SONS AND DOTTIRS: THE SEARCH FOR VIKING GENES

Rental records, held at St. Werburgh's Abbey in Chester record that in the year 1398 for Great Sutton Parish in Wirral an *Agnes Hondesdoghter* and a *Johanne Hondesdoghter* rented a cottage each for 2 shilling. These records, from about the same time as the supposedly Cheshire poet was compiling *Sir Gawain and the Green Knight*, also record in the same parish that a certain *Richard Hondesson* rented 2 bovates for 20 shilling and 3 acres for 4 shilling. Nearby, a similar rental agreement for Childer Thornton, also in Wirral records that *Mabilla Raynaldesdoghter* was renting a cottage for 1 shilling. This is rather remarkable in that the "daughters of Hondes", the "son of Hondes" and the "daughter of Raynald" all show that in parts of Merseyside as late as the turn of the 15th-Century Scandinavian customs were still being practised. This form of naming children is identical to that still practised in Iceland - for example a recent President of Iceland was Vigdís Finnbogadóttir: the daughter of Finnbogi. This local custom on Merseyside was surprising when it was almost contemporary with Henry V fighting at Agincourt and not long before Richard III was losing his crown at Bosworth Field. As far as we know there are no other examples of this practice occurring so late in mainland Britain. Intriguingly, also in nearby Whitby parish, one of the fields is recorded in 1440 as *Rawnuesfeld*, which probably preserves the same root name Ragnaldr (not necessarily the same man) as the father of Mabilla.

What remains of the Scandinavian settlers? We have already seen in the early Chapters of this book that they have left behind an abundance of place-names, stonework, and archaeology, together with a rich and colourful history in the Ingimund tradition, the skirmishes over Chester and the likely location of the Battle of Brunanburh. The dialect of the region has also preserved their influence, with words like rakes, carrs, slacks and arrowes used in the context of lanes, marshes, cuttings and pastureland respectively, commonplace until Victorian times. The local Mersey dialect - *Scouse* - and the nearby dialect of *Lancastrian* have both been influenced by the Vikings, in common with all the northern dialects. It was therefore of some irony that, centuries later, when Liverpool had become a major seaport, Norwegian sailors walking the docks introduced the stewy dish called *Labskaus* or

"Scouse" to the community, from which the term "Scouser" arose to describe the locals. In everyday English speech, words like egg (ON *egg*) and window (ON *vind-augr* "wind eye") preserve a broader influence of the Scandinavian tongue. And we have the local by-laws (ON *býr* or ODan *by*). But can we find some clues of Viking ancestry from the people, namely the present day population? The traditional association of fair hair and blue eyes with Scandinavians isn't unfortunately an acceptable criterion, since many Scandinavians don't have this, and many people from outside Scandinavia do: the traditional perception of Anglo-Saxons is for example the same. Fortunately there are more objective ways to assess Scandinavian influence.

Surnames

The simplest way, at least in principle, of looking for traces of Scandinavian influence in people is in their surnames. There are many surnames which have Scandinavian origins, and Kay Rogers has produced two short books describing many of these[163]. These names derive from one of six main sources:

(i) the name of a place, such as RABY 'boundary settlement' WHITBY, TARBOCK, HESKETH, from *hesta-skeið* 'horse race track' and local field-name in Irby, Thornton and a major name in West Lancashire; KIRK, from *kirkja*, 'church'; KIRKBY, means 'the settlement of or at the church'; LUNT, from *lundr* - 'The Grove'; TARLETON, from '*Thórald's tún*' which means 'Thórald's farmstead', and SCARISBRICK which comes from *Skar's brekka* (hill slope).

(ii) the name of a topographical feature. Some examples are BECK, from *bekkr* 'stream'; CARR, from *kjarr* 'marsh' or 'brushwood in marshy ground', HOLME, HULME etc., from *holmr* 'island on marshy ground', GILL, from *gil* 'ravine or dip' or TASKAR, from *skógr*, which means 'wood', and possibly WHARTON from *varðr-tún* "farmstead with the beacon or look-out" and BARKER, from *bjarg* 'hill cliff' or the personal name *Bokr*.

(iii) The name of a material item or weapon, or colour, such as BRANT, from *brandr* 'sword'; and RATHBONE, from *rauðr* - red.

(iv) The name of a profession or trade: SKINNER, from *Skinnr* 'worker in leather', GILL, from *gilli* 'servant' (also from a topographical feature, as in (ii) above), GRICE, from *gríss* - to

---

[163] K.H. Rogers (1995) *Vikings and Surnames*, William Sessions Ltd., York, 1991, and *More Vikings and Surnames*, Local History Press, Nottingham.

Winter Walkabout: Red Rocks, West Kirby, Caldy, Fra...

The last of the Wirral Vikings.

by Jim Barrow

*Gordon Tottey:
Article from the Liverpool
Daily Post, 15th March
1971, page 5.
Courtesy of the
Liverpool Daily
Post and Echo.*

STORYTIME

. . . at Heswall library with 23-year-old Christine Payne at Irby.

THE NORSEMAN

Mr Gordon Tottey, his forefathers landed with Vikings invaders.

GOOD OLD DAYS

Mr and Mrs William Gates of Caldy in search of Old England.

RED ROCKS is a tiny finger of sandstone pointing out into the Irish Sea from the extreme western point of the Wirral Peninsula.

Bright sunshine warmed the soft redrock and glinted on the tiny waves breaking on them, as Eddie Barford, and I started our walk—with more than 100 miles of Cheshire and North Wales ahead of us.

Red Rocks, our starting point, looked east to Hoylake, and a deserted sweep of beach. To the West on Hilbre Island, in the Dee Estuary, now a bird sanctuary, the building sparkled while in sunshine.

The island, said to have been the home of a recluse monk, 900 years ago, was undergoing close scrutiny from two ladies sitting on the bare rock and looking out to sea.

We spoke briefly to 73-year-old Mrs Lucy Weston and 69-year-old Mrs Mary Winters, who were staying at Wirral Point, a Cheshire County Council holiday home for old age pensioners.

As they clambered back over the rocks we followed the sweep of sand south to West Kirby, where the village nestles beneath a hill surrounded by a tall column of stone.

In front of us we saw an elderly man, his trousers tucked into wellington boots, and well muffled against the wind swinging a golf club, and driving a ball hard down the sand before marching after it.

With difficulty we managed to catch up with our beach golfer, who turned out to be 72-year-old Mr Gordon Tottey, whose family are known to have lived in West Kirby at the time the Domesday Book was compiled.

He told us: "I've been told I'm descended from the Vikings who went to Ireland, and then came over here to West Kirby, but I don't see how anyone can know."

Although Mr Tottey scoffs at the possible link with the Vikings, he does recall the shock he got while working on a Norwegian ship. He says: "One of the men on board, who was a Norwegian, came up to me and said: 'I might be your cousin', I looked at his face and I might have been looking into a mirror—his name was Tottey."

Mr Tottey was born in a black and white timbered cottage on the site of the present railway station, and for more than 30 years he ran a sweets and tobacconist's shop.

He pointed to the promenade and told us: "One of the houses was used by a man called Mr Mines who used it to build a very frail looking aircraft to compete in the Manchester Air Race of 1906."

Mr Tottey still fishes the Dee, but says that there aren't half as many fish as there used to be and blames the pollution in the Dee and the seals which get into the estuary.

VILLAGE POSTMAN

A little further on we met 77-year-old Mr Thomas Shortman and his 76-year-old wife, Grace who live at Banks Road, West Kirby.

They have now retired from the grocer's shop they took over 5 years ago. Mr Shortman, a former professional concert pianist, came from Portsmouth with no experience of do with farming pigs.

(v) The name of an animal, such as SCARFF, from *Skarfr* 'cormorant'

(vi) A Norse or Danish personal name, e.g. COLLEY, CALEY etc, from the personal name *Koli*; SWAIN, from the personal name *Svein*.

A good example of an old Merseyside family bearing a Viking name is the TOTTY or TOTTEY family, whose name derives from the Old Norse/ Old Danish personal name Tostig. Totty and Tottey is a name characteristic of North Wirral, but rare in other parts of Britain, and the Totty brand was once a famous Ice Cream in West Kirby. In 1971 the family was the subject of considerable press interest because of the Viking roots of the name and its near-peculiarity to Wirral.

There are however some problems in using surname alone as "proof" of Viking ancestry. Firstly it can only be applied to males, since it is only the male line that preserves the surname. Secondly, it assumes there has been no illegitimacy across the hundreds of years the surname has been passed from father to son, to his son and to his son etc.: there have been approximately forty generations since the time of the Scandinavian settlements of the area. Most seriously however surnames - in the form we now know them - were not in common use until the 14th/15th centuries! However, what these surnames do is to give us an idea of the local speech and customs of the bearer, and also we can assess the chances of the ancestors of a particular person being present in the area in medieval times by seeing if his surname - or an earlier form of it - was in use on Merseyside all those years ago.

There is however something else which is passed virtually unchanged from generation to generation, father to son *etc.*, and allowing us to penetrate right back to the time of the settlements - this is DNA on the male Y-chromosome.

Y-chromosome Polymorphisms

In 1971, Peter Sawyer writing in his book *The Age of the Vikings* (pages 255-6) had indicated the potential of population genetics as an indicator of population movements, if an appropriate genetic tool could be found. The potential for using the male Y-chromosome as a tool for genealogical research was first revealed with two research papers published in 1985[164], but it was not until the last few years that the technology has advanced significantly to enable the easy study of special patterns of DNA on it, called polymorphisms to throw light on the origins and migrations of populations.

[164] M. Cassanova et al (1985) *Science*, 230, 1403-1406 and G. Lucotte and N.Y. Ngo (1985) *Nuleic Acids Research*, 13, 8285. For a review, see M.A. Jobling and C. Tyler-Smith (1995) Fathers and Sons: the Y chromosome and human evolution, *Trends in Genetics*, 11, 449-456.

The Y-chromosome. It consists of a huge length of DNA (deoxyribonucleic acid) with about 60,000,000 units called bases (given the symbols A,T,C,G) linked together into a long chain and wrapped around another long chain with a complementary sequence of bases to give a double helix. The order in which the bases occur characterize an individual's Y-chromosome. In the example given, Mr Hyde and Dr Jekyll clearly have different Y-Chromosomes.
Courtesy of Mark Jobling and Turi King.

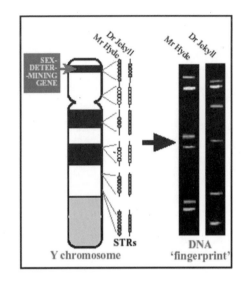

Y-chromosome Jargon

Polymorphism. A difference between the DNA of two Y-chromosomes due to a rare error in the body's genetic replication machinery.

Base Of 4 types: adenine (symbol A), thymine (symbol T), cytidine (C), and guanine (G). These are linked together into a long chain. The sequence of bases on the chain characterizes a person's DNA.

Base pair DNA has 2 long chains of bases wrapped around each other into a double helix in such a way that the A residue of one chain pairs with a T on the other chain, and a C residue pairs with a G.

STR Short Tandem Repeat. A sequence of 3-5 bases, e.g. TAGA, which is repeated typically 8-30 times in a row on a man's Y-chromosome

Binary marker A difference between Y-chromosomes involving a very slowly changing process, such as base substitution, the change of one base for another. Groups of chromosomes characterized by these kinds of markers can be very plentiful in populations, and so they are not the markers of choice for discriminating between individuals.

PCR Polymerase chain reaction. Technique which amplifies sections of DNA from an individual, allowing markers such as STRs or binary markers to be analyzed.

Haplotype Detailed classification of a man's Y-chromosome based on the numbers of tandem repeats for a chosen set of at least 6 STRs, and/or binary markers.

Haplogroup Overall classification of a man's Y-chromosome based on the binary markers.

Genetic material in humans - in the form of DNA - is packaged in structures called chromosomes. Every cell (apart from red blood cells) in both men and women contains 22 pairs of chromosomes, called autosomes. Apart from these, in the cells of women there is a pair of chromosomes called X-chromosomes, and in the cells of men there is one of these X-chromosomes, but also one male-specific chromosome called the Y-chromosome. In fact, the Y-chromosome is the reason that a man is male - it carries a gene which switches on the pathway of male sex determination early in development. Apart from the essential sex-determining gene, very little of the DNA on the Y-chromosome defines anything about how we look or what diseases we might suffer from, and most is what the experts call "junk DNA". However, unlike

DNA on the autosomes and X-chromosomes, the DNA on the Y is passed from generation to generation only along the male line, from father to son. Another important difference between the Y and the other chromosomes is that it escapes from a reshuffling process (called recombination) which occurs every generation. This means that the message in the DNA sequence that we get from our Y-chromosomal ancestors is much clearer to read than the message from the ancestors who bequeathed their autosomes and X-chromosomes to us. Changes on Y-chromosomes only occur through a mistake or "mutation" in the body's normally impeccable copying machinery, and this produces a difference between different Y-chromosomes in the population, known as a *polymorphism*. These changes or polymorphisms are however very rare - some occur over a course of hundreds of years, and some over thousands or longer. Some (such as base substitutions, where one letter of the DNA code changes for another) have probably happened only once in the history of man - these are "unique event polymorphisms" and are not useful for giving clues on paternal ancestry over the last few hundred years. The most useful are polymorphisms involving what the geneticists call *short tandem repeats* "STR's" or "*microsatellite markers*", since these can change over a period of hundreds of years, as opposed to multi-millennia. For example, a particular STR known as DYS19 contains a motif of four DNA bases, TAGA, repeated 10-17 times in a man's Y-chromosome. If a man has 14 repeats, this number is then passed on faithfully from generation to generation along the male line, father to son and so on, until suddenly, due to a rare error in the body's genetic replication machinery, the next generation might receive a Y-chromosome with only 13 repeats. DNA analysis technology known as "PCR" (Polymerase Chain Reaction) now allows the analysis of a set of 19 of these microsatellite markers[165], given the names DYS19, DYS385, DYS388, DYS389, DYS390, DYS391, DYS392, DYS393, DYS434, DYS435, DYS436, DYS437, DYS438, DYS439, DYS460, DYS461 and DYS462.

Though the Y-chromosome has many advantages in its male-specificity, relatively simple passage down the generations, and wide range of different markers that it carries, it is not a perfect tool for distinguishing population origins. While individual men coming from different continents carry Y-chromosomes which are so distinct that they are easily told apart, populations having common ancestral origins going back only millennia - such as the Germanic or "Invader" group (which includes North Germany - the homeland of the Anglo-Saxons - Denmark, Sweden and Norway - the homeland of the Vikings) - will have similar spectra of Y-chromosomes in their populations which makes discrimination between populations on this

[165] E. Bosch, A.C. Lee, F. Calafell, E. Arroyo, P. Henneman, P. deKnijff, M.A. Jobling (2002) High resolution Y-Chromosome typing: 19 STRs amplified in three multiplex reactions. *Forensic Science International*, 125, 42-51.

scale very difficult (in fact the Y-chromosomal populations of Denmark and North Germany are virtually identical, based on the markers currently available). Y-chromosome spectra in populations are likely to be considerably different, however, where common ancestors are much further back in time - such as comparing the Germanic group with the Celtic group of populations.

A recent illustration of this point came from a study which attempted to address a hugely important debate concerning the Dark Ages that has rumbled for years: was there a mass migration of Anglo-Saxons into England, driving the Celts away, as has been thought over the centuries, or was the sudden change to an Anglo-Saxon culture due to a military takeover by a relatively small number of German immigrants, leaving the indigenous population largely unmolested? The recent opinion of scholars has tended to favour the latter theory[166]. To examine this[167] a transect was taken of seven towns in a line from east to west across the UK: North Walsham, Fakenham, Bourne, Southwell and Ashbourne in England, and Abergele and Llangefni (Angelsey) in Wales, and the Y-chromosome distributions were compared, using Friesland in Holland as an 'Anglo-Saxon' control. The distributions were found very similar for the five English towns and Friesland, but very different when compared with the two Welsh towns, and the authors used this as evidence for strong Anglo-Saxon immigration into England, but an abrupt transition at the Welsh border, which was more of a barrier to migration than the North Sea. The latter may well be well be true, but evidence for Anglo-Saxon migration into England was not convincing, since unfortunately all the English towns sampled were in the old Danelaw. The differences with Wales may well have been due to the Y-chromosomes of Danish invaders rather than Anglo-Saxons, and it is also worth pointing out that the inland Welsh sample comprised only 12 men, and the Western sample was taken from a single village on an island (Angelsey), and so may have been strongly affected by what scientists call 'genetic drift' - the random variations of frequency of types of Y-chromosomes from one generation to the next that can occur in small populations.

The question of the strength - or weakness - of the Anglo-Saxon settlements in relation to the Celts in England will become clearer once data for other parts of England unaffected by the Danish or Norse settlements becomes available - such as the South-west Midlands and the South-West.

What *is* clear is that research using Y-chromosome polymorphisms is most powerful when used in conjunction with other data - such as surnames, place-name distributions (called "philology") - historical and archaeological

---

[166] N. Higham (1992) *Rome, Britain and the Anglo-Saxons*. Seaby, London; Arnold, C.J. (1974) *From Roman Britain to Saxon England*. Croom Helm, London; Hodges, R (1989) *The Anglo-Saxon achievement: Archaeology and the beginnings of English Society*, Duckworth, London.

[167] M.E. Weale, D.A. Weiss, R.F. Jager, N. Bradman and M.G. Thomas, (2002) Y Chromosome evidence for Anglo-Saxon mass migration, *Molecular Biology and Evolution* 19, 1008-1021

data[168], together with knowledge of the flux or expansion in populations. The latter is for example critical for Merseyside which has undergone an enormous population expansion since the growth of the Port of Liverpool. Taking Wirral as an example, the population at the 1801 census was approximately 10,000. The population today is now approaching 400,000, a population increase in 200 years of 40 times: this is six times the national average increase. This means that the majority of men on Merseyside are not carrying Y-chromosomes of ancestral people in the area 1000 years ago.

Sampling an individual's DNA

DNA sampling is normally done from a mouth swab of the buccal cells lining the cheek. Having taken the swab, a volunteer then washes it into a tube containing preservative solution, the tube is sealed and the samples are then extracted and analysed in groups of up to 100 in the laboratory using a technique known as the Polymerase Chain Reaction (PCR) which provides the STR data. An excellent web site describing the principles of PCR with an interactive display is:

   http://allserv.rug.ac.be/~avierstr/principles/pcrani.html

Preliminary survey of Merseyside and Cheshire

A preliminary survey was done in 2001 involving 66 individuals from North Wirral, 26 from South Wirral, 49 from West Lancashire (Ormskirk and Skelmersdale area) and 46 from Mid-Cheshire (based around Northwich). This was part of the BBC 'Blood of the Vikings' Project, and the sampling was done by two students from the University of Nottingham, Emma Compton and Giles Pergl Wilson as part of their Master of Science in Applied Biomolecular Technology. A number of dentists also helped with sample collection and the analyses were performed by these students in the laboratories of Professor David Goldstein at University College London. The national survey, led by Goldstein, involved two thousand volunteers. The criterion used for a volunteer to take part was the same as the national survey: his paternal grandfather had to come from the area to which his sample was assigned. Unfortunately this criterion proved insufficient, in that only a small proportion of the volunteers (e.g. six from North Wirral) possessed surnames that were present in the area before the Industrial Revolution, too small a number to comment on possible Viking ancestry. However, the preliminary survey did appear to show a strong similarity between the populations of North Wirral, West Lancashire and South Wirral, but which appeared very different from Mid-Cheshire and very

---

[168] M.P. Evison (2000) All the Genes? Evaluating the biological evidence of contact and migration. In *Cultures in Contact* (ed. D.M. Hadley and J.D. Richards) Brepols, Belgium, 277-294.

Distribution of Y-Chromosome types "2.47+" and "3.65+" which are prevalent in the "Invader" group (Norway, Denmark and North Germany), but absent from the Celtic group (Wales and Ireland). The highest levels of these chromosomes are found in Norway, with 38% of men surveyed having 2.47+ and 22% of 3.65+.

This preliminary survey was done in 2001 as part of the BBC Blood of the Vikings project. The data for Wales and Norway is from Wilson and co-workers[169]

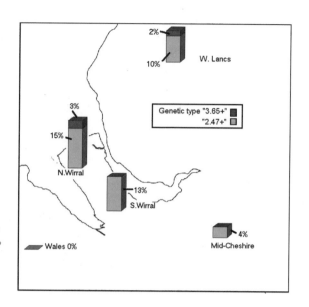

Corresponding density map of Scandinavian place-names (from Wainwright[170]).

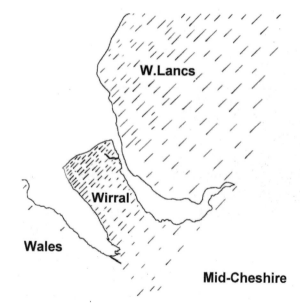

[169] J.F. Wilson, D.A. Weiss, M. Richards, M.G. Thomas, N. Bradman and D.B. Goldstein (2001), Genetic evidence for different male and female roles during cultural transitions in the British Isles, *Proceedings of the National Academy of Sciences*, USA, 98, 5078-5083.

[170] F.T Wainwright (1942) North West Mercia 871-924, *Trans. Hist. Soc. Lancashire, Cheshire* 94, 3-55.

different from recently published data for Wales. By contrast, the Mid-Cheshire result showed a high-correlation with Wales, a result consistent with the view that the Anglo-Saxon influence on the population was not major.

These differences (coincidentally or otherwise) appeared to map to the differences in Scandinavian place-name density between the Wirral and West Lancashire group and Mid-Cheshire and Wales, as defined by Wainwright over 60 years ago. Remarkably, one of the individuals tested in North Wirral was presented in the BBC series as one of the best examples of the 2000 individuals tested nationally, of a Y-chromosome match with individuals sampled in Norway - this was Bill Housley, from a family of fishermen going back many generations in Meols. One morning in June 2001, Bill visited his dentist, Barry Marsden, who was one of the dentists we had asked to help with the survey. A few months later a phone-call came from Sam Roberts, producer, with Paul Bradshaw, of the BBC Blood of the Vikings series. Bill recalls his experience in an interview with Per Anders Todal of the Norwegian newspaper *Dag og tid*, when we visited his house on a Sunday afternoon the following January.

Bill Housley with the author

Interview with Bill Housley by Per Anders Todal

"When the BBC rang me I was absolutely gobsmacked. It came as a shock to me. It all started with a routine visit to the dentist. He told me about this survey on behalf of London University, and asked me if I'd like to take part, by giving a sample of my DNA.

Later I had a phone call from Sam at BBC2. I was told "we've found something unique about you", and they wanted to come and see me. I met with the people from the BBC. They said they weren't allowed to tell me what they'd found yet, but they filmed this little interview down at the promenade. Then we visited the Anglo-Saxon centre, and in the final interview they presented what they'd found out in general. Then Julian Richards said "we believe there's something special about Bill. We are 99 percent certain he's of Viking origin.

They told me about the ancestors in Ireland that came to the Wirral. So Julian said: "you could say Bill is a Viking." Soon after, the press got hold of it. There were articles in *The Echo, Daily Post, The Mail* and *The Sun*. When the guy from the *Post* wanted me to put on a Viking helmet, I refused absolutely. This was far more serious to me. If I had done that, my sons would never have forgiven me.

Previously, I never had a great deal of interest in the history of the Vikings in this country. But since the BBC contacted me, I've become interested. It's fascinating. I knew there had been Viking settlements in this area, in places like Meols. I am very happy to be able to contribute to this research. People stop me in the street now, telling me they've seen me in the paper. I have become Bill the Viking...

I've been associated with the fishing industry for 30 odd years, and I come from a family of fishermen. My family goes way over a hundred years back in this area. My great-great-grandfather drowned at sea on July 13 1910. He was in a dinghy transferring fish. His son and cousin were also on board. It was a sunny day, but suddenly it turned over. He'd never learnt to swim. Three of them drowned that day, and all were buried in the same grave.

Now I'm wondering if my family's involvement in the fisheries is because of the Norwegian heritage. We have all been connected with fishing. Myself, I've moved around a bit, but I've never lived away from the sea. I wouldn't be able to. I just love the sound of the sea. I've also noticed that I always tend to drive along the promenade when I am able to, to see the tide. Maybe it's a sea gene I've got.

Through my work, I've also had great ties with Norway through the fishing industry, and Norwegian companies like Findus. We've always looked upon the Norwegians as allies. There's always been a bond across the North Sea, a maritime connection. I went into shipping after leaving school, as an apprentice to become a broker. In 1960 I went into National Service for two years. After the army I just wanted to work with boats, I didn't want to work in an office. But the fisheries here were in decline. So I got into the selling side of the fisheries. I joined Findus as a representative salesman. Then I moved on to Young Seafood, an international seafood company, and worked there for 11 years. Later I set up my own company, selling Norwegian fish. We had an annual turnover of around one million pounds a year. But my companion backstabbed me and squeezed me out. I had taken him on although I didn't really need anyone; I think we should trust people. It was a blow, but I've put it behind me now. There's no point in being bitter. I'm turning 63 in August, and I still work in the industry, as a sales manager for a seafood company called M & J Seafoods. I've got four sons - Matthew (20), Luke (16), Mark (38) and Graham (35).

My father used to work all his life as a fisherman, and his father before him. Their boat was called a nobbie, a 30 foot prawner. They were fishing boats, but also yachts, with a beam and sails. My Granny and her mother used to sell fish at the promenade. The men would land the fish, and the women would sell it. What they couldn't sell there, they'd put on a cart and take it to the station".

The full survey based on medieval surnames

It was a great stroke of luck for Bill, the BBC, Wirral and Merseyside that he took a trip to Barry Marsden's dental surgery in Moreton at just the right time. The discovery of Bill was exceptional in that to detect evidence for Viking ancestry one normally needs to study the Y-chromosome distribution across a whole population. Because of the huge population explosion in the area since 1801 as referred to above, in order to get the clearest possible picture of the genetic make up of medieval Wirral and West Lancashire it is absolutely necessary to focus on the Y-chromosomes of people bearing surnames that were present in the region either in or shortly after the medieval period.

Surnames in the form as we know them now were not passed from father to son in early medieval times: it was not until the 14th-Century that it became commonplace, and as we have seen with the Great Sutton and Thornton Rentals above, this practice was still not followed in some areas. However we can make the reasonable assumption that the existence of a surname in the 14th/15th or 16th centuries which corresponds to anything other than the name of a place outside the region, is representing someone whose family has been there for generations. And if we make the additional assumption there has been no illegitimacy in a surname line from this period to the present then by replacing the inappropriate BBC criterion of two paternal generations with a criterion of someone possessing an old Wirral or West Lancashire name, we can focus on a much more representative set of Y-chromosomes for the region. A similar surname criterion was applied in a recent survey of the Orkneys[171].

Old Wirral and West Lancashire surnames

We can use the 1542 subsidy rolls of all households in Wirral paying taxes recorded during the reign of Henry VIII, together with other medieval records and court proceedings (see Chapter 4 where a namesake of the author is accused of killing a dog) to compile the following list of medieval names (this list excludes those bearing names coming from outside the Wirral/West Lancashire region):

> Adam, Allin, Alleyne, Andrew, Aspinall, Ball, Barber, Barker, Barrell, Barrow, Bailiff, Beck, Bennett, Bergs, Billing, Bird, Blackburne, Boland, Brant, Bratherton, Browne, Brunt, Burscough, Bryde, Burrows, Bushell, Caley, Carr, Carlile, Carlisle, Challoner,Charnock,Chantrell,Coley, Colley, Colton, Coke, Corf, Corfe, Corness,Cotton, Cowper, Cross, Dalby, Dane, Danold, Davey, Davy, Denham, Denson, Dobb, Doe, Done, Duke, Dunn,Edmonds, Edmunds, Ellcock, Fazackerley,

Fiddler, Fidler, Foreshaw, Forshaw, Fox, Francis, Gallie, Gardener, Gardiner, Gardner,Garratt, Garrett, Gibson,Gill, Gleave, Glegg, Goodacre, Grace, Gray, Gregory, Grey, Grice,Hale,Hancock, Hand, Harding, Hare, Harper, Harrison, Harvey, Heath, Helsby, Hender, Hesketh, Hey, Heyward, Hide, Hill, Hogg, Hole, Holme, Holmes,Home, Hough, Hulme, Hulmes, Humphrey, Huntington, Hynes, Jennion, Jensen, Jeunds, Johnson, Jump, Kemp, Kirk, Kirkby, Lancelyn, Leck, Ledsham, Leighton,**Lennard,** Leonard, Ley, Lightfoot, Linacre, Little, Lunt, Macklin, **Massie,** Massey, Matthew, Mayle, Mayles, Middleton, Milner, Molyneuz, Moss, Moulding, Mutton, Nelson, Newbold, Newton, Otter, Otty, Page, Parr, Pearson, Pemberton, Pendleton, Pennington, Penketh, Penney, Philip, Phylip, Pigot, Pinnington,Plumbe, Poole, Potter, Prenton, Pye, Pyke, Radcliffe, Rathbone, Ravenscroft, Richardson, Rider, Ridley, Rimmer, Robinson, Rogerson, Russell, Rutter, Saddler, Sadler, Sampson, Scaife, Scarff, Scarffe, Scarisbrick, Sclater, Scriven, Sefton, Sharpe, Shephard, Shepherd, Sherlock, Skinner, Smalley, Smythe, Spenser, Stones, Swain, Swaine, Swarbrick, Swindley, Tarleton, Taskar, Tellett, Thomason, Thomasson, Thomson,Threadgill, Threadgold, Tottey, Totty, Tumath, Tyldesley, Wade, Wainwright, Walley, Walton, Warburton, Waring, Warington, Watmough, Watt, Whalley, Wharton, Wilkinson, Williamson, Whitby, Whitehead, Whitelaw, Whitfield, Whitmore, Whittle, Whyte, Williamson, Willoughby, Worral, Woods, Woodward, Wilcock, Wise, Wyse, Young, Yoxon.

For the West Lancashire survey, the list of surnames is based on a fascinating 14th-Century document listing all those inhabitants of the Parishes of Ormskirk, Scarisbrick with Hurlton, Bickerstaffe, Burscough with Marton, Westhead with Lathom and Skelmersdale who promised to contribute to the stipend of the priest of the altar of Our Lady at Ormskirk, in the year 1366. The document, at the Lancashire Record Office, Preston, was reproduced in the Ormskirk & District Family Historian, Spring 1991 (ISBN 0 947915 28 1). The transcription to modern day names was done by Stephen Roberts:

Bakhous (Backhouse), *Balsagh* (Balshaw), *Barett* (Barret-t), *Benyood*, *Bere* (Bere/Bear etc.), *Beyson* (Benson?), *Blanchard* (Blanchard), *Bron* (Brown), *Byld* (Bold), *Byrd* (Bird), *Cadyk* (Cadick), *Carles* (Charles), *Cauns*, *Cay*, (Kay), *Childesfadre*

(Childsfather), *Coly* (Coly), *Davy* (Davy), *de Adburgam,* *de Aghton* (Aughton), *de Asshurst* (Ashurst), *de Aykescogh* (Aikscough), *de Balshagh* (Balshaw), *de Barton* (Barton), *de Beulond, de Blyth* (Blythe), *de Blythe* (Blythe, Bligh etc.), *de Boold* (Bold), *de Bretherton* (Bretherton/Brotherton), *de Bronburgh* (Bromborough), *de Bronylegh* (Bronley, and variants), *de Burscogh* (Burscough), *de Bykerstath* (Bickerstaff), *de Cole* (Cole), *de Couper* (Cooper), *de Depdale* (Deepdale), *de Dewicar* (Dewacre), *de Eggeacr* (Eggacre), *de Ellerbek* (Ellerbeck), *de ffourokshagh, de Fletcher* (Fletcher), *de Goldicar* (Goodacre), *de Gosfordsich, de Greceby* (Greasby), *de Halsagh* (Halshaw), *de Hamelton* (Hamilton), *de Haskeen* (Haskin(s)/Askin(s)/Astin/Ashken/ Haskings etc.), *de Haylegh, de Holand* (Holland), *de Holbrok* (Holbrook), *de Horscar* (Horsecarr), *de Hurlton* (Hurlton), *de Hyllome, de Hyton* (Huyton), *de Irby* (Irby), *de Kirkeby* (Kir(k)by), *de Ledebeter* (Leadbetter), *de Legh* (Leigh/Lee/Lea), *de Leyland* (Leyland), *de Longebak* (Longback), *de Longeton* (Longton), *de Marton* (Marton), *de Mell* (Mell), *de Mellyng* (Melling), *de Milner* (Milner), *de Morcroft* (Moorcroft), *de Mosbury* (Mossbury), *de Moscar* (Mossock), *de Mosok* (Mossock), *de Mourehyles* (Moorhills), *de Oldome* (Oldham), *de Olton* (Olton/Oulton), *de Orell* (Orrell), *de Owatton* (Overton), *de Owynbrek* (Owenbreck Overbeck), *de Par* (Parr), *de Penwytham* (Penwortham), *de Prestcotte* (Prescot), *de Raynford* (Rainford), *de Raynhull* (Rainhill), *de Ruynacre, de Shirwallaacrs, de Stryvelyn, de Sutton* (Sutton), *de Tailour* (Taylor), *de Teulond de Tildeslegh* (Tyldesleigh), *de Westheved* (Westhead), *de Wynmarleigh* (Winmarleigh), *de Wyresdale* (Wyresdale), *del Abbay* (Abbey), *del Aspynwall* (Aspinall/Aspinwall/Astmole), *del Bakhous, del Barwe* (Barrow), *del Brodfeld* (Broadfield), *del Brodheved* (Broadhead), *del Brokefeld* (Brookfield), *del Car* (Carr), *del Crosse* (Cross), *del Grene* (Green), *del Greves* (Greaves), *del Halle* (Hall), *del Helmes* (Holmes), *del Heth* (Heath), *del Hyles, del Lone* (Lone), *del Marhalgh* (Marhall?), *del Mor* (More/Moore), *del Mosse* (Moss), *del Outsich, del Platt,* (Platt), *del Rydyng* (Riding), *del Scoles* (Scholes/Scales), *del Shagh* (Shaw), *del Strenger* (Stranger), *del Syche* (Such/Sutch/Souch/Zouch/Chuck/Chucks), *del Tou, del Wall* (Wall), *del Warinawro, del Wodes* (Woods), *del Wolfall* (Wo(o)lfall), *del Yate* (Yate-s), *Dobbeson* (Dobson), *Doggeson* (Dodgeson), *Drake* (Drake), *Dykounson* (Dicconson/

Dickinson), *Ekirgarth, Elot* (Elliott), *fe Copphull* (Copphull, Coppell), *fel Vale* (Vale), *ffaber* (Smith), *Ffarwys, Ffox* (Fox), *fi Robti* (Roberts/Robertson), *fil Alex* (Alexson), *fil Beco, fil Carpent* (Carpenter), fil *Elyn* (Ellin), *fil ffabri* (Smithson), *fil Hankok* (Hancock), *fil Henr* (Henry-son), *fil Johis* (Jones-son), *fil Johis Becokson* (Becokson), *fil Maryot* (Marriott), *fil Nicholl* (Nicholson), *fil Thom* (Thomas/Thompson etc.), *fil Walt'i* (Walterson), *fil Willi* (Williams-son), *filia Boold* (Bold-son), *fillia Nutricus* (Foster-son), *Foluler*(?) (Fuller), *Garc Thom* (Thomasman), *Gillseson* (Gilson), *Gray* (Grey/Gray), *Hawot, Hennson* (Henson), *Hertblod* (Hartblood), *Hopcrone, Horbert* (Hubert), *Jakson* (Jackson), *Johis* (Jones), *Kemp* (Kemp), *Lagard* (Lagard), *le Bagger* (Badger), *le Bakster* (Baxter), *le Barker* (Barker), *le Blawer* (Blower), *le Bower* (Bower), *le Brabayn* (Brabourn), *le Breton* (Bre(re)ton), *le Cart* (Carter), *le Chalonner* (Chalonner/Challener/Challender, Challenor etc.), *le Clerk* (Clerk), *le Coudrey* (Cowdrey/Cowdray/Cowdroy etc.), *le Cropper,* (Cropper), *le ffreshe* (Fresh), *le Halleknave* (Hallknave), *le Hunt* (Hunt), *le Kekker* (Checker), *le Kyng* (King), *le Lauder* (Lauder), *le Long* (Long), *le Mercer* (Mercer), *le Parker* (Parker), *le Porter* (Porter), *le Prestesmon* (Priestman), *le Reder* (Reader), *le Salter* (Salter), *le Scuster* (Shuster), *le Sergeant* (Serjeant/Sargeant etc.), *le Smyth* (Smith), *le Spenc* (Spence), *le Spencer* (Spencer), *le Spicer* (Spicer), *le Sporier* (Spurrier), *le Swoon* (Swan), *le Tasker* (Tasker, Taskar), *le Turnour* (Turner), *le Walker* (Walker), *le Walsh* (Walsh), *le Warner* (Warner), *le Webster* (Webster), *Lenne, Mabbeson, Madok* (Madoc-k), *Materei, Messenger* (Messenger), *Milde, Moubyn* (Maulby), *Nykson* (Nickson), *Oety* (Otti/Oti/Otty), *Olyf* (Ollif), *Owasen* (Owenson), *Owitheved* (Outhead), *Pacok* (Peacock), *Page* (Page), *Parlement* (Parliament), *Paweson* (Pawson), *Penydale* (Penidale/Pennydale), *Pety* (Petty), *Pye* (Pye/Pie), *Pygyn* (Pigeon), *Pykhare* (Pickhare), *Relict. Ade Osmarshagh, Robynson* (Robinson), *Ryout* (Rideout), *Ryvelyng, Shakelauedy* (Shakalady), *Shakerewet, Smalshagh* (Smallshaw), *Sowerby, Spurwyn Spynk* (Spink-s), *Staynes* (Staynes), *Steell* (Steele), *Stotfoldshagh* (Stotfoldshaw), *Stykk, Tabart* (Tarbert), *Tewe* (Tew), *Thomasmon* (Thomasson), *Todd* (Todd), *Toppyng* (Topping), *Tynkeler, Tysing, Waryng* (Waring), *Willison* (Wilson), *Wodeloft* (Woodloft), *Wyld* (Wild), *Wyldebold* (Wildbold/Wildblood), *Wynmenske.*

What the new survey is trying to address

The distribution of Y-chromosome types for Wirral and West Lancashire based on the above surnames will be compared with the distributions in the Viking homelands of Norway and Denmark together with Germany, Ireland and Wales along with published data for other areas of the United Kingdom including the Danelaw, and used in conjunction with place-name, historical, and archaeological data. It will first of all see if the strong "Invader" influence in the area from the early survey is reinforced, and then see if a Norwegian Viking signal can be picked out from the other Germanic signals. If the Anglo-Saxon contribution to Y-chromosomes across England as a whole is shown by other studies to be weak, the strength of the "Invader" signals compared to "Celtic" may also give us an indication of the Danish contribution to West Lancashire and Ingimund's Wirral.

The survey team

To address these issues a multi-disciplinary survey team has been assembled consisting of experts in Y-chromosome genetics, local and national history and place-names (philology) and consists of Dr. Mark Jobling and Turi King at the University of Leicester, Department of Genetics, the author and Ziff Hansen at the School of Biosciences, University of Nottingham, and Professor Judith Jesch at the School of English. The expertise encompassed by these researchers is reinforced by the expert local history knowledge of Stephen Roberts, author of *A History of Wirral*[72] and Patrick Waite, Chairman of the West Lancashire Heritage Association. As we have seen, neither a study of Y-chromosome polymorphisms, nor place-name evidence performed in isolation are sensitive enough to address the questions above: a multi-disciplinary approach is essential. Dr. Jobling's group has been responsible for developing much of the Y-chromosome methodology, including the recent extension of the sensitivity of the procedure to 19 STRs. The Genetics Department including Professor Sir Alec Jeffreys is internationally famous for developing the DNA fingerprinting methods used in forensic science. Judith Jesch is an internationally famous Viking expert and philologist and has taken over from the late Christine Fell as head of English at Nottingham, which also has the English Place Name Society and its research fellow Paul Cavill conveniently located in it.

[72] Chichester U.K. In Particular, Chapter 3 for History of the Dark Ages and Chapter 5 for analysis of 1545 surnames and implied origins of Wirral people.

Maternal chromosome polymorphisms

Apart from the Y-chromosome, passed from father to son with little change, there is an analogous maternally inherited piece of DNA, mitochondrial DNA, which passes from mother to children, and this too can be used to compare population movements. In a fascinating study recently published by Helgason and coworkers[173] on Iceland it was shown that whereas the male population showed a strong correlation with Norway the female population had a high affinity with the Gaelic countries leading to much interesting discussion as to why that should be so. This was mirrored in a similar study on the Orkneys.[174] This could also prove a very fruitful area of research for Merseyside, although it would have to be without the use of surnames as a guide.

[173] A. Helgason, S. Sigurdardottir, J. Nicholson, B. Sykes, E.W. Hill, D.G. Bradley, V. Bosnes, J.R. Gulcher, R. Ward and K. Steffanson (2000) Estimating Scandinavian and Gaelic ancestry in the male settlers of Iceland. *American Journal of Human Genetics*, 67, 697-717.

[174] See footnote 169

Chapter 15
2002AD: AN ANNIVERSARY NOT FORGOTTEN!

It was not long after that before they came back ...again
Irish Chronicler, circa 902AD

The year 2002 marked the 1100th anniversary of the expulsion of the Norsemen from Ireland. We don't know how long it took for the first batch of settlers to arrive in Wirral after their unsuccessful attempt to settle in Anglesey, or how long it took them to colonise north of the Mersey and coastal West Lancashire. Chester was still controlled by the Saxons at least until the attacks of 907AD, but as we have seen, eventually the Vikings established a strong presence in the south of the city. However, 2002 seemed as good as any for Merseyside and Chester to celebrate the anniversary of the start of the colonisation: so it did!

2001: A Viking Odyssey

Anniversary Logo

Anniversary Web Site:
http://www.nottingham.ac.uk/~sczsteve

The build up started in February 2001 at Birkenhead Town Hall with the launch of *Wirral and its Viking Heritage,* and *Ingimund's Saga,* an event hosted by Wirral Borough Council and attended by a hundred guests including His Excellency Thorstein Pálsson, Ambassador of Iceland, Mrs Anne Ulset, Director of Cultural Affairs at the Royal Norwegian Embassy in London, Ms. Liv Sandven Deputy Mayor of Trondheim and Gerhard Dalen, Minister of Cultural Affairs, together with the Deputy Mayoress of Wirral, Pauline Cocker. The event was widely covered by not only the local North-west press but also most of the main newspapers in Norway and Iceland such as *Adresseavisen, Dagsavisen, Aftenposten, Nationen, Nytt frå Norge, The Norway Post* and *Morgunblaðið,* together with BBC Radio Merseyside, BBC North West Tonight and Channel One (North-west Cable TV): even the radio station NRK2 in Norway held a discussion on it involving the Oslo based Archaeologist Arne Emil Christensen. The interest was primarily because most people have associated Merseyside with many other things in the past, such as the football clubs and the Beatles, but not Vikings. For many people, the connection of the area with the Vikings is both new and surprising.

Lørdag 24. februar 2001 **5**

De fant Tors hammer

Trønderske utsendinger i vester-veg har gjenfunnet Tors ham-mer. Det skjedde ikke langt fra Liverpool der et helt lite sam-

Thors hammer "gjenfunnet"

After the launch, the guests were shown around the area. One of the Norwegian newspapers captured the moment when Ms. Sandven and Gerhard Dalen visited Thors Stone at Thurstaston with a BBC TV crew, with the headline *De fant Tors Hammer* (They founds Thor's Hammer): the article by Hermann Hansen told how the delegation from Trondheim Norway had visited their former "Tronder" colony and had rediscovered (gjenfunnet) their Thors hammer. However they were satisfied that the locals had been looking after it properly and so "they would not be taking it back with them on this occasion".

St. Olave Festival "Olsok" in Chester revived - after a gap of a mere 950 years

The delegation then visited Chester. Upon arrival at St. Olave's Church, Lower Bridge Street (now the Cheshire Revival Centre) in the old Viking sector of the city the party was greeted by a small padlock on the gate. Despite an unsuccessful attempt at opening it by Dalen, the Trondheim Director of Cultural Affairs, who, summoning the power of St.Olav and the Church of Norway tried to command the lock to open, the idea of reviving a celebration of St.Olav in the city after a gap of a mere 950 years or so was hatched, thus mirroring a celebration held every year in Norway.[175]

February 2001: Padlocked gate stops Norwegian delegation from Trondheim Kommune entering St. Olave's. "But it was not long before they came back again."

---

[175] The lock was later found to have been open all the time.

St.Olave Festival 2001

This consisted of two parts. First of all there was a Viking encampment day held at Arrowe Park, Wirral, on 5th August, an event covered by the BBC

North-West TV cameras. The event, organized by the local Park Ranger service in conjunction with the local Viking re-enactment group - the *Wirhalh Skip-Felag,* was attended by thousands of people (with a maximum of about 3000 at its peak) and consisted of craft displays, games and a re-enactment of the arrival of the Scandinavian settlers from Ireland. Whilst Ingimund is away negotiating with Æthelflæd, Lady of Mercia, the Vikings arrive to set up a farmstead at Arrowe only to be confronted by a curious group of Saxon fighters from Chester. A small skirmish ensues, until word gets through of the agreement between Ingimund and the Queen. The English warriors withdraw, grudgingly allowing the refugees to stay.

July 2001: A solitary Viking with a humble warning at the Wirral Show in Wallasey of the forthcoming anniversary year and another possible invasion.

Part two of the revived St. Olave event was at Chester the following Saturday (11th August) and started with a lunchtime service at St. Olave's church led by the Norwegian Pastor, Oddgeir Bolstad, of the Scandinavian Church in Liverpool. Some forty people squeezed into the small but homely church, including the Mayor and Mayoress of Wirral, Councillor John and Pauline Cocker. The event was concluded with talks at the Grosvenor Museum also in the former Viking south of the City. The day's events were extensively covered by the November 2001 edition of the BBC History Magazine.

Pastor Oddgeir Bolstad leads the first revived Olsok Service, 11th August 2001.

New Scandinavian arrivals reach Arrowe Park where they are confronted by a small Saxon force from Chester. 5th August 2001. Courtesy: Pip Shedden

The author gets drawn into the skirmish. He tries to reason, but there is a language barrier.

Viking craft displays, 5th August 2001. Courtesy: Pip Shedden

May-Day Dawn Celebration 2002.

The first major event of the anniversary year itself was held at daybreak on May 1st at Thors stone, Thurstaston, and built on a tradition of May 1st dancing at the stone by the Mersey Morris Men. The event was preceded by a special reception at Wallasey Town Hall the evening before put on by the Mayor and Mayoress of Wirral, Councillor John and Pauline Cocker, whose guests included Liv Sandven, now Mayor of Trondheim, Gerhard Dalen, Per-Olav Uddu (Director of the St.Olav Festival Olavfestdagene in Norway) and the Mayoress of South Wirral (Ellesmere Port and Neston), Councillor Moira Andrews. The guests of honour, together with 100 other brave souls were then up to join the Mersey Morris Men, Mockbeggar Morris Ladies, members of the Wirhalh Skip-Felag and Teachers, parents and youngsters of Thingwall Primary School in Wirral. As dawn broke at about 5.30AM, a blast of the horn by Hrolf Douglasson of the Wirhalh Skip-Felag heralded the dancing, followed by the capture of the stone by Thingwall school. The event finished in the car park with bacon sandwiches for all - courtesy of the Borough Council and the Morris Men, and then a breakfast reception at the Leasowe Castle Hotel, the allerged site of the King Canute attempt at turning back the waves. The event was covered in full by BBC Radio Merseyside and the local Press. May 1st finished with the Trondheim partyentering Chester and finally negotiating the padlock at St. Olave's Church.

"It was not long before they came back again". May 1st 2002, this time saw a successful entry into St.Olave's church by the Norwegian delegation of the Mayor of Trondheim, Liv Sandven (centre), the Director of Cultural Affairs (including Religion), Gerhard Dalen (right) and the Director of the Olavfestdagene (the Festival of St. Olave in Norway) Per-Olav Uddu.

1100 years on: Daybreak May 1st 2002 at Thor stone. Top left. Hrolf Douglasson sounds the horn. Bottom left. The dancing commences. Top right. Hrolf shows some trainees a trick or two. Bottom right. The Children of Thingwall School then capture the rock.

Top: May 1st: Morris men recruit Mayors: Mayor of Ellesmere Port and Neston, Moira Andrews (left), Mayor and Mayoress of Wirral, John and Pauline Cocker (centre) and Liv Sandven, Mayor of Trondheim (right) join the Morris Men.

Bottom: The Author with members of the Wirhalh Skip-Felag. Photos courtesy of Pip Shedden.

April 29th 2002: Children of Thingwall School present a delegation from Trondheim Norway with certificates and special School cups.

Opposite: April 29th 2002: The Mayor of Trondheim presents the Mersey Morris Men at Irby Mill with their National 2002 bronze medals won at a recent tournament.

Exchange of gifts, and an Education link-up
The day before the May-day event Liv Sandven, together with Gerhard Dalen and Per-Olav Uddu had been special guests of the Headmaster, teachers and children of Thingwall Primary School, and in the evening the Mayor also presented the Mersey Morris Men with bronze medals, won at the recently held all-England Rapper Tournament in Sheffield.

Unveiling of the 1100th anniversary Viking Mural, Thingwall
For several months the children of Thingwall School had been preparing a special mural, led by their artist-in residence Brian Edmundson. June 28th saw the official unveiling by the Norwegian Consul of Liverpool, Mr. Peter Copland. The School prides itself in its historic name and connections with the Viking past.

Burning of a Viking Ship, Anglesey
We don't know when Ingimund's Viking refugees were driven out of Anglesey at the battles of *Osmeliaun* or *Ros Meilon*. In the absence of a known date for this battle, Saturday 20th July was deemed as good as any to commemorate it, and sunset at 9.45pm hundreds witnessed the burning of a Viking vessel at Amlwch, as part of Anglesey's highly successful annual Viking event.

St. Olave's Festival 2002: Three Mayors and a Pilgrim Master!
This was the second year of the revived Merseyside and Chester St.Olave's Fest, and started as previous with the Viking Encampment at Arrowe Park, but this time run over two days (July 27th& 28th). The event was attended by thousands of people, including the newly elected Mayor of Wirral, Councillor Patricia Williams .and was covered in full by BBC Radio Merseyside. As in the previous year, this was followed by the more formal Chester event on August 10th. The format was altered somewhat compared to 2001. The eight hundred or so visitors who successfully crossed the Viking guard at the front entrance of the Grosvenor Museum witnessed an

June 2002: Mr. Peter Copland, Norwegian Consul of Liverpool with staff and pupils of Thingwall school after the unveiling of the Anniversary Mural (top) and (bottom) an earlier photograph taken in May of children from the school working on it.

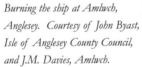

Burning the ship at Amlwch, Anglesey. Courtesy of John Byast, Isle of Anglesey County Council, and J.M. Davies, Amlwch.

*August 10th 2002:
Vikings introduce the concept
of Bouncers to Chester.*

impressive array of Viking displays and crafts. This was supplemented by talks on the city's Viking heritage, and a presentation by Norway's St.Olav Pilgrim Priest, Kjell Skartseterhagen on the life and achievements of St. Olav, and how these are celebrated every year in Norway. Guests included the Lord Mayor and Mayoress of Chester, the Mayor and Mayoress of South Wirral (Ellesmere Port and Neston) and the Mayor of Wirral and her Consort.

The party of dignatories, protected by a Viking "Varangian style" guard of honour led a procession across the former Scandinavian south of the city from the Grosvenor Museum to St. Olave's Church, Lower Bridge Street, where for the second successive year a service in commemoration of St.Olav and the Christian Viking Community on Merseyside and Chester. The service was led by Kjell Skartserhagen.

Kjell told of the warrior King Olav's conversion to Christianity and how he subsequently changed much of Scandinavia from following Messrs. Odin, Thor and colleagues towards the Man from Nazareth. He also explained the importance of the St. Olav Pilgrimage to Scandinavians. As a result plans for a similar annual Pilgrimage, run over the summer weekend in July or August nearest St. Olav's Day (29th July) have now been made for Merseyside, which will run from West Kirby, along the Wirral Way to St. Olave's.

The 2002 Mersey-Chester Olsok event finished with a tour of the area, including a visit by Kjell to St. Hilary's Church in Wallasey, where he saw the 17th-Century manuscript recording the Viking *klint* at one of the many

*St. Olav Pilgrimprest, Kjell
Skartseterhagen, leads the 2nd
revived Olsok service, August
11th 2002.*

brekka on both sides of the Mersey. The entry of 1642 in Wallasey's Parish Register at St. Hilary's records the unfortunate death of two girls by something falling on them at *ye Clynsse*. This is the last reported use of this word in Wallasey. Now the rock is known as the "Granny rock". The 1642 entry was the subject of some interesting

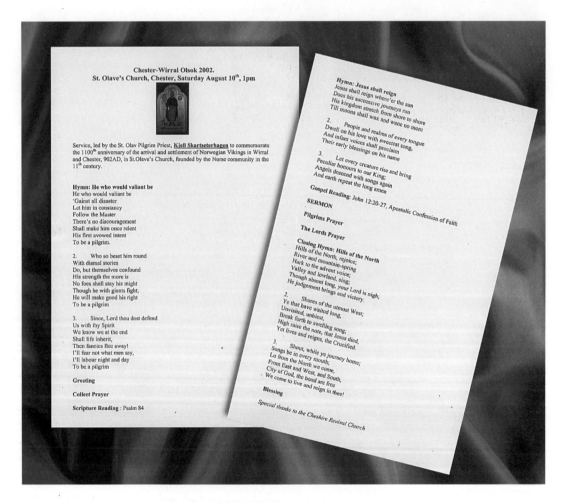

Chester-Wirral Olsok 2002.
St. Olave's Church, Chester, Saturday August 10th, 1pm

Service, led by the St. Olav Pilgrim Priest, **Kjell Skartseterhagen** to commemorate the 1100th anniversary of the arrival and settlement of Norwegian Vikings in Wirral and Chester, 902AD, in St.Olave's Church, founded by the Norse community in the 11th century.

Hymn: He who would valiant be
He who would valiant be
'Gainst all disaster
Let him in constancy
Follow the Master
There's no discouragement
Shall make him once relent
His first avowed intent
To be a pilgrim.

2.   Who so beset him round
With dismal stories
Do, but themselves confound
His strength the more is
No foes shall stay his might
Though he with giants fight;
He will make good his right
To be a pilgrim

3.   Since, Lord thou dost defend
Us with thy Spirit
We know we at the end
Shall life inherit,
Then fancies flee away!
I'll fear not what men say,
I'll labour night and day
To be a pilgrim

Greeting

Collect Prayer

Scripture Reading : Psalm 84

Hymn: Jesus shall reign
Jesus shall reign where'er the sun
Does his successive journeys run
His kingdom stretch from shore to shore
Till moons shall wax and wane no more

2.   People and realms of every tongue
Dwell on his love with sweetest song,
And infant voices shall proclaim
Their early blessings on his name

3.   Let every creature rise and bring
Peculiar honours to our King;
Angels descend with songs again
And earth repeat the long amen

Gospel Reading: John 12:20-27, Apostolic Confession of Faith

SERMON

Pilgrims Prayer

The Lords Prayer

Closing Hymn: Hills of the North
Hills of the North, rejoice;
River and mountain-spring
Hark to the advent voice;
Valley and lowland, sing;
Though absent long, your Lord is nigh;
He judgement brings and victory.

2.   Shores of the utmost West;
Ye that have waited long,
Unvisited, unblest,
Break forth to swelling song;
High raise the note, that Jesus died,
Yet lives and reigns, the Crucified.

3.   Shout, while ye journey home;
Songs be in every mouth;
Lo from the North we come,
From East and West, and South,
City of God, the bond are free
We come to live and reign in thee!

Blessing

Special thanks to the Cheshire Revival Church

Order or service, St. Olave's Church, August 10th 2002.

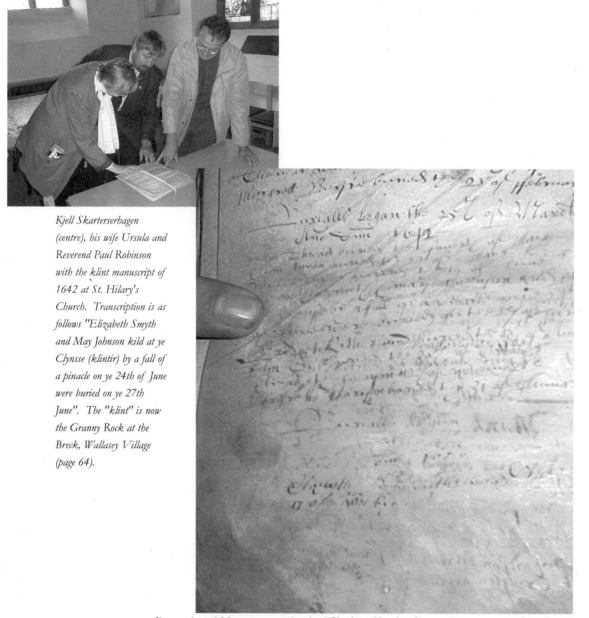

Kjell Skarterserhagen (centre), his wife Ursula and Reverend Paul Robinson with the klint manuscript of 1642 at St. Hilary's Church. Transcription is as follows "Elizabeth Smyth and May Johnson kild at ye Clynsse (klintir) by a fall of a pinacle on ye 24th of June were buried on ye 27th June". The "klint" is now the Granny Rock at the Breck, Wallasey Village (page 64).

discussion 100 years ago in the *Cheshire Sheaf*, a discussion recounted in detail in the book *Ingimund's Saga*. In that discussion it was concluded that the case for the Red Noses on the sea front was unlikely as an alternative location for *ye Clynsse*.

Volunteers at the DNA sampling session at Ormskirk, November 13th 2002., the 100th Anniversary of the St. Brice's Day Massacre. Courtesy of the Ormskirk Advertiser Series, and Abacus Healthcare.

In attendance at the sell-out St. Brice's ay Event was local Viking Kevin Taylor from Scarisbrick who has constructed an authentic Viking house in his back garden.

November 13th, Ormskirk

The final major event of 2002 celebrating 1100 years of Viking history of 2002 was held at Hurlston Hall, Ormskirk and consisted of Y-chromosome sampling of volunteers from Old West Lancashire families followed by the Ormskirk Advertiser Lecture on Blood of North-west Vikings, an event covered handsomely by the North-west Media. The date - 13th November - coincided with the St. Brice's day massacre, in 1002AD when King Æthelred 'ordered to be slain all the Danish men who were in England'.

1100 years on: Mersey Viking and a new ferry link

2002 saw the extension of ferry links between Merseyside with Ireland, with the opening of the £25million Twelve Quays terminal on Wirral. June 17th saw the opening of the Belfast - Wirral link, followed by the Dublin -Wirral link. One of its ferry boats is appropriately named… the Mersey Viking. The original vessels transporting the Viking refugees from Dublin in 902AD or thereabouts were probably less elaborate.

The first Viking settlers came in boats from Dublin. 1100 years later they are able to travel back again with the opening of a £25million ferry link with Dublin and Belfast: and the ferry boat Mersey Viking. The original vessels of 902AD were probably less elaborate, as was the quayside. Courtesy of Wirral Borough Council.

It will not be long before they come back again

2002 did not mark the end of celebratory activities. As the Chronicler of the Three Fragments said at the end of his description of the events a millennium ago: It was not long before they came back again. Preparations are already underway for 2037AD, and then 2902AD.

FURTHER READING

1. Wirral and its Viking Heritage (Paul Cavill, Stephen Harding and Judith Jesch), paperback, English Place Name Society, Nottingham (2000)

2. Ingimund's Saga: Norwegian Wirral (Stephen Harding, with Foreword by Magnus Magnusson), paperback, Countyvise, Birkenhead (2000).

3. Blood of the Vikings (Julian Richards), hardback - especially pages 176 to 179, Hodder and Stoughton (2001)

4. Women in the Viking Age (Judith Jesch) Boydell Press (1991).

TV AND RADIO BROADCASTS

Many of these can be accessed using broadband connection from the Web site:

> http://www.nottingham.ac.uk/-sczsteve, or
> http://www.nottingham.ac.uk/~sczsteve.

Those that cannot be downloaded please contact steve.harding@nottingham.ac.uk

1. BBC Radio Merseyside, Tony Snell show, 5/2/01 ("The Vikings" - 20 min).
2. BBC North West Tonight Broadcast 23/2/01 (News item by Mark Edwardson - launch of two new Wirral/Mersey Vikingbooks, 3 min)
3. Channel One (SW Lancashire Cable) 26/3/01 (Feature by Cathy Henderson - 7 min).
4. Channel One 7/6/01 (Feature by Cathy Henderson 7 min)
5. BBC North West Tonight 5/8/01 (News item by Ralph Blunsom - Viking re-enactment at Arrowe Park - 2 min).
6. Granada Reports, 9/10/01 (News Item by Rachel Bullock: Derek Mellor from Neston - 3 min).
7. BBC Radio Merseyside, Andy Ball Sunday Lunchtime show, 14/10/01 (10 min).

8. BBC North West Tonight, 22/10/01 (News item by Alan Urry. Keith Sherratt from Frankby - 2 min).

9. BBC Blood of the Vikings, 13/11/01 (Clip from programme 2 - Brunanburh, 1 min).

10. BBC Blood of the Vikings, 20/11/01 (Clip from programme 3 - Genetic survey volunteers from West Kirby, 1 min).

11. BBC Blood of the Vikings, 4/12/01 (Clip from programme 5 - Bill Housley from Meols, 3 min).

12. BBC Radio Merseyside, Roger Phillips Show, 5/12/01 (5 min)

13. Channel One, 3/1/02 (News item by Nicola Dixon - 1100th anniversary of Viking settlements, 3.5min).

14. BBC Radio Lancashire, 8/3/02 Patrick Waite talks about the forthcoming genetic survey of W. Lancashire.

15. BBC Radio Merseyside, 1/5/02 Lucinda Smith describes the 1100th anniversary May Day celebrations at Thor's stone, Thurstaston, 5am, with the Mersey Morris Men and Mockbeggar Morris Ladies, the children of Thingwall School and the Wirhalh Skip Felag (Viking reenactment group): hear how Thor miraculously lifts the clouds! (6 min).

16. BBC Radio Merseyside, 1st broadcast 28/5/02 Where's Wirral? - BBC Sense of Place series, 30 min. Roger Phillips. Pauline McAdam. Includes interviews with Lorraine Rogers (Chairman Tranmere Rovers), Steve Harding, Ben Harrison, Helen Renner and Scirard Lancelyn Green.

17. NEW:BBC Radio Lancashire, 5/5/02 Patrick Waite and Wigan MP Ron Rigby talk further about the forthcoming genetic survey of W. Lancashire.

Newspaper articles

Many of these can be accessed using broadband connection from the Web site:

http://www.nottingham.ac.uk/-sczsteve, or
http://www.nottingham.ac.uk/~sczsteve

1. The last of the Wirral Vikings, (Article by Jim Barrow about Mr. Gordon Tottey from West Kirby) *Daily Post*, 15/3/1971, page 5

2. When Wirral was under Viking rule, (Article by David Charters) *Daily Post*, 11/12/00, page 10.

3. Focus on Viking Settlers (Article by Chris Bartley), *Wirral Life*, January 2001, page 19.

4. The Vikings are back - in peace (Article by Alan Weston), *Daily Post*, 24/2/01, page 14.

5. De fant Tors Hammer (They found Thor's Hammer - article by Hermann Hansen) *Adresseavisen* (Norway) 24/2/01, page 5.

6. Vikinger fram fra glemselen (Vikings rescued from oblivion- article by Trine Andersen) *Dagsavisen* (Norway), 27/02/01, page 21.

7. I engelske Wirral snakket de norsk til utpå 1400-tallet (in Wirral, England they spoke a type of Norwegian up to the 15th Century - article by Trine Andersen) *Aftenposten* (Norway), 27/2/01.

8. De glemte vikinger (the forgotten Vikings- article by Trine Andersen) *Nationen* (Norway), 1/3/01, pages 16, 17.

9. Nordvest-Englands glemte vikinger (Northwest England's forgotten Vikings - article by Trine Andersen) *Nytt fra Norge* (Norway) 6/03/01.

10. Wirral's Viking legacy (Article by Louise Powney), *Wirral News Group*, 7/3/01.

11. Bætt við breska víkingaafarinn (a rediscovered British Viking Place - article by Sigrun Davidsdottir) *Morgunblaðið* (Iceland) - lesbók section, 10/3/01, p17.

12. New book reveals Wirral's Viking past, (Article by Stuart Hughes), *Wirral Globe*, 14/3/01.

13. Help Trace our Heritage (Article by Stuart Hughes) *Wirral Globe* 4/04/01.

14. Let's Talk Vikings (Article by Stuart Hughes), *Wirral Globe* 25/04/01.

15. Are you part of Wirral's early Viking Heritage?, (Article by Louise Powney) *Wirral News Group* (Wirral News, Wallasey News, Birkenhead News, Hoylake News, Neston News, West Kirby News, Bebington News) 16/5/01, page 11.

16. Man on a mission to crack our Norse code, (Article by Alison Dando) *Liverpool Echo*, 28/5/01.

17. Viking Invasion, *Wirral Globe* 1/08/01.

18. UK St. Olave's Festival resurrected to mark 1100th anniversary of Norwegian influx (Article by Rolleiv Solholm), *The Norway Post*, 22/9/01, page 1.

19. Scouse Key to Norse Code (Article by Nick Baty), *The Times*, September 20th, Weekend section, p17 - see also Genetics and Genealogy - Article 22.

20. Weekend Feature: British hunt for Viking genes (Article by Rolleiv Solholm), *The Norway Post*, 13/10/01, page 1.

21. Steeped in rich Viking history (Article by Louise Powney), *Wirral News Group*, 19/09/01, p9, Wirral News Group Anniversary special.

22. By gum, I'm a Viking (Article by Emma Bird and Rob Brady), *Daily Post*, 4/12/01.

23. Are we Viking descendents? (Article by Louise Powney) *Wirral News Group*, 5/12/01, p4.

24. Found on the Wirral, a man with the blood of a warrior (Article by Adam Powell), *Daily Mail*, 5/12/01, p32.

25. Cheeky way to research Viking past! (Article by Lloyd Jones) *Ormskirk Advertiser*, 13/12/01, p3 - see also Cheeky way to research Viking past.

26. Important birthday for the Vikings (Article by Louise Powney), *Wirral News Group*, 16/01/02, p5.

27. Viking fan Steve says Thanks , *Wirral Globe* 22/01/02.

28. The search for Wirral's Viking blood line, (article by Phil Fleming) *Wirral Globe* 23/04/02.

29. Do you still have the blood of the Vikings. (Article by Mike Hornby) *Daily Post*, 24/04/02, p3, and Do you still have the blood of the Vikings. (Article by Mike Hornby) *icLiverpool*, 24/04/02, and Key Names, *ic Liverpool*, 24/04/02.

30. Was your ancestor a viking? (Article by Louise Powney), *Wirral News Group*, 24/04/02, p3, Wirral News Group.

31. Home Swede home to Vikings (Lead Article), *Ormskirk Advertiser*, 24/04/02.

32. Search is on for a Viking (Article by Sarah Burdon), *Ormskirk Champion*, 24/04/02, p1.

33. Dawn tribute to Viking Invaders (Article by Claire Lane), *The Chronicle*, 26/04/02.

34. Battle Stations. *Daily Post/ Liverpool Echo*, 29/04/02.

35. Viking horn sounds start of a celebration (Article by Mike Hornby), *Daily Post*, 1/05/02, p7.

36. *The Wirral Chronicle*, 3/5/02, page 3 (article by David Harding):"Sounding off about our long Viking heritage", and "Youngsters join in and do their Thing", and "Norwegian delegation joins in festivities".

37. City gets set for Viking 'invasion' (Article by Clare Wildman), *Chester Evening Leader*, 7/05/02, p32.

38. Youngsters get back in touch with Viking roots (Article by David Harding), *Chester Chronicle*, 5/07/02.

39. Pupils keen to pass Viking DNA tests (Article by Louise Powney),

Wirral News Group, 17/07/02.

40.   Modern Vikings!: swab tests, *Wirral Globe,* 24/07/02, p21.

41. Do you have a Viking for Wirral's History (Article by Louise Powney), *Wirral News Group, 24/07/02*, p32.

42. City to Celebrate its long Viking History, *Chester Chronicle,* 9/08/02, p19.

43. Vikings return in force to Chester...one thousand years on, *Daily Post,* 13/08/02, p7.

44. Viking invasion wins over Town, *Chester Chronicle,* 16/08/02, p13.

45. Church's Viking Past, *The Mail* (Chester), 21/08/02, p2.

46. Peaceful invaders from across the sea (article by Clifford Burchall), *Ormskirk Advertiser,* 21/11/02, p25.

Magazine & Journal Articles

Many of these can be accessed using broadband connection from the Web site:

http://www.nottingham.ac.uk/-sczsteve,

http://www.nottingham.ac.uk/~sczsteve.

1. 1,000 years ago...What evidence for a Wirral Viking invasion? (Article by Fiona Philpott) *Wirral Journal,* Summer 1990.

2. Viking Wirral. A second Millenium Viking Nation, *Wirral Journal* No. 5, Spring 2001.

3. Viking Wirral (article by Barbara Jones) *Rovers Rearguard,* 5th January 2001.

4. Wirral's wild rovers return Article by *Cheshire Life* August 2001, pages 186-189.

5. 1100th anniversary of Viking Wirral and Chester: Olsok is resurrected!, *Wirral Champion,* September 01, p22 .

6. The Blood of the Vikings (Article by Emma Head) *The University of Nottingham Newsletter*, Number 228, October 29 2001, pages 8-9.

7. Norse festival revived on Merseyside (Article by Nigel Jones) *BBC History,* Vol. 2., November 2001, p8 .

8. Meols (Article by David Griffiths) *British Archaeology,* Issue 62., December 2001, p8.

9. What's in a Name?: As in Our Name (Article by Tony Coombes) *Rovers Review* (Tranmere official programme vs Cardiff City, FA Cup 4th Rd.), 27/1/02, p33.

10. May Day Horn Blast Starts Viking 1100th Anniversary Celebrations, *Wirral Champion*, June 02, p29.

11. Vikings return to Chester, *FORUM* (Chester), September 2002, p3.

12. Viking Day takes city back in time, *Chester News*, Autumn 2002, p18.

GENERAL REFERENCES

The reader is also referred to the many references in the footnotes

Anderson, A. (1964) *The Story of Bromborough* (locally published: copies in the local library).

Biddle, F. and Fellowes, A. (1992) *Moreton Wirral: A Pictorial History*,Volume 2 (see pages 46 & 53) Countyvise Ltd., Birkenhead U.K.

Chitty, G. *Wirral Rural Fringes Survey*. Journal of the Merseyside Archaeological Society, 2, 1-22 (1978). The archaeological finding at Bromborough Court is reported as "A Further Note" on p81.

Cohat, Y. (1992) *The Vikings - Lords of the Seas*, Translated by Ruth Daniel, Thames and Hudson Ltd., London, U.K.

Dawson, G. (1998) *Wirral Gleanings*, Dawson Publishing, Irby U.K.

Dawson, G. (1992) *Tingvelle: A History of Thingwall and other North Wirral farming villages* (see page 2), Dawson Publishing, Irby U.K.

Dodgson, J. McN. (1972) *The Place-Names of Cheshire Part IV,* English Place-Name Society Vol. 47., Cambridge University Press, Cambridge U.K
Comprehensive list of Cheshire Place Names.

Ellison, N.F. (1955) *The Wirral Peninsula*, Redwood Burn Ltd., Trowbridge & Esher, U.K.

Fellows-Jensen, G. (1992) *Scandinavian Place-Names of the Irish Sea Province*. In (Graham-Campbell, J., editor) *Viking Treasure from the North*

West, page 39, National Museums and Galleries on Merseyside Occasional Papers, Liverpool Museum Number 5, Liverpool, UK

Glendening, P.J.T. (1961) *Icelandic* (1961) Hodder and Stoughton, London, U.K.

Gordon, E.V. (1957) *Introduction to Old Norse.* 2nd edition, revised by A.R. Taylor, Oxford University Press, Oxford U.K.

Graham-Campbell ed. (1992) *Viking Treasure from the North West. The Cuerdale Hoard in its Context.* Liverpool Museum, Liverpool, U.K.

Griffiths, D. (1992) *The Coastal Trading Ports of the Irish Sea.* In (Graham-Campbell, J., editor) *Viking Treasures from the North West.* (pages 63-72). National Museums and Galleries on Merseyside, Liverpool U.K.

Griffiths, D. (2003-4) *Vikings of the Irish Sea* (Tempus, forthcoming). Haugen, E. (1976) The Scandinavian Languages. London.

Higham, N.J. (1993) *The Origins of Cheshire.* Manchester University Press, Manchester U.K.

Jochens, J. (1995) *Women in Old Norse Society,* Cornell University Press, Ithaca, New York. U.S.A.

Kristín Bragadóttir and Stevens, P.J. (2000) Living and Reliving the Icelandic Sagas *Stefnumót við Íslenska Sagnahefð,* Landsbóksafn Íslands - Háskólabókasafn, The Library of Congress, Cornell University Library USA, The University of Manitoba Libraries, Canada.

Laura Goodman Salverson (1923) *The Viking Heart,* Toronto, Canada.

Magnus Magnusson (1976) *Hammer of the North.* Orbis Publishing Limited, London.

Magnus Magnusson (1973) *Viking Expansion Westwards,* Bodley Head, London.

Magnus Magnusson (1980) *Vikings!* Elsevier-Dutton Pub. Co.,

Amsterdam, Holland/London. U.K./New York, USA.   Second Edition. 2000 (Harvill Press).

Magnus Magnusson and Hermann Pálsson (translators, 1965) *The Vinland Sagas. The Norse Discovery of America*. Penguin Classics, Harmondsworth, U.K.

Magnus Magnusson and Hermann Palsson (translators, 1966) *King Harald's Saga*. Penguin Classics, Hammondsworth: Penguin.

Meehan, A. (1996) *The Dragon and the Griffin: The Viking Impact*. Thames and Hudson, London.

Omerod G. (1882) *The History of the County Palatine and City of Chester*. 2nd edition revised by Thomas Helsby. George Routledge & Sons, London.

Orchard, A. (1997) *Dictionary of Norse Myth and Legend*. Cassel, London U.K.

Roberts, S.J. (2002) *A History of Wirral,* Phillimore, Chichester, U.K.

Snorri Sturluson Heimskringla: *Sagas of the Norse Kings*. Translated by S. Laing, revised with footnotes P. Foote. (1961) Everyman's Library, Dent (London, U.K.) and Dutton (New York U.S.A.).

Snorri Sturluson *Egils Saga* : Translated and edited by Christine Fell and includes peoms by John Lucas (1975) Everyman's Library, Dent (London, U.K.) and Dutton (New York U.S.A.).

Snorri Sturluson *The Poetic Edda*. Translated by Carolyn Larrington (1996). Oxford University Press, Oxford U.K.

Snorri Sturluson *The Prose Edda:* Tales from Norse Mythology. Translated by Jean I Young (1954). Bowes and Bowes (Cambridge) and University of California Press (Berkeley, Los Angeles and London).

Thacker, A.T. (1987) *Scandinavian Settlements in Cheshire*. In The Victoria History of the County of Chester vol I, eds B.E. Harris and A.T.

Thacker, p254-260, Oxford University Press, Oxford, U.K.

Wainwright, F.T. (1975) *Scandinavian England,* Edited by H.P.R. Finsberg, Philimore Press, Chichester.

WEBSITES

Main Wirral/West Lancashire/Chester Viking web page:
http://www.nottingham.ac.uk/-sczsteve
Contains links to other relevant pages, TV and radio broadcasts and Newspaper/Magazine reports, as well as a comprehensive guide to events

Genetic Survey:
http://www.nottingham.ac.uk/-sczsteve/survey.htm
Contains link to BBC Blood of Vikings Page

Arctic Images: Ragnar Th. Sigurðsson's website containing superb digital images of the North.
http://www.artic-images.com/

Hnefatafl: play the Viking board game!:
http://www.expomedia.se/tablut/eng/history.htm

PCBT Photograpy: Website of Patrick Trollope
http://www.pcbtphotography.co.uk
Patrick also runs the Southport Reporter:
http://www.southportreporter.com

Polymerase Chain Reaction:
http://allserv.rug.ac.be/~avierstr/principles/pcrani.html

St. Bridget:
http://catholic.org/saints/saints/ brigidireland.html

St. Olav
http://viking.no/e/people/st.olav/e-olav.htm

Trani (crane bird) web page:
http://europa.eu.int/comm/environment/nature/directive/grus_grus.htm

INDEX

Back cover illustration by J.M. Davies, 24 Salem St, Amlwch, Anglesey

Also by the Author

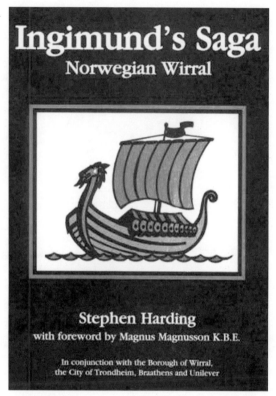

1100 years ago a group of Viking settlers from Norway arrived somewhere between West Kirby and Meols on the shores of north Wirral, having been driven out of Ireland. This initiated a mass migration of their fellow countrymen into the area and soon they had established a community with a clearly defined border, its own leader, its own language, a trading port, and at its centre a place of assembly or government - the Thing at Thingwall. This community was answerable to nobody else: the English, the Welsh, the Dublin Norse, the Isle of Man, Iceland, and not even Norway. The Wirral Norse settlement therefore satisfied all the criteria of an independent, self-governing Viking State - albeit a mini one!

This book is about these people, why they left Norway, where they settled, their religion, their pastimes - such as horse-racing at Irby and rock-climbing at Wallasey - and the legends that have been attributed to them - including the awesome Thór's Stone at "Thorsteinn's farmstead". Wirral was also probably witness to one of the greatest battles in the history of the British Isles - Brunanburh.

Published by Countyvise Ltd., 14 Appin Road, Birkenhead, CH41 9HH, U.K. cv@birkenheadpress.co.uk

Size A5 paperback, 226 pages, fully illustrated/ colour., ISBN 1 871201 09 8.

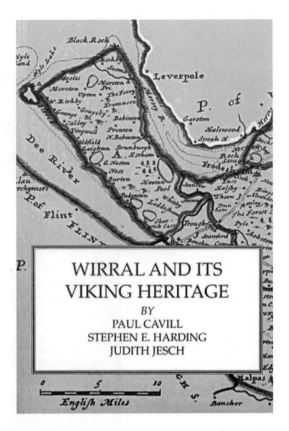

This book is a guide to the Viking impact on the Wirral. It includes reprinted illustrated essays from F. T. Wainwright, John McN. Dodgson, J. D. Bu'lock and W. G. Collingwood, on the history, art and names of the region. And the work is brought up to date by original contributions from Simon C. Bean, Stephen E. Harding, Judith Jesch and Andrew Wawn on recent developments in the history, archaeology, scholarly and popular interest in the Wirral. It is completed by a gazetteer examining the origins of the major names, which also forms an index to the volume.

The book provides absorbing reading and is an important resource for anyone interested in the past of the Wirral and the origins of its names.

Published by the English Place-Name Society, School of English Studies, University of Nottingham, Nottingham NG7 2RD. bonnie.millar@nottingham.ac.uk
Registered Charity No. 257891.Popular Series, ISBN 0 904889 59 9

Paperback, 235 x 157 mm, ix + 149 pp.